Wildlife
Madagascar

Ken Behrens &
Keith Barnes

PRINCETON
press.princeton.edu

Published by Princeton University Press,
41 William Street, Princeton, New Jersey 08540
In the United Kingdom: Princeton University Press, 6 Oxford Street,
Woodstock, Oxfordshire OX20 1TR
nathist.press.princeton.edu

First published 2016

British Library Cataloging-in-Publication Data is available

Library of Congress Control Number 2016930334
ISBN 978-0-691-16171-6

Production and design by **WILD**Guides Ltd., Old Basing, Hampshire UK.
Printed in China

10 9 8 7 6 5 4 3 2 1

Ken: To my wife

Keith: For my Dad and Mom, who taught me
to love nature. And to my wife Yi-fang and son
Joshua, who allow me the time to enjoy it.

Contents

A brief introduction to Madagascar

Madagascar is so different from the rest of the world that it is sometimes called 'The Eighth Continent'. Not only does it have the high level of endemism (species not found elsewhere) that is typical of an island, but it also boasts remarkable diversity, which for some groups approaches that more typical of a whole continent.

Madagascar is the land of lemurs, a radiation of our own primate order that evolved into exhilarating diversity on this island. These endearing creatures are the ambassadors for Malagasy nature; many people who have no idea where this island is located immediately recognize the Ring-tailed Lemur. Madagascar is also a land of fabulous birds, ancient reptile lineages, and six of the world's nine species of baobabs.

All naturalists find Madagascar fascinating as a treasure-trove of biodiversity and a 'laboratory of evolution', much like the Galápagos but on a grander scale. And for travelling naturalists, Madagascar is a 'must-visit' place. Although Madagascar has long been known for birds and mammals, its reptiles, amphibians, insects and plants are just as unique.

Madagascar is a land of distinctive and odd creatures, a whole different track of evolution from the rest of the world. A good example of this is the Mossy Leaf-tailed Gecko, a master of disguise whose mossy fringes and colour changing abilities allow it to blend into the tree trunks where it sleeps during the day.

About this book

This is the first field guide that has attempted to cover the whole range of diversity of this 'mini-continent' in one book. It obviously cannot be comprehensive, but rather aims to cover the species and groups that are most likely to be encountered in the most frequently visited sites. Madagascar's most popular natural sites are listed on *page 10*, ranked by the approximate number of visitors each receives every year.

As an example of the way that species selection for this book was weighted towards the most frequently visited sites, an especially common or interesting species that is found only at the island's most popular natural site of Andasibe might be included, whereas a species that is found only in Marojejy National Park is more likely to be excluded since that site is much less visited, albeit wonderful. A few exceptionally interesting species that can be found only in sites that are off the main tourist routes have been included in the hope of inspiring people to visit new sites. Also included are some especially interesting species that do occur within the most-visited sites, but which are hard to find. These are included to inspire visitors to seek them out with the help of skilled guides.

Focused birders will locate a few species not covered in this book; keen mammal enthusiasts might visit remote forests and find lemurs that, similarly, have not been included; and fanatical herpetologists who spend their nights stalking the forest and digging in the leaf-litter will find many reptiles and amphibians that are not featured. However, this book aims to cover the vast majority of the birds, mammals, reptiles and butterflies (plus a few other arthropods and plants) that a casual visitor or a general naturalist will see. Visitors with a strong interest in one particular group will want to bring a thorough reference that covers it, but will still find this guide valuable for its broad coverage of other wildlife. Finally, naturalists who might never travel to Madagascar should find this guide a fascinating exhibition of the island's wild riches.

To some degree, this book reflects the mammal and bird bias of the average visitor, covering those groups more thoroughly than others. But at the same time, visitors are encouraged to broaden their horizons. It is hoped that the extensive coverage of Madagascar's truly incredible reptiles, amphibians and insects (butterflies in particular) will make these seem more accessible.

One of the countless odd and unique facets of Madagascar is that you are required to hire a local guide to visit almost any natural site. While this might be frustrating for some 'lone wolf' naturalists, it also has great benefits. Most Malagasy local guides are passionate and knowledgeable, and their expertise will enhance your trip and increase the number of species that you see. The information in the 'where to see' section will be useful in planning your trip, especially if you have key targets. Once you arrive in Madagascar, you can refer to this book when directing the efforts of your local guides. Most local guides specialize in lemurs, but there are many fascinating birds, reptiles and frogs that they probably know, but would not focus on finding unless you mentioned your interest.

Map of Madagascar showing biogeographic zones and most-visited natural sites

This map shows the distribution of Madagascar's remaining natural habitats. The major division is between the wet east, where rainforest is the natural habitat, and the dry west, with deciduous forest. The central High Plateau is virtually deforested. For more information on biogeographic zones, see *pages 12–13*.

Madagascar's most-visited natural sites

Rank	GENERAL TOURISTS	SERIOUS NATURALISTS	BIRDERS
1	Andasibe area (Andasibe-Mantadia NP, *etc.*)	Andasibe area (Andasibe-Mantadia NP, *etc.*)	Andasibe area (Andasibe-Mantadia NP, *etc.*)
2	RN7 south: Toliara / Isalo NP	Ranomafana NP	RN7 south: Toliara / Ifaty / Isalo area / Zombitse-Vohibasia NP
3	Nosy Be	Isalo NP	Ranomafana NP
4	Far north: Ankarana and Amber Mountain NPs, *etc.*	Berenty / Fort Dauphin	Ankarafantsika NP / Betsiboka Delta (Mahajanga)
5	Tsingy de Bemaraha NP	Kirindy Forest	Masoala NP
6	St. Marie Island	Tsingy de Bemaraha NP	Berenty
7	Berenty / Fort Dauphin	Nosy Be	Anjozorobe area (Anjozorobe-Angavo forest)
8	Masoala NP	Far north: Ankarana and Amber Mountain NPs, *etc.*	Far north: Ankarana and Amber Mountain NPs, *etc.*
9	Kirindy Forest	Masoala NP	Marojejy NP
10	Ankarafantsika NP	Ankarafantsika NP	Kirindy Forest
11	Ranomafana NP	Marojejy NP	Tsingy de Bemaraha NP
12	Marojejy NP	Toliara / Anakao / Ifaty	Nosy Be
13	Anjozorobe area (Anjozorobe-Angavo forest)	Anjozorobe area (Anjozorobe-Angavo forest)	St. Marie Island

Key to the sites

1. Amber Mountain NP
2. Anakao
3. Andasibe-Mantadia NP
4. Anjozorobe-Angavo forest
5. Ankarafantsika NP
6. Ankarana NP
7. Berenty Reserve
8. Betsiboka Delta (Mahajanga)
9. Fort Dauphin (Tôlanaro)
10. Ifaty
11. Isalo NP
12. Kirindy Forest
13. Marojejy NP
14. Masoala NP
15. Nosy Be
16. Ranomafana NP
17. Sainte Marie Island
18. Tsingy de Bemaraha NP
19. Toliara (Tulear)
20. Zombitse-Vohibasia NP

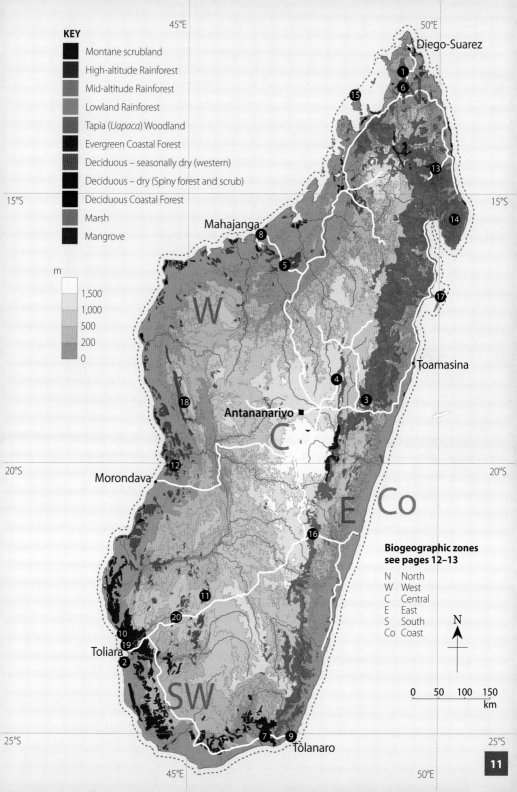

KEY

- Montane scrubland
- High-altitude Rainforest
- Mid-altitude Rainforest
- Lowland Rainforest
- Tapia (*Uapaca*) Woodland
- Evergreen Coastal Forest
- Deciduous – seasonally dry (western)
- Deciduous – dry (Spiny forest and scrub)
- Deciduous Coastal Forest
- Marsh
- Mangrove

m

- 1,500
- 1,000
- 500
- 200
- 0

Diego-Suarez

Mahajanga

Antananarivo

Toamasina

Morondava

Toliara

Tôlanaro

W

C

E

Co

SW

N

Biogeographic zones see pages 12–13

N   North
W   West
C   Central
E   East
S   South
Co Coast

N

0   50   100 150
km

Biogeographic zones of Madagascar

The zones presented here are reflected in the range icons that accompany each species account.

East [E]

- Predominant natural habitat is humid forest ('rainforest'), Madagascar's most species-rich habitat.
- Rainforests stay lush and green year-round. They are watered by moisture off the Indian Ocean that is precipitated by the eastern escarpment. Trees very tall in lowlands, but shorter in higher-elevation forest.
- Species distribution within eastern rainforest is complex. Many lemurs and frogs, and some reptiles, have small and localized distributions, often within specific elevations.
- Vast deforestation; much of eastern zone now covered in scrubby secondary forest and artificial savannah. Lower-elevation forests have been most drastically impacted.
- The highest mountains support open heath and grassland above treeline. These habitats are species-poor.
- Eastern marsh is one of Madagascar's most special and most threatened habitats. It supports several endemic birds and many frogs.

West [W]

- The western two thirds of Madagascar, comprising the central highlands and the western lowlands, are much drier than the east, lying in the rain shadow of the eastern mountains.
- Originally covered in dry deciduous forest, which has lower diversity than rainforest, but is still rich, with many endemics. Lemurs and reptiles are especially rich in the west, while frog diversity is low.
- Most of the west is now savannah in which mango and palms are prominent. Large areas have also been converted to rice cultivation.
- Most (although not all) of the trees in the western forest are deciduous: they lose their leaves during the dry season. The abundant leaf-litter and more open character of this habitat make it very different from eastern rainforest.
- The west holds extensive wetland habitat: marshes, lakes and wide rivers. Most have been degraded by humans.

North [N]

- The north is essentially a mix of the eastern and western zones. Here the island tapers to a point, while general climatic trends are also disrupted by Tsaratanana, Madagascar's highest mountain massif. The Sambirano region around Nosy Be is the only area on the west coast that sees almost as much rainfall as parts of the eastern zone.
- Some parts of the north, such as Amber Mountain and Lokobe National Parks (NPs), hold rainforest. This forest lacks the diversity of eastern rainforest, but does support many localized endemics.
- Much of the north, such as Ankarana NP, holds dry forest like that of the western zone. Large stretches are also covered in human-created savannah habitat.

Centre [C]

- Mostly above 800 m (2,600') elevation.
- Before humans arrived, Madagascar's central highlands probably supported a mix of savannah and forest. But this is the part of Madagascar that has been most heavily impacted by human activity and is now dominated by arid grasslands and eroded gullies.
- Another feature of the centre is vast areas of rice cultivation. Rice paddies do support some birds and frogs.
- Forest persists in a few places, mainly in valleys where it is shielded from burning. Such forest resembles eastern rainforest, although it is drier and supports fewer species.

Southwest [SW]

- The southwest is the driest part of Madagascar. Its aridity has given rise to the island's most distinctive habitat, the spiny forest. There is also some gallery forest and wetland.
- Least diverse of Madagascar's zones, but supports many endemic species. The plants are fascinating, with most endemic not just to Madagascar, but to this zone.

Coast [Co]

- Madagascar's 10,000 kilometres (6,200 miles) of coastline encompass mangroves (mainly in the west and north), mudflats, rocky and sandy beaches, and salt marshes.
- Supports many species of birds, along with sea turtles and marine mammals. Coral reefs are beyond the scope of this book, but Madagascar's reefs are world-class.

Human-modified grasslands, rice paddies and villages
South of Ambositra, Central Zone

Hamerkop
p. 96

Mascarene Martin
p. 136

Spotted Blue Swallowtail p. 288

Jewelled Chameleon p. 192

Black Kite
p. 100

Common Myna *p. 176*

Madagascar Fody *p. 178*

Mascarene Ridged Frog *p. 248*

Cattle Egret *p. 92*

Rufous Mouse Lemur *p. 32*

Giraffe-necked Weevil *p. 284*

Comet Moth *p. 314*

Trees become more stunted at higher elevations; lush year-round.

Stripe-throated Jery *p. 160*

Satanic Leaf-tailed Gecko *p. 234*

Elongate Ancient Leaf Chameleon *p. 188*

Low-elevation eastern rainforest
Masoala NP, Eastern Zone

Helmet Vanga *p. 172*

White-fronted Brown Lemur *p. 46*

Common Leaf-tailed Gecko *p. 236*

Cream-lined Swallowtail *p. 286*

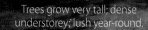

Trees grow very tall; dense understorey; lush year-round.

Speckled Day Gecko *p. 222*

Red Ruffed Lemur *p. 52*

Scaly Ground-roller *p. 144*

Lowland Streaked Tenrec *p. 76*

Northern rainforest is very similar to eastern rainforest, but has lower species diversity.

Madagascar Paradise Flycatcher
p. 152

Orange-backed Mantella *p. 254*

Red-legged Plated Lizard *p. 212*

Lesser Frigatebird
p. 118

Sanford's Brown Lemur
p. 46

Lesser Crested / Roseate Terns *p. 116*

The west coast is generally richer than the cyclone-scoured east coast.

Green Sea Turtle *p. 184*

Bottlenose dolphin *p. 80*

Western dry forest and freshwater marsh
Lake Ravelobe, Ankarafantsika NP, Western Zone

Coquerel's Sifaka *p. 56*

Fosa *p. 68*

Madagascar Swordtail *p. 288*

White-faced Whistling-duck *p. 84*

Western dry forest is desiccated in the dry season, but lush in the wet season, although the understorey is often open. Very similar dry forest can also be found in the northern zone.

Leaf-nosed snake *p. 240*

Schlegel's Asity *p. 148*

Cuvier's Madagascar Swift *p. 208*

Western marshes are Madagascar's richest for birds, although they are poorer in terms of endemics than the eastern marshes.

Grey Heron *p. 88*

Spiny forest
Parc Mosa, near Ifaty, Southwestern Zone

Madagascar's most visually distinctive habitat; almost barren in the dry season, but sees a wet season flush of green.

Octopus trees *p. 318* are found only in the spiny forest.

Grey-brown Mouse Lemur *p. 32*

Madagascar Giant Swallowtail *p. 290*

Long-tailed Ground-roller *p. 146*

Baobabs *pp. 320–323* are found throughout the southwest, west, and north, but are especially prominent here.

White-lined Chameleon *p. 204*

Madagascar Keeled Plated Lizard *p. 214*

How to use this book

Headings

Closely related and/or similar species are grouped together onto page-spreads. Each such spread has a heading. The headings in the mammal and butterfly sections include scientific family names, as family differences are fundamental to understanding these groups. Scientific family names are less useful for other groups, and are therefore not included.

SECTION INTRODUCTIONS

There is a two-page introductory spread for each of the four major vertebrate groups. These include information on the way to approach identification within a given group (*e.g.* mammal identification should be approached in a very different manner than frog identification).

Names

Each species account starts with a common name. With good reason, biologists prefer scientific names for their greater precision and lesser variability. But casual naturalists generally find common names easier to understand and process, so this guide includes them for all species. In some cases, as with birds and mammals, common names are fairly standardized. The source for bird names was *The Birds of Africa: Volume VIII*, for lemur names was *Lemurs of Madagascar*, and for other mammals was *Mammals of Madagascar*. Finding standardized common names for reptiles, amphibians, insects and plants was more challenging. For reptiles and amphibians, the main source used was *Complete Guide to Scientific and Common Names of Reptiles and Amphibians of the World*. For butterflies, *Field Guide to Butterflies of South Africa* was followed for the species and genera covered in that book, the other names being those in general use. See Further reading (*page 327*) for more details of all of these volumes. Other species have one or more well established common names, often from the pet trade, in which case these were used. For many species, there is simply no established common name, or the existing names are misleading or otherwise inadequate, in which case the only option was to invent new ones (marked with asterisks). All naturalists are encouraged to pay attention to both the common and scientific names, and to realize that most Malagasy local guides will not know common names for reptiles or amphibians.

The scientific names are included and, where relevant, the subspecies name if it is endemic to Madagascar. In some cases, a whole subgenus, genus, cluster of genera, or family is treated with a single account.

As well as the common and scientific names, most accounts also include Malagasy and French common names. It is hoped that these will be useful both to non-English-speaking visitors and to Malagasy guides and researchers. They can also be helpful in interacting with Malagasy people who are not directly involved in tourism, but whose goodwill is essential to preserving natural places. Malagasy and French mammal and bird names are mainly from the same sources as English common names. Malagasy reptile names come from the

Malagasy edition of *Amphibians and Reptiles of Madagascar*. Other names come directly from Malagasy researchers and naturalists. Widespread species tend to have many different Malagasy names, depending on the region, but it is beyond the scope of this book to include them all. There is also wide overlap in the usage of Malagasy names, with one name often used for many different species. To avoid confusion, the use of the same Malagasy name for more than one species is generally avoided in this book. As a result, the preferred Malagasy name for certain species in a given location may not be included, or may be applied to a different species.

Icons

STATUS

Each account features several icons. The numbers correspond to the adjacent photographic plate, allowing easy correlation of the text and the photos. There are also icons for species that are endemic or introduced, and a coloured bar for species that are considered globally threatened (Critically Endangered, Endangered, Vulnerable) or near threatened on the International Union for Conservation of Nature (IUCN) Red List (see www.iucnredlist.org for more information). The icons and codes are summarized in the panel to the right.

DISTRIBUTION

Each species account includes a distribution map that shows the broad biogeographical zones where that species occurs. There are six zones (East, Southwest, West, Centre, North and Coastal), each of which is subdivided into three sections (northern, central and southern). These sections are shaded to indicate relative abundance as shown in the key. These are not true range maps, but rather a shorthand way of representing approximate distributions. Those interested in detailed information about the ranges of Malagasy species should look to more in-depth references to individual groups. However, for even the most casual visitor, quick reference to range is one of the best ways to narrow down a species that you are trying to identify.

Status

E   **Endemic Family** – the species and the whole family to which it belongs are found only on Madagascar

E   **Endemic** – a species found only on Madagascar

B   **Breeding endemic** – only breeds on Madagascar

R   **Regional Endemic** – found only in the Malagasy region

e   **Endemic subspecies** – subspecies in Madagascar is (or are) endemic to the island

I   **Introduced** – a species introduced to Madagascar by humans

IUCN Red List Status

CRITICALLY ENDANGERED
ENDANGERED
VULNERABLE
NEAR THREATENED

Distribution

▦   common to fairly common
▦   uncommon to rare

Other icons and codes

♀   female
♂   male
br   breeding
nb   non-breeding
im   immature
ju   juvenile

M   Malagasy name
F   French name

Boxes

DIMENSIONS

A grey box contains the species' dimensions. The default dimension, unless noted otherwise, is the total length from the tip of the nose to the tip of the tail. For many reptiles, the distance from the tip of the nose (snout) to the vent (at the base of the tail), the snout to vent length [SVL] is more useful; these instances are marked. For butterflies, wingspan [WS] is the most useful measurement. When males and females are significantly different in size, separate dimensions for the sexes have been included. For mammals, weights are also given.

WHERE TO SEE

This box aims to go beyond abstract ideas of range to give you a substantial idea of where you might find a given species. It might include tips on the best sites for that species, and what times of day and season are best for a search. In mentioning the best sites for each species, a deliberate distinction is made between national parks proper (*e.g.* Andasibe-Mantadia NP) and areas that include a national park (*e.g.* Andasibe area). Finding certain species requires entering a national park, while others can be found both in and around a given park, including disturbed secondary habitat, community forests, and smaller satellite reserves run by community associations or NGOs.

Main Text

DISTRIBUTION: This section goes beyond the information in the range icon to provide more details of where a species is found, both worldwide and within Madagascar. Terms such as 'west' and 'north' used in this section don't necessarily correspond to the names of the biogeographic zones that form the basis for the maps. For example, 'west coast' might refer to the entire west coast of the island, which includes portions of the southwestern and northern zones in addition to the coast of the western zone proper. The distribution section also contains information about what habitat a species prefers.

IDENTIFICATION: This section isn't intended as a detailed description of each species, but rather a quick condensation of the best ways to recognize it and separate it from similar species. Differences between males and females are mentioned here if useful. In some cases, range and habitat information that is immediately relevant to identification is also included.

VOICE: If a species is vocal, its most frequent and distinctive vocalizations are described.

BEHAVIOUR: This variable section includes some further details about how a species lives: whether it's social or solitary, nocturnal or diurnal, arboreal or terrestrial. When they are known, details of diet and reproduction are also often included here.

Inset Boxes

Inset boxes are interspersed throughout the book; these usually highlight something interesting or unusual about a species or group covered by that particular page spread. There are also a few boxes that mention similar species that aren't covered in the main text. This kind of information is also included in the identification section of the main text in some instances.

Photos

The photos on each plate are scaled to illustrate the real size relationship between the species. Sometimes smaller photos of a different scale, such as birds in flight, are included, but these cases should be obvious. Photos included within boxes are at a different scale from the others.

For most species in which males and females are very different, there are captioned photos illustrating the two. In some cases where only one photo is included, but the individual shown can be reliably sexed, this is captioned. Most of the photos were taken by the authors. Photos by other photographers are credited on *pages 328–331*.

Visiting Madagascar

Seasoned international travellers with lots of time and the ability to be flexible can backpack around Madagascar and see most of its wonders. But most people will prefer to visit the country with the help of a tour company. Many international companies run natural history or birding tours to Madagascar. Both of the authors work for Tropical Birding (www.tropicalbirding.com), which offers birding, natural history and photography tours all over the world. Another way to visit Madagascar is with the help of a Malagasy tour operator. Two such companies that are reliable and professional are 8th Continent Expeditions (www.8thcontinentexpeditions.com) and Za Tour (www.zatours-madagascar.com).

Green Bright-eyed Frog *p. 260*

Mammals

About 240 species of mammal have been described from Madagascar, but the basic inventory of its mammal species is ongoing: dozens of new species have been described in recent decades.

- One-third of Madagascar's mammals are considered to be either Critically Endangered or Endangered on the latest IUCN Red List (see *page 27*).

- There are eight orders of mammal represented on Madagascar. The most important groups are illustrated below.

Lemurs (*pages 32–65*). A massive radiation of primates that is endemic to the island. There are five living families, plus a further three that have become extinct.

Tenrecs (*pages 74–77*). Family endemic to Madagascar, apart from a couple of otter-shrews found on the African mainland. Tenrecs have radiated into incredible diversity, ranging from shrew, hedgehog and mole, to otter-like in form.

Rodents (*pages 78–79*). Madagascar supports an endemic sub-family of rodents, whose most remarkable member is the rabbit-like Giant Jumping Rat.

Bats (*pages 70–73*). These flying mammals have colonized the island with relative ease. About 80% of the species are endemic.

Malagasy Carnivorans (*pages 66–69*). These predators comprise an endemic family of ten species, that vary from puma-like to mongoose-like in form.

Whales and dolphins (*pages 80–81*). The warm waters around Madagascar are relatively poor in marine mammals, but a few species are frequently sighted.

- Each of Madagascar's major terrestrial mammal groups: tenrecs, lemurs, rodents and carnivores, seems to have originated from a single colonizing event, most likely animals that rafted their way onto the island. For example, the whole range of lemurs, from tiny mouse lemurs up to the extinct 'gorilla' lemurs, are likely to have evolved from a single common ancestor.

- Several species of mammal appear to have reached Madagascar with human assistance, namely: Asian Musk Shrew *Suncus murinus*, Small Indian Civet *Viverricula indica*, Black Rat *Rattus rattus* and Brown Rat *Rattus norvegicus*, House Mouse *Mus musculus* and Bush Pig *Potamochoerus larvatus*. Of these, the rats and mice are by far the most frequently seen.

- Lemurs are Madagascar's most celebrated biological treasure. Fifteen percent of the world's primate species and subspecies, 20% of its primate genera, and one third of its primate families, are endemic to this island. Lemurs form one of the most prominent voices in the Malagasy forest. Most species are vocal and produce many different calls.

- The majority of Madagascar's mammals are nocturnal. Three of its five lemur families consist of nocturnal species, while bats, tenrecs and rodents are either mainly or entirely nocturnal. The Malagasy carnivorans vary from being mainly diurnal to entirely nocturnal.

- Local guides in all protected areas invariably prioritize lemurs, and are very good at finding their quarry. Seeing most tenrecs, rodents, carnivorans and bats is a matter of luck and the amount of time spent in the forest, particularly on night walks.

- Most lemur species time their breeding for the flush of food that becomes available during the wet season, so most eastern species give birth between September and November, and western species slightly later. One of the reasons to visit Madagascar between October and February is to see lemur babies.

- The identification of most Malagasy mammals is made easier by reference to their ranges. Confusing groups, like woolly lemurs and sportive lemurs, often have only a single species in any one location.

Indri *p. 62* is the largest living lemur

These tiny nocturnal lemurs include the smallest living primate in the world: Madame Berthe's Mouse Lemur *Microcebus berthae*. They closely resemble the galagos, or 'bushbabies', of Africa. Modern taxonomy has seen the number of recognized species increase dramatically from two to 18, and more species may yet be described.

Although mouse lemurs are occasionally found sleeping during the day (resembling tiny fur balls), most sightings are during the night, usually in the form of a pair of eyes bounding about the forest at remarkable speed.

There is some variation in size and colour (from grey to rufous), but all mouse lemurs look very similar, especially with a typical night walk view. According to current information, most can be identified simply by where you are, so refer to the locality and species table on this page.

E **1** # Mouse lemurs *Microcebus* spp. [18 species]

M Tsidy
F Microcèbe

DISTRIBUTION: Found throughout the island in forest and some human-modified habitats such as scrubby secondary forest and plantations.

| Length: | 23–31 cm \| 9–12" |
| Weight: | 30–110 g \| 1–4 oz |

WHERE TO SEE: Almost any Malagasy forest, and many degraded areas, will support at least one species.

ID: Tiny size and near-constant activity separate them from most other lemurs. When seen at close range, the long tail is conspicuous. See giant mouse lemurs (*page 36*) for separation from those species. Most areas of the west hold two species: **Grey Mouse Lemur** **1b** plus one other species (*see below*). Identification in these cases can be very difficult, but compared with Grey Mouse Lemur, **Golden-brown Mouse Lemur** **1f** has warmer brown colour on its back and a longer tail; **Grey-brown Mouse Lemur** **1e** has a rufous stripe along its back, and a more contrasting pale grey-and-rufous facial pattern; and **Madame Berthe's Mouse Lemur** is smaller, with more rufous coloration.

VOICE: High-pitched, squeaky and rather rodent-like.

BEHAVIOUR: Feed mainly on fruit, supplemented with invertebrates and tree gum. Species that are well studied have been shown to give birth to 1–3 young from September to May.

WHICH MOUSE LEMUR AM I LOOKING AT? The most frequently visited sites in Madagascar and the mouse lemur species that can be expected there:

Amber Mountain NP	Montagne d'Ambre Mouse Lemur	*M. arnholdi*
Andasibe-Mantadia NP	Goodman's Mouse Lemur	*M. lehilahytsara*
Andringitra NP	**1a** Rufous Mouse Lemur	*M. rufus*
Anjozorobe-Angavo forest	Goodman's Mouse Lemur	*M. lehilahytsara*
Ankarana NP	**1d** Tavaratra Mouse Lemur	*M. tavaratra*
Ankarafansika NP	**1b** Grey Mouse Lemur	*M. murinus*
	1f Golden-brown Mouse Lemur	*M. ravelobensis*
Berenty	**1b** Grey Mouse Lemur	*M. murinus*
	1e Grey-brown Mouse Lemur	*M. griseorufus*
Isalo NP	**1b** Grey Mouse Lemur	*M. murinus*
Kirindy Forest	**1b** Grey Mouse Lemur	*M. murinus*
	Madame Berthe's Mouse Lemur	*M. berthae*
Marojejy NP	uncertain; Mittermeier's Mouse Lemur?	*M. mittermeieri?*
Masoala NP	undescribed species	*M. sp. nova*
Nosy Be / Lokobe NP	Nosy Be Mouse Lemur	*M. mamiratra*
Nosy Mangabe	**1c** uncertain; Anjiahely Mouse Lemur?	*M. macarthurii?*
Ranomafana NP	**1a** Rufous Mouse Lemur	*M. rufus*
Tsingy de Bemaraha NP	Peters' Mouse Lemur	*M. myoxinus*
Toliara / Ifaty	**1b** Grey Mouse Lemur	*M. murinus*
	1e Grey-brown Mouse Lemur	*M. griseorufus*
Zombitse-Vohibasia NP	**1b** Grey Mouse Lemur	*M. murinus*

Mouse lemurs are fond of licking tree gum, or bananas in the case of the famous Rufous Mouse Lemurs of Ranomafana!

1a

1b

1c

1d

Mouse lemur of uncertain species from Nosy Mangabe

1e

1f

During the day mouse lemurs sleep in tree holes and dense vegetation

Dwarf lemurs are small nocturnal lemurs in the same family as mouse lemurs. They are remarkable as the only primates known to go into a hibernation-like torpor during the dry season (approximately May to September), during which they live off the reserves of fat stored in their tails. Dwarf lemur taxonomy is still imperfectly understood, and there are several undescribed species. There seems to be little overlap in the range of most species, so tentative identifications can be based on the location of a sighting. Refer to the locality and species table on this page.

E **1** Dwarf lemurs *Cheirogaleus* spp. [7+ species]

M Tsidihy, Hataka, Matavirambo
F Cheirogale

DISTRIBUTION: Found almost throughout in forest and some human-modified habitats such as secondary forest and plantations. Generally absent from the High Plateau, and scarce in the southwest.

ID: Larger and slower-moving than mouse lemurs. Smaller and more horizontal than sportive lemurs. Superficially similar to fork-marked lemurs, but with smaller ears, no fork mark on the back, slower movements, and much less vocal. Separation of individual dwarf lemur species can be difficult, with range the best guide. There are three widespread groups. The western and northern *medius* complex (including **Fat-tailed Dwarf Lemur** **1c**) is fairly distinctive: cold grey above and white below, with no warm tones. The eastern and northern *crossleyi* complex (including **Montagne d'Ambre Dwarf Lemur** **1b**) has broad black eye rings and shows a considerable amount of rufous-brown on the head, as well as on the body in some individuals. The eastern *major* complex (including **Greater Dwarf Lemur** **1a**) has intermediate coloration, with colder brown on the head and body, and less black on the face than the *crossleyi* complex.

| Length: | 40–55 cm \| 16–22" |
| Weight: | 0·1–0·5 kg \| 0·3–1·1 lb |

WHERE TO SEE: Amber Mountain, Masoala, and Ankarafantsika NPs, Kirindy Forest, and the Andasibe area are some of the easiest places to find a dwarf lemur.

VOICE: Generally quiet. Calls that have been noted include screams during territorial confrontations, a rising squeak, and a high *"kak-kak-kak..."* similar to the call of the diurnal Broad-billed Roller (*page 140*).

BEHAVIOUR: Move slowly through the trees, with a mainly horizontal posture. Give birth during the wet season to 1–4 young, with 2–3 being the most common. Diet consists of fruit, nectar, leaves, buds, and insects.

WHICH DWARF LEMUR AM I LOOKING AT? The most frequently visited sites in Madagascar and the dwarf lemur species that can be expected there:

Amber Mountain NP	**1b** Montagne d'Ambre Dwarf Lemur	*C. andysabini*
Andasibe-Mantadia NP	Crossley's (or Furry-eared) Dwarf Lemur	*C. crossleyi*
Andringitra NP	undescribed species – *crossleyi* complex	*C.* sp. *nova*
Anjozorobe-Angavo forest	Crossley's (or Furry-eared) Dwarf Lemur	*C. crossleyi*
	Sibree's Dwarf Lemur	*C. sibreei*
Ankarana NP	undescribed species – *medius* complex	*C.* sp. *nova*
Ankarafantsika NP	**1c** possible **undescribed species** – *medius* complex	*C.* sp. *nova?*
Kirindy Forest	Fat-tailed Dwarf Lemur	*C. medius*
Marojejy NP	possible undescribed species – *crossleyi* complex	*C.* sp. *nova?*
Masoala NP / Nosy Mangabe	**1a** Greater Dwarf Lemur	*C. major*
Ranomafana NP	undescribed species – *crossleyi* complex	*C.* sp. *nova*
Sainte Marie Island	**1a** Greater Dwarf Lemur	*C. major*
Tsingy de Bemaraha NP	Fat-tailed Dwarf Lemur	*C. medius*
Zombitse-Vohibasia NP	Fat-tailed Dwarf Lemur	*C. medius*

1a Species in the *major* group have colder tones and a smaller black 'mask' than those in the *crossleyi* group. This is a Greater Dwarf Lemur from Maroantsetra.

1b Species in the *crossleyi* group show some warm rufous tones. This individual is a Montagne d'Ambre Dwarf Lemur.

Species in the *medius* group (including Fat-tailed Dwarf Lemur) are cold grey on back, with no warm tones. This individual is from a possible undescribed species in Ankarafantsika NP.

1c

Giant mouse and fork-marked lemurs are also members of the nocturnal Cheirogaleidae family. In general, they are seen much less frequently than mouse or dwarf lemurs.

E **1** # Giant mouse lemurs *Mirza coquereli / Mirza zaza*

M Tsiba
F Microcèbe Géant

DISTRIBUTION: Coquerel's Giant Mouse Lemur *M. coquereli* **1a** is found in the southern half of western Madagascar, in dry forest. **Northern Giant Mouse Lemur** *M. zaza* **1b** is found in forest fragments and plantations in the northwest.

ID: Combination of size, large ears, and active habits will normally identify them. The long, reddish tail is dark towards the end.

VOICE: Makes a quiet *"swiiick"* call, especially at the start of the wet season.

BEHAVIOUR: Nocturnal and typically solitary. Move actively, although not as frenetically as typical mouse lemurs (*page 32*). Diet is catholic: fruit, flowers, tree gum, invertebrates, and even small vertebrates. Give birth to twins.

ENDANGERED	
Length:	54–57 cm | 21–22"
Weight:	0·3 kg | 0·7 lb

WHERE TO SEE: Although uncommon **Coquerel's Giant Mouse Lemur** can be seen during night walks in Kirindy Forest. Also occurs in Zombitse and Tsingy de Bemaraha NPs. **Northern Giant Mouse Lemur** does not occur in any frequently visited protected areas, but can be seen in plantations around the town of Ambanja.

E **2** # Fork-marked lemurs *Phaner* spp. [4 species]

M Tanta
F Phaner

DISTRIBUTION: Pale Fork-marked Lemur *P. pallescens* **2a** is found in the west, **Sambirano** *P. parienti* (not illustrated) and **Montagne d'Ambre Fork-marked Lemurs** *P. electromontis* **2b** in the north, and **Masoala Fork-marked Lemur** *P. furcifer* (not illustrated) in the northeast. Fork-marked lemurs are found both in forest and some disturbed habitats like plantations.

ID: If seen, the fork marks on the back of the head are diagnostic.

VOICE: One of the most vocal groups of nocturnal lemurs. The most common call is a piercing *"wheet"* much like the 'laser gun' call of Crested Coua (*page 126*). Also give chattering and squirrel-like calls.

BEHAVIOUR: Move faster than all other lemurs except the mouse lemurs (*page 32*). Often found in small groups. Specialize in eating tree sap and gum.

ENDANGERED / VULNERABLE	
Length:	52–66 cm | 20–26"
Weight:	0·3 kg | 0·7 lb

WHERE TO SEE: **Pale Fork-marked Lemur** is common during night walks in Kirindy Forest, and also occurs in Zombitse and Tsingy de Bemaraha NPs. The rarely seen **Masoala Fork-marked Lemur** is found around Masoala. **Sambirano Fork-marked Lemur** occurs in the northwest, and is sometimes seen around Ambanja. **Montagne d'Ambre Fork-marked Lemur** is occasionally seen on Amber Mountain.

2b

1a

1b

Large ears and long bushy tail

Dark line on back which forks on the head

2a

Sometimes sits horizonally, but at other times is more vertical

Sportive lemurs are classified as an entirely separate family. They are rather chunky, with big eyes and ears, and have a vertical posture. These nocturnal lemurs are often seen during the day, roosting in tree cavities or dense tangles. At night, they move about with impressive leaps, while retaining their vertical posture.

This is another group, like the mouse lemurs, where the number of recognized species (currently 26) has increased dramatically in recent years, and new species may yet be described. These species look very similar, especially at night, but show some variation in size, colour, prominence of the ears, and other traits. However, it is unusual for two species to coexist, and so most can be identified by location (see table below).

E **1** ## Sportive lemurs Lepilemur spp. [26 species]

M Hataka, Boengy, Apongy
F Lépilémur

DISTRIBUTION: Throughout the island, in forested habitats, including spiny forest.

Length:	43–64 cm | 17–25"
Weight:	0·5–1·2 kg | 1–2·6 lb

ID: Similar in size to dwarf lemurs (page 34), but have a vertical rather than horizontal posture. They also tend to sit most of the time, making occasional leaps, rather than constantly moving about in a tree. Often confused with woolly lemurs (page 54), which are also nocturnal and regularly seen in habitual sleeping sites during the day. However, woolly lemurs have less prominent ears and have pale stripes on the back of their thighs; they are also more likely to be found during the day in a family huddle than the more solitary sportive lemurs.

WHERE TO SEE: Night walks in forest almost anywhere on the island can result in sightings.

1g

VOICE: Quite vocal, especially at the beginning of the wet season. Calls are emphatic grunts, squeals, and screams.

BEHAVIOUR: During the day, they sleep in tree cavities and forks, and dense tangles. Local guides often know the whereabouts of sportive lemur sleeping sites and are able to show them to visitors. Feed on leaves, nectar, and fruit. The breeding habits of most species are poorly known, but they are thought to give birth to a single young at the beginning of the wet season.

Small-toothed Sportive Lemur from Ranomafana NP, one of the darker species

WHICH SPORTIVE LEMUR AM I LOOKING AT?
The sportive lemur species that occur at the most frequently visited sites in Madagascar:

Site		Species
Amber Mountain NP	**1a** Ankarana Sportive Lemur	L. ankaranensis
Andasibe-Mantadia NP	Weasel Sportive Lemur	L. mustelinus
Andringitra NP	**1g** Small-toothed Sportive Lemur	L. microdon
Anjozorobe-Angavo forest	Weasel Sportive Lemur	L. mustelinus
Ankarana NP	**1a** Ankarana Sportive Lemur	L. ankaranensis
Ankarafansika NP	**1f** Milne-Edwards' Sportive Lemur	L. edwardsi
Berenty	**1c** White-footed Sportive Lemur	L. leucopus
Isalo NP	**1d** Red-tailed Sportive Lemur	L. ruficaudatus
Kirindy Forest	**1d** Red-tailed Sportive Lemur	L. ruficaudatus
Marojejy NP	Seal's Sportive Lemur	L. seali
Masoala NP	Masoala Sportive Lemur	L. scottorum
Nosy Be / Lokobe NP	**1e** Nosy Be Sportive Lemur	L. tymerlachsonorum
Ranomafana NP	**1g** Small-toothed Sportive Lemur	L. microdon
Tsingy de Bemaraha NP	Bemaraha Sportive Lemur	L. randrianasoloi
Toliara / Ifaty	Uncertain; Petter's Sportive Lemur?	L. petteri?
Zombitse-Vohibasia NP	**1b** Zombitse Sportive Lemur	L. hubbardorum

1a Occasionally has a horizonal posture

1b Usually sleeps in tree holes or tangles during the day

1c Long, bushy tail. Some species of sportive lemur show a dark line on the back

1d

1e

1f

Bamboo lemurs are members of the 'true lemur' family, all of which are active during the day. As their name suggests, bamboo lemurs eat bamboo and are usually found in stands of it. Three of the six Malagasy species are covered here.

E **1** # Greater Bamboo Lemur *Prolemur simus*

M Varibolo, Godroka
F Grand Hapalémur

DISTRIBUTION: Formerly widespread, but now restricted to a few patches of rainforest in the central and southern parts of eastern Madagascar.

ID: Much larger than other bamboo lemurs. Has a broad face and white ear-tufts.

VOICE: Gives quiet *"chuck"* notes and a short, rising, raspy trill.

BEHAVIOUR: Like Golden Bamboo Lemur, eats mainly Giant Bamboo *Cathariostachys madagascariensis*, although it prefers the pith inside the canes, leaving impressively mangled bamboo stalks in areas where it has fed. One baby is born in October or November.

WHERE TO SEE: Ranomafana NP is famous for this species, but the small population that is normally seen by visitors is under threat and may soon vanish, for reasons that are poorly understood. Another place to see this species is Torotorofotsy, a site near Mantadia NP that is managed by Association Mitsinjo. Entrance tickets and a local guide can be arranged at their office near Andasibe.

CRITICALLY ENDANGERED	
Length:	85–90 cm | 2·9'
Weight:	2·2–2·5 kg | 4·9–5·5 lb

The main food is the pith inside Giant Bamboo stems

Broad face and white ear-tufts

E ① **Grey Bamboo Lemur** *Hapalemur griseus*

M Bokombolo, Kotrika
F Petit Hapalémur Gris

DISTRIBUTION: Found in rainforest with bamboo throughout the central and southern parts of eastern Madagascar. Also found in dry forest in the west, although rarely seen by visitors there.

ID: Reminiscent of a sportive lemur, but active during the day, and their ears and eyes are much smaller. The very similar **Northern Bamboo Lemur** *Hapalemur occidentalis* (not illustrated) is found in the north and northeast, and is occasionally seen in Marojejy and Masoala NPs.

VOICE: Not very vocal. Sometimes gives a quiet grunting similar to that given by brown lemurs, and a plaintive squeal.

BEHAVIOUR: Sometimes feeds sluggishly for long periods, but highly active at other times, making impressive leaps. Usually alone or in small groups. Feeds on bamboo and other plant material. One infant is born at the beginning of the wet season.

VULNERABLE	
Length:	67 cm | 2·2'
Weight:	0·7–0·8 kg | 1·5–1·9 lb

WHERE TO SEE: Easiest to see in Andasibe-Mantadia NP, with tame individuals often along the main trail in the Analamazaotra section of the park. Also fairly common in Ranomafana NP. Occasionally seen in Tsingy de Bemaraha NP.

E ② **Golden Bamboo Lemur** *Hapalemur aureus*

M Bokombolomena
F Hapalémur Doré

DISTRIBUTION: Very small range in the rainforest of the southeast.

ID: The golden colour of this species distinguishes it from both the smaller Grey Bamboo Lemur and the larger Greater Bamboo Lemur (*page 40*).

VOICE: Vocal. Gives a quiet grunting similar to that of brown lemurs. The territorial call is a complicated clucking and whistling.

BEHAVIOUR: Usually seen in small groups, feeding placidly within a thick stand of Giant Bamboo *Cathariostachys madagascariensis*. One infant is born in November or December.

CRITICALLY ENDANGERED	
Length:	70–80 cm | 2·3–2·6'
Weight:	1·3–1·7 kg | 2·9–3·7 lb

WHERE TO SEE: Ranomafana NP, which exists in large part due to the discovery of this species there in 1985. Local guides are skilled at tracking this flagship species.

2

Golden Bamboo Lemur has an amazing ability to process the potent poison cyanide, which is found in large quantities in its favourite food: the young shoots and leaves of Giant Bamboo.

1

The race around Andasibe (*right*) is rich brown in colour; the race in the west and southeast (*below*) is paler and greyer

2

Young shoots of Giant Bamboo are a favourite food

This handsome member of the 'true lemur' family is the best-known Malagasy creature, the face of the island's biodiversity. It is also the best-studied of the island's lemurs, and even gives its name to a popular souvenir shop.

E **1** # Ring-tailed Lemur *Lemur catta*

M Maky
F Maki

DISTRIBUTION: Found in the southern third of Madagascar in a range of habitats, from spiny forest up to the high mountains of Andringitra. Despite its extensive range, its actual distribution is quite fragmented.
Like most lemurs, it is threatened by forest clearance for charcoal, pasture and agriculture; hunting for food; and capture as pets.

ID: Black eye patches and a ringed tail make it unmistakable.

VOICE: Plaintive hoots and raucous chattering, often given in concert by groups.

BEHAVIOUR: Lives in mixed-sex groups of up to 30, in which females are dominant. Typically, a single infant is born in September. Diet consists of a large variety of plant material, plus small animals.

> Although females are socially dominant, male Ring-tailed Lemurs still vie for the attention of females. They stage 'jumping fights' in which they slash at each other with their upper canines. They also engage in 'stink fights' in which they ritually waft scent at each other.

ENDANGERED	
Length:	95–110 cm | 3–3.5'
Weight:	2.2–3.5 kg | 4.8–7.7 lb

WHERE TO SEE: Berenty is famous for this species. It can also be found in Isalo and Andringitra NPs, as well as in the small community-run Parc Anja near Ambalavao along the RN7 highway.

Lemur feet are leathery, with long toes

1

1

Commonly seen in trees

The most terrestrial lemur

Vocal

Black nose and rings around the eyes

Brown lemurs are a large genus (*Eulemur*) within the 'true lemur' family, and include some of the lemur species most frequently seen by visitors. There are 12 species, of which eight are covered in this guide.

Brown lemurs are medium-sized, vocal, and generally found in groups. Unusually for lemurs, the male and female of most species have obviously different coloration. They are generally diurnal, but can also be active at night. Fruit is their most important food, although other plant parts and small animals are also eaten. This is another group in which the number of species has increased in recent years, due to the recognition of several species that were formerly considered subspecies of Brown Lemur.

E **1** Sanford's Brown Lemur *Eulemur sanfordi*

M Ankomba, Beharavoaka
F Lémur de Sanford

DISTRIBUTION: Found in both rainforest and dry forest in the far north.

ID: The male has white tufts around the face, while the female is quite plain. Occurs alongside the similarly sized Crowned Lemur (*page 50*), but has a very different facial pattern.

VOICE: Makes a guttural grunting, often imitated by local guides, and also gives a squealing call.

BEHAVIOUR: Active during both day and night, usually in small groups. Young are born in September or early October. Feeds on fruit, leaves, and flowers. Often found in mixed groups with Crowned Lemur.

ENDANGERED	
Length:	88–95 cm | 3'
Weight:	1·8–1·9 kg | 4 lb

WHERE TO SEE: Not hard to find in Amber Mountain and Ankarana NPs.

E **2** White-fronted Brown Lemur *Eulemur albifrons*

M Varikosy
F Lémur à Front Blanc

DISTRIBUTION: Rainforest in the northeast, with distribution centred on Maroantsetra.

ID: The male has a mostly white head and is unmistakable, although the female is drabber. This is the only brown lemur likely to be seen in most of the sites where they occur.

VOICE: Similar to Sanford's Brown Lemur.

BEHAVIOUR: Similar to Sanford's Brown Lemur.

ENDANGERED	
Length:	89–96 cm | 2·9–3·2'
Weight:	~2 kg | 4·4 lb

WHERE TO SEE: Fairly common on Nosy Mangabe, on Masoala, and in Marojejy NP.

1

1♀ 1♂

Male (*right*) shows pale tufts on head; female (*left*) is plainer

2♀ 2♂

Male (*right*) shows a mostly white head; female (*left*) has a dark head

E **1** (Common) **Brown Lemur** *Eulemur fulvus*

M Varika
F Lémur Brun

DISTRIBUTION: Common in rainforest in the central and northern parts of the east, dry forest in the northwest, and forest fragments on the High Plateau. Introduced to Mayotte.

NEAR THREATENED

Length:	84–101 cm | 2·7–3·3'
Weight:	1·7–2·1 kg | 3·7–4·6 lb

WHERE TO SEE:
Common around Andasibe. Less common but still easy to see in Ankarafantsika NP.

ID: A medium-sized brownish lemur with a blackish face. Male and female look similar. In the east, occurs with Red-bellied Lemur, which is darker red-brown overall, with a black tail, and white marks in front of the eyes of males. In Ankarafantsika NP, occurs alongside Mongoose Lemur (*page 50*), which is greyer overall, and has different male and female facial patterns, both of which are different from Brown Lemur.

VOICE: Fairly vocal. Most distinctive call is a mechanical rasping wail that is often given in concert by a whole group at the same time. Also gives a pig-like grunt which is often imitated by local guides.

BEHAVIOUR: Found in small to medium-sized groups which feed on fruits, leaves and flowers, often remaining in one small area; capable of rapid movement through the forest.

E **2** **Red-fronted Brown Lemur** *Eulemur rufifrons*

M Gidro
F Lémur à Front Roux Méridional

DISTRIBUTION: Fairly common though local both in eastern rainforest and western dry forest, in the southern half of Madagascar.

NEAR THREATENED

Length:	85–103 cm | 2·7–3·4'
Weight:	average 2·3 kg | 5 lb

WHERE TO SEE: Ranomafana, often along the main road through the national park. Also common in Kirindy Forest.
Red-fronted Brown Lemur and Red-collared Brown Lemur *Eulemur collaris* (not illustrated) have both been introduced to Berenty, where they hybridize.

ID: Male has a bright rufous patch on top of the head and a greyish back. Female is brownish with dull rufous on the head. In the east, occurs alongside Red-bellied Lemur, which is darker red-brown overall, with a black tail, and a different facial pattern. In Tsingy de Bemaraha NP, replaced by the very similar **Rufous Brown Lemur** *Eulemur rufus* (not illustrated).

VOICE: Similar to Brown Lemur.

BEHAVIOUR: Similar to Brown Lemur.

E **3** **Red-bellied Lemur** *Eulemur rubriventer*

M Tongona, Barimaso
F Lémur à Ventre Rouge

DISTRIBUTION: Widespread in eastern rainforest, although absent from Masoala Peninsula.

VULNERABLE

Length:	78–93 cm | 2·6–3·1'
Weight:	1·6–2·4 kg | 3·5–5·3 lb

WHERE TO SEE: Ranomafana NP, including along the main trails. Also occurs in Andasibe-Mantadia NP, but much less common there.

ID: Male has a reddish-brown body and bold white 'teardrop' marks on its face. Female has a pale belly and less distinct 'teardrops'. Both sexes have a black tail, and are more reddish in overall coloration than other brown lemurs.

VOICE: Rising, quizzical *"whooey"* that sounds like some calls of Common Myna (*page 176*). Also gives quiet grunts and a series of pure, whistled notes.

BEHAVIOUR: Similar to Brown Lemur, although generally more retiring and difficult to see.

1

Medium-sized brownish lemur with mostly blackish face

2♀

2♂

Male grey on back with rufous on top of head; female brownish

3♀

Female has pale belly

3♂

Male shows white 'teardrops'

E **1** # Black Lemur *Eulemur macaco*

M Komba
F Lémur Macaco

DISTRIBUTION: Found in a small area of northern Madagascar in primary and secondary Sambirano forest, timber plantations, and areas of mixed cultivation and forest. Seems more tolerant of disturbance than many lemurs.

ID: All-black male is unique. The female with its overall brown coloration and white facial tufts is also unmistakable within its range.

VOICE: Most common call is a distressed squeal, often given by a group in concert.

VULNERABLE	
Length:	90–110 cm | 2·9–3·6'
Weight:	1·8–1·9 kg | 4 lb

WHERE TO SEE: In Lokobe NP on Nosy Be, or on a tourist excursion to Nosy Komba, where a tame group of lemurs seems to subsist mainly on handouts.

BEHAVIOUR: Much like other *Eulemur* species. Feeds mainly on fruit, and is active both day and night. A single young is born between September and November.

E **2** # Crowned Lemur *Eulemur coronatus*

M Ankomba Fiaka
F Lémur Couronné

DISTRIBUTION: The most northerly of Madagascar's lemurs, almost reaching Cap d'Ambre at the island's northern tip. Uses both moist and dry forest, including degraded forest.

ID: Male is rufous-grey, and female pale grey. Both show a diagnostic crown patch, which is black in the male and rufous in the female.

VOICE: Gives a distressed squeal, very similar to that of Black Lemur.

ENDANGERED	
Length:	75–85 cm | 2·5–2·8'
Weight:	1·1–1·3 kg | 2·4–2·9 lb

WHERE TO SEE: Fairly common and conspicuous in Amber Mountain and Ankarana NPs. Often around the camping sites in both national parks.

BEHAVIOUR: Much like other *Eulemur* species. Found in small groups up to about 15 individuals. Often associates with Sanford's Brown Lemur (*page 46*). Eats mainly fruit, and is active both day and night. Young are born between mid-September and October.

E **3** # Mongoose Lemur *Eulemur mongoz*

M Dredrika
F Lémur Mongoz

DISTRIBUTION: Dry forest in the northern part of western Madagascar. Also introduced to the Comoros.

ID: Found alongside the similar Brown Lemur (*page 48*) in Ankarafantsika NP. Mongoose Lemur is paler and greyer overall, and shows strong white patches on the snout, whereas Brown Lemur has an all-black face.

VOICE: Fairly quiet. Gives a long, pig-like snore, and a rasping hiss.

CRITICALLY ENDANGERED	
Length:	75–83 cm | 2·5–2·7'
Weight:	1·1–1·6 kg | 2·4–3·5 lb

WHERE TO SEE: Fairly common in Ankarafantsika NP. Watch the mango trees around the park headquarters, both during the day and at night.

BEHAVIOUR: Generally similar to other *Eulemur* species, although found in smaller groups and generally less conspicuous. Young are born in October.

1♂

1♀

Both sexes have tufts on the sides of the head.
All-black male very different from female

2♂

2♀

Male is rufous-grey, with black on top of the head; female is pale grey, with a rufous 'crown'

3♂

3♀

Male grey, with rufous on the face; female mostly grey, with white below

E 1 Black-and-white Ruffed Lemur *Varecia variegata*

M Varikandana
F Vari Noir-et-blanc

DISTRIBUTION: Lowland and middle-elevation rainforest in the east. Its range is patchy and fragmented.

ID: Large, long-tailed, black-and-white lemur. Similar in size and coloration to Indri (*page 62*), but that species has a very short tail.

VOICE: Extremely loud and distinctive: aggressive and almost agonized screaming, often given by a whole group in concert, and answered by neighbouring groups.

BEHAVIOUR: Generally found high in the canopy. Capable of tremendous leaps, but they often do not move much for long periods. Normally found in small groups. Feeds mainly on fruit, often hanging by its back legs to feed. Female gives birth to twins, which are placed in a nest when young. Ruffed lemurs seem to be unique among primates in this nesting behaviour.

CRITICALLY ENDANGERED

Length:	1·1–1·2 m | 3·5–3·9'
Weight:	3·1–3·6 kg | 6·8–7·9 lb

WHERE TO SEE: Can usually be found in the Mantadia sector of Andasibe-Mantadia NP with some effort. Also in Ranomafana NP, where it can often be heard on the farther (southeastern) reaches of the main trail system, but is difficult to see due to the precipitous terrain.

E 2 Red Ruffed Lemur *Varecia rubra*

M Varimena, Varignena
F Vari Roux

DISTRIBUTION: Primary rainforest on the Masoala Peninsula, in the northeast.

ID: Large size and red colour render it unmistakable.

VOICE: Similar to Black-and-white Ruffed Lemur: very loud and vocal.

BEHAVIOUR: Similar to Black-and-white Ruffed Lemur. Female gives birth to 2–3 young between September and early November.

CRITICALLY ENDANGERED

Length:	1–1·2 m | 3·3–3·9'
Weight:	3·3–3·6 kg | 7·3–7·9 lb

WHERE TO SEE: Fairly common and conspicuous in and around Masoala NP. Sometimes in forest along the beach near the tourist lodges, but more commonly in the adjacent primary forest.

There is a large amount of variation in the pattern of black and white on the Black-and-white Ruffed Lemur. There are three different subspecies described, which some experts consider full species: '**Variegated**' *Varecia variegata*, '**Southern**' *V. editorum*, and '**Northern**' *V. subcincta*. '**Southern**' can be seen in Ranomafana and Andasibe-Mantadia NPs, while '**Northern**' may be encountered on Nosy Mangabe. '**Variegated**' is best seen in Betampona Special Nature Reserve, well off the normal tourist circuit. '**Northern**' shows the most black, with an all-black rump and half-black hindlegs. '**Southern**' has a white rump, and a smaller patch of black on the hindlegs. '**Variegated**' is similar to Southern, but with a white band along its back.

1

1

1

'Northern' Black-and-white Ruffed Lemur (*below*) has much black on its back half

2

2

The 'red panda' of Madagascar!

Ruffed lemurs are extremely loud and vocal, and often hang upside down

Woolly lemurs are members of the family Indriidae, which also includes the sifakas (*pages 56–61*) and the Indri (*page 62*). All Indriidae are characterized by vertical clinging and leaping behaviour, resting upright against a support, and moving through the forest in impressive leaps of up to 10 m (33 feet). Woolly lemurs are quite different from the rest of the family, being much smaller, and nocturnal rather than diurnal. They are often pointed out at day roosts by local guides in national parks. As in many other groups of lemur, there has been a flurry of new species recognized in recent decades. There are now nine described woolly lemurs, and that number may grow further. Several species are very local and will be seen only by visitors heading to remote parts of the island. All woolly lemurs are similar, with only subtle differences between them; fortunately, most locations have only a single species, which can be identified by reference to the table below.

E **Woolly lemurs** *Avahi* spp. [9 species]

M Fotsife, Avahy, Ampongy
F Avahi

DISTRIBUTION: Found in forest, including secondary forest. Six of the nine species are found in the eastern rainforest, one in the Sambirano forest of the north, and two in the dry forest of the west.

ID: Superficially similar in size and shape to sportive lemurs (*page 38*). The easiest way to distinguish a woolly lemur is normally the white stripes on the back of the thighs. Woolly lemurs found at a day roost are often in huddles of multiple family members, whereas this is uncommon in sportive lemurs. Dwarf lemurs (*page 34*) are smaller, have a more horizontal posture, and tend to crawl rather than leap when on the move.

VOICE: A high-pitched, grunted *"avahi"*, which gives the genus its name. Also produces a long, descending series of quavering whistles.

BEHAVIOUR: Generally sluggish, perhaps due to its nutrient-poor diet of leaves. Groups sleep huddled together during the day. The single young is born in August or September.

ENDANGERED / VULNERABLE	
Length:	48–70 cm | 19–28"
Weight:	0·9–1·4 kg | 2–3 lb

WHERE TO SEE: Eastern Woolly Lemur is often found at day roosts or at night in the Andasibe area. **Western Woolly Lemur** is frequent in Ankarafantsika NP. **Peyriéras' Woolly Lemur** is occasionally found in Ranomafana NP.

WHICH WOOLLY LEMUR AM I LOOKING AT?
The woolly lemur species that occur at the most frequently visited sites in Madagascar:

Site		Common name	Species
Andasibe-Mantadia NP	1b	Eastern Woolly Lemur	A. laniger
Andohahela NP		Southern Woolly Lemur	A. meridionalis
Andringitra NP		Peyriéras' Woolly Lemur	A. peyrierasi
Anjozorobe-Angavo forest	1b	Eastern Woolly Lemur	A. laniger
Ankarafansika NP	1c	Western Woolly Lemur	A. occidentalis
Marojejy NP	1b	Eastern Woolly Lemur	A. laniger
Masoala NP	1a	Masoala Woolly Lemur	A. mooreorum
Ranomafana NP		Peyriéras' Woolly Lemur	A. peyrierasi
Tsingy de Bemaraha NP		Bemaraha Woolly Lemur	A. cleesei

Nocturnal lemurs can be easily spotted at night by their conspicuous eye shine

1a

1b

Typical daytime sighting of a 'ball' of half-asleep Eastern Woolly Lemurs

1c

1b

Vertical posture is typical of all Indriidae, including woolly lemurs

Smaller ears than sportive lemurs; conspicuous white stripe on thighs

Sifakas are among the biggest, best-known, and most engaging of the island's lemurs. Seeing all nine species is something of an accomplishment for lemur-watchers, as the species are scattered all around the island, and some of them are very rare and local. Although all species are similar in diet and behaviour, the sifakas in the eastern rainforest tend to live at lower densities, in smaller groups with larger home ranges.

E **1** Decken's Sifaka *Propithecus deckenii*

M Sifaka Fotsy*
F Propithèque de von der Decken

DISTRIBUTION: Dry forest in the central part of western Madagascar.
ID: A large white sifaka with a black face.
VOICE: Explosive *"see-fak"* similar to Verreaux's Sifaka.
BEHAVIOUR: Similar to Verreaux's Sifaka.

Crowned Sifaka (*page 60*) has a small range, wedged between those of Decken's and Coquerel's Sifakas.

ENDANGERED	
Length:	0·9–1·1 m | 3–3·6'
Weight:	3–4·5 kg | 6·6–9·9 lb

WHERE TO SEE: Easy to see at Tsingy de Bemaraha NP. Also common and tame in the remote Beanka Forest, north of Bemaraha.

E **2** Coquerel's Sifaka *Propithecus coquereli*

M Sifaka Mena Sandry*
F Propithèque de Coquerel

DISTRIBUTION: Dry forest in the northwest.
ID: A large chestnut, black and white lemur.
VOICE: Explosive *"see-fak"* similar to Verreaux's Sifaka.
BEHAVIOUR: Found in groups of 3–10. Diet and most behaviours similar to other sifakas. Single young born in June or July.

ENDANGERED	
Length:	0·9–1·1 m | 3–3·6'
Weight:	3·7–4·3 kg | 8·1–9·5 lb

WHERE TO SEE: Ankarafantsika NP, often around the headquarters.

E **3** Verreaux's Sifaka *Propithecus verreauxi*

M Sifaka
F Propithèque de Verreaux

DISTRIBUTION: Spiny forest and other kinds of dry forest in the southwest.
ID: A large, mostly white lemur with a dark brown crown. Occasionally shows dark grey on limbs and back. Unmistakable within its range.
VOICE: The harsh *"see-fak"* alarm call gives this group of animals its common name.
BEHAVIOUR: Found in groups from 2–14, averaging 5–6. They move through trees by making often-spectacular leaps, and sometimes also along the the the ground with an extraordinary 'dancing' motion. The diet consists of leaves, fruit, and flowers. The single young is born in July or August.

ENDANGERED	
Length:	0·9–1·1 m | 2·9–3·6'
Weight:	3–3·5 kg | 6·6–7·7 lb

WHERE TO SEE: This is one of the lemurs for which Berenty is famous, and that is where most 'dancing lemur' photos have been taken. Also easy to find in Kirindy Forest, and occurs in Zombitse and Isalo NPs, although it can be more elusive in those parks.

Despite jumping powerfully between octopus trees (*page 318*) in the spiny forest, Verreaux's Sifakas seem to avoid damage to their hands and feet.

1 Whitest of the western sifakas

2 Mostly white; dark brown crown

Dark brown marks on limbs; white head, black face

3

1 All sifakas are capable of incredible leaps (*above*); sifakas 'dance' to cross treeless areas (*below*).

3

Sifaka coloration The nine species of sifaka vary from all-white (Silky) to all-black (Perrier's), these two extremes living in fairly close geographical proximity to each other in northern Madagascar. There is also considerable colour variation within some species. The taxonomic status of the sifakas is still controversial, and some experts recognize fewer than nine species.

E ① Silky Sifaka *Propithecus candidus*

M **Simpona Fotsy**
F **Propithèque Soyeux**

DISTRIBUTION: Rainforest on and around the Marojejy Massif of the northeast.
ID: The whitest of the sifakas, with a black face, which in some individuals is mottled with pink.
VOICE: Similar to Milne-Edwards' Sifaka.
BEHAVIOUR: Diet consists of leaves, fruit, and seeds. A single infant is born in June or July.

CRITICALLY ENDANGERED	
Length:	0·9–1·1 m | 3·1–3·4'
Weight:	5–6 kg | 11–13 lb

WHERE TO SEE: In Marojejy NP. Usually not too difficult to find around Camp Marojejia, the middle of the park's three camps. This rare beauty is worth the hike.

E ② Milne-Edwards' Sifaka
Propithecus edwardsi

M **Simpona Mainty***
F **Propithèque de Milne-Edwards**

DISTRIBUTION: Middle- and high-elevation rainforest in the southern part of eastern Madagascar.
ID: A large, dark sifaka that cannot be confused with anything else in its range.
VOICE: Not very vocal, but makes an explosive sneezing *"simpona"*, which gives it its Malagasy name, and also a series of grunts and a plaintive whistle.
BEHAVIOUR: Social habits and diet similar to other sifakas. Young are born in June and July.

ENDANGERED	
Length:	0·8–1·0 m | 2·6–3·3'
Weight:	5·0–6·5 kg | 11–14 lb

WHERE TO SEE: With some effort, can be found in Ranomafana NP, either on the main trails or the Vohiparara Trail.

E ③ Diademed Sifaka *Propithecus diadema*

M **Simpona**
F **Propithèque à Diadème**

DISTRIBUTION: Rainforest in the north-central part of eastern Madagascar.
ID: A large grey, gold, and white sifaka.
VOICE: Similar to Milne-Edwards' Sifaka.
BEHAVIOUR: Similar to other sifakas.

CRITICALLY ENDANGERED	
Length:	0·9–1·1 m | 3·1–3·4'
Weight:	6–8·5 kg | 13–19 lb

WHERE TO SEE: Andasibe-Mantadia NP. The reintroduced sifakas in the Analamazaotra part of the park are the easiest to see.

Can show pink on face

Mostly black

Whitest sifaka

Most colourful sifaka

E ① **Perrier's Sifaka** *Propithecus perrieri*

M Ankomba Joby
F Propithèque de Perrier

DISTRIBUTION: Small area of dry forest in the far north.
ID: An unmistakable all-black sifaka.
VOICE: Gives an explosive sneezing call.
BEHAVIOUR: Similar to other sifakas, although groups are smaller: from 2–6 individuals.

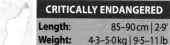

CRITICALLY ENDANGERED	
Length:	85–90 cm | 2·9'
Weight:	4·3–5·0 kg | 9·5–11 lb

WHERE TO SEE: Requires a special visit to the Andrafiamena protected area, run by the NGO FANAMBY. For accommodation, there is a community campsite and a newly constructed lodge called 'Black Lemur Camp'. Also found in the Analamerana Special Reserve, administered by Madagascar National Parks.

E ② **Tattersall's** (Golden-crowned) **Sifaka**
Propithecus tattersalli

M Ankomba Malandy
F Propithèque de Tattersall

DISTRIBUTION: Small area of dry forest in the far north.
ID: A mostly white sifaka with gold on top of the head, which gives this species its alternative English name.
VOICE: Various calls include a *"see-fak"* call similar to that of Verreaux's Sifaka (*page 56*).
BEHAVIOUR: Found in groups of 3–10. Young are born in July and August.

CRITICALLY ENDANGERED	
Length:	87–94 cm | 2·8–3·1'
Weight:	average 3·5 kg | 7·7 lb

WHERE TO SEE: Will require a visit to the remote Daraina region of the far north. There is a protected area run by FANAMBY where this sifaka can easily be found. Visitors can bring their own camping gear or stay at the Camp Tattersalli tented camp. Visits should be coordinated through FANAMBY.

E ③ **Crowned Sifaka** *Propithecus coronatus*

M Sifaka Mainty Loha*
F Propithèque Couronné

DISTRIBUTION: Small area of dry forest in the northwest.
ID: Separated from Decken's Sifaka (*page 56*) by its all-dark head.
BEHAVIOUR: Not well known, but generally similar to other sifakas.

ENDANGERED	
Length:	0·9–1 m | 2·8–3·3'
Weight:	3·5–4·3 kg | 7·7–9·5 lb

WHERE TO SEE: One accessible site is the tiny Antrema Forest, near the lighthouse a few kilometres north of Katsepy, and across the Betsiboka River from Mahajanga. Another site is the Bombetoka-Belemboka Forest, near the village of Boanamary, south of Mahajanga. This site is managed by FANAMBY, and visits should be coordinated through them.

2

A Tattersall's Sifaka demonstrating the astounding leaping abilities typical of all the sifakas.

1 Blackest sifaka

3 All-dark head

2 Tufty ears and gold crown

3 All sifakas have long, powerful hind legs

The Indri is one of Madagascar's best-known creatures and is classified as the sole member of its genus within the sifaka family.

E **1** **Indri** *Indri indri*

DISTRIBUTION: The central and northern portions of the eastern rainforest. Absent from the Masoala Peninsula.

ID: This is the heaviest living lemur. Although its colour is variable, the Indri's size, short tail, and bushy ear-tufts make it unmistakable.

VOICE: One of the world's great natural sounds. Groups start calling with a breathless hooting, and then break into long, slurred, remarkably loud notes, almost deafening at close range. Indris are most vocal during the morning and in the wet season, but may call at any time, even at night.

BEHAVIOUR: Lives in small groups of 2–6, with females seemingly the dominant individuals. Like other members of the sifaka family, it generally sits in a vertical position, but is capable of incredibly powerful leaps through the forest. Eats leaves, along with some fruit, flowers, seeds, bark, and a daily dose of soil. Female gives birth every two or three years to a single infant, born in May or June.

CRITICALLY ENDANGERED	
Length:	69–77 cm | 2·2–2·5'
Weight:	6–9·5 kg | 13–21 lb

WHERE TO SEE: The flagship species of Andasibe-Mantadia NP. The habituated Indris of the Analamazaotra portion of the park are usually easy to find. Although the Indris in Mantadia are often shy, that sector of the park offers the wonderful experience of hearing several groups counter-sing across a rugged landscape. The black form of Indri can be found in the Anjozorobe-Angavo forest, accessed via Saha Forest Camp.

Extinct Megafauna The Indri, as the largest living lemur, is a reminder of Madagascar's lost megafauna. At least 17 extinct lemur species have been identified from subfossils. All of these were larger than the Indri, some much larger. There were three 'koala lemurs', weighing as much as 85 kg (187 lb); a whole family of 'sloth lemurs', many of which climbed through trees upside down, in sloth fashion, and probably weighed almost 200 kg (441 lb); and even a giant aye-aye. Human activity contributed to the extinction of these giant lemurs, although they may have survived until well after the first Europeans visited Madagascar.

The Malagasy name for Indri, Babakoto, roughly translates as 'father of man'

Very short tail

Extremely vocal

This remarkable creature is one of the world's most bizarre animals. Its strangest features are its perpetually growing incisor teeth and its thin, elongated middle fingers, which are used to extract larvae from dead wood. Although it was sometimes considered to be a rodent in the past, recent genetic studies have placed it firmly in the lemurs. It forms its own family (one of Madagascar's five lemur families), whose exact relationship to the other lemurs is still uncertain. An extinct giant aye-aye is known from subfossils.

E **1** **Aye-aye** *Daubentonia madagascariensis*

M Hay-Hay
F Aye-aye

DISTRIBUTION: Perhaps the most widely distributed lemur. Found in most of the forested environments on the island, although absent from the southwestern spiny forest.

ENDANGERED	
Length:	74–90 cm | 2·4–2·9'
Weight:	2·5 kg | 5·5 lb

ID: The large eyes and ears, and grizzled black fur are distinctive. Larger than other nocturnal lemurs.

VOICE: Rarely heard *"aye-aye-aye"* that gives the species its name.

BEHAVIOUR: Nocturnal and generally solitary. One of its most important foods is the nut of the Ramy tree *Canarium madagascariense*, but it feeds on a variety of larvae, seeds, nectar, and fruit. Signs of Aye-aye feeding, such as gnawed nuts and holes in trees, are seen much more often than the animals themselves. Nests are often used for sleeping during the day. The birth of a single young does not seem to be seasonal; the female gives birth every 2–3 years.

WHERE TO SEE: A remarkably shy and elusive nocturnal creature. Although Aye-aye is present in most national parks, it is very rarely seen. The best chance is on Ile Roger, or 'Aye-aye Island', which hosts an introduced population. This island is located off Mananara-Nord, in the northeast. Visits can be arranged by the owner of Chez Robert in Mananara-Nord, who owns the island. Nosy Mangabe, off Maroantsetra, was formerly good for Aye-aye, but the current ban on night walks in national parks has made it virtually impossible to find there. Some visitors have found Aye-aye on night walks around the town of Maroantseta.

Nightlife of the Eighth Continent

A visit to Madagascar would not be complete without at least one night walk in dry forest and another in rainforest. This is the best way to see a remarkably high proportion of the island's wildlife. About half of the lemurs, several birds, and many geckos, snakes, and frogs are best sought at night, and chameleons are easiest to find when they sleep on conspicuous low tree limbs.

Good local guides have flashlights, but keen visitors should bring a headlamp, and perhaps a more powerful light.

Most mammals are easily spotted by their 'eyeshine' and local guides are remarkably good at finding amphibians and reptiles. Night walks inside the national protected area system have been prohibited for the last few years and visitors are now restricted to walks along main roads, in peripheral zones, or in community forests and other alternative reserves.

Huge ears; mix of black and white hairs

The incisors grow constantly, like those of a rodent (*above*); the middle finger is almost skeletal (*below*)

There are 11 species of Malagasy carnivorans, of which the four most likely to be seen by visitors are covered here. Sighting even one of these four species takes some luck, as these are scarce and retiring creatures.

E **1** **Ring-tailed Vontsira** *Galidia elegans*

M Vontsira
F Vontsira à Queue Annelée

DISTRIBUTION: Found in most of the island's rainforest, and in Sambirano forest. Scarce in the western dry forest, and absent from the spiny forest.

ID: Dark reddish coloration and long, ringed tail easily identify it: formerly called Ring-tailed Mongoose.

VOICE: The most frequently heard call is a high-pitched whistle. Also gives a low-pitched, quiet chattering.

BEHAVIOUR: Generally diurnal, and found alone or in small groups, on the ground or in trees. Its diverse diet includes small mammals, birds, reptiles, amphibians, fish and invertebrates. Young are born between November and January.

| Length: | 55–69 cm | 22–27" |
| Weight: | 0·8–1·1 kg | 1·7–2·4 lb |

WHERE TO SEE: Fairly tame individuals can be seen around the campsites in Ankarana and Amber Mountain NPs. Also seen regularly in eastern rainforest, especially Ranomafana NP, and in western dry forest in Tsingy de Bemaraha NP.

E **2** **Northern Bokiboky** *Mungotictis decemlineata*

M Bokiboky
F Mungotictis

DISTRIBUTION: A small area of western dry forest centred on Morondava.

ID: Mongoose-like shape, with long nose and bushy tail. Eight to ten fine lines on the back and sides: formerly called Narrow-striped Mongoose.

VOICE: Quiet *"tok tok tok"* calls, given by members of group to stay in touch.

BEHAVIOUR: Generally diurnal and social, found in groups of up to 12. Most often on the ground, but also climbs trees. Eats mainly insects, but also other invertebrates, small mammals, and reptiles. The single young is born between October and December.

ENDANGERED		
Length:	45–56 cm	18–22"
Weight:	0·4–0·5 kg	0·9–1·2 lb

WHERE TO SEE: Fairly common in Kirindy Forest, often in the camp itself.

E **3** **Spotted Fanaloka** *Fossa fossana*

M Fanaloka
F Fanaloka Tacheté

DISTRIBUTION: Mainly in eastern rainforest, although also occurs in drier forest in the north.

ID: Heavily spotted and striped on the back. Quite similar to the introduced **Small Indian Civet** *Viverricula indica* (not illustrated), but the civet is larger, with thicker legs, a longer body, and a tail with complete rings.

VOICE: Not frequently heard, but does make a contact call described as *"coq-coq"*.

BEHAVIOUR: A shy, nocturnal species that is found singly or in pairs, usually on the ground or low in trees. Feeds on small mammals, reptiles, frogs and invertebrates. The single young is born during the wet season.

VULNERABLE		
Length:	62–71 cm	24–28"
Weight:	< 1·9 kg	4·2 lb

WHERE TO SEE: Extremely shy. Formerly habituated at 'Belle Vue' along the main trails at Ranomafana NP, but the current night walk ban precludes seeing this species there. Occasionally spotted elsewhere in Ranomafana NP, in Ankarana NP, and in other parks, but seeing this animal requires luck.

1 Northern individuals (pictured) very red; darker in the east; black legs and belly in the west

Long and low to ground; complete bands on tail

Fine lines on back; pointed face

2

3

Rows of spots on back; incomplete bands on tail

E **1** **Fosa** *Cryptoprocta ferox*

M Fosa
F Cryptoprocte

DISTRIBUTION: Although rarely seen, the Fosa is found in virtually all of the intact forest on the island, and will even venture out of forest into agricultural areas and villages during the night.

ID: This long-tailed, heavy-jawed, puma-like carnivoran is the largest living indigenous land mammal in Madagascar, and is unlikely to be mistaken for anything else.

VOICE: Most common call is a quiet, ominous, grunted *"meow"*. During the mating season, the male gives a low roar, while the female makes a wild, higher-pitched howling.

BEHAVIOUR: Active both day and night. Equally at home on the ground and high in trees, the Fosa is the feared predator of Madagascar, preferring mammals, including the largest lemurs and the introduced **Bush Pig** *Potamochoerus larvatus* (not illustrated). It will also eat smaller carnivorans, Giant Jumping Rat, tenrecs, reptiles, birds, amphibians, invertebrates and domestic animals. Between two and four young are born during the wet season.

VULNERABLE	
Length:	1·4–1·7 m | 4·6–5·6'
Weight:	5–10 kg | 11–22 lb

WHERE TO SEE: Generally hard to find. Kirindy Forest is the best location. Sightings there are likely between May and October, and almost guaranteed during the November mating season. Also regularly seen in Ankarana, Andasibe-Mantadia, and Zombitse-Vohibasia NPs, most often during November, when pairs may mate for hours high in the trees.

Con-fosa-ing Two animals are often called 'fosa' in Malagasy: the **Fosa** proper (alternately 'fosa varika'), and the **Spotted Fanaloka** (*page 66*). Adding to the confusion, the scientific name of the Spotted Fanaloka is *Fossa fossana* due to some confusion when this species was described. The rare **Falanouc** *Eupleres goudotii* (not illustrated) may also be referred to as 'fosa', so care is needed when when discussing carnivoran sightings, especially with local guides who are helping you to search for these creatures.

Male Fosas have the largest penis bone in relation to their size of any land mammal, and pairs engage in snarling bouts of mating that can last for hours.

1

Shaped like a stretched-out mountain lion

Equally at home in trees and on the ground

Powerful feet and jaws

There are at least 45 species of bat in Madagascar, of which nearly 80% are endemic. Most Malagasy bat lineages originated from Africa, but at least one Asian group is also represented. Many of these species are virtually impossible to distinguish based on typical night-time views in flight. The few species that are distinctive even in flight, or that are frequently seen when roosting, are the ones covered here. For most bats, wingspan (WS) is given as well as length.

E **1** # Madagascar Straw-coloured Fruit Bat
Eidolon dupreanum

M Angavo
F Roussette Paillée de Madagascar

DISTRIBUTION: Throughout Madagascar, in a variety of habitats.
ID: Large, but smaller than Madagascar Flying Fox. Shows duller buff coloration, a narrower snout, and narrow whitish wings in flight.
VOICE: High-pitched squeals and chatters.
BEHAVIOUR: Forms roosts during the day, which often contain hundreds of individuals. At night, ventures out to feed on fruit, nectar and pollen.

VULNERABLE	
Length:	19–22 cm | 7–9"
WS:	75–95 cm | 2·5–3·1'
Weight:	0·2–0·3 kg | 0·6–0·8 lb

Narrower muzzle than flying fox

WHERE TO SEE: At night may be seen in many places. Well-known day roosts include *Raphia* palms in Tsimbazaza Zoo, Tana, caves in Ankarana NP, and cliffs in Tsingy de Bemaraha NP.

E **2** # Madagascar Flying Fox *Pteropus rufus*

M Fanihy
F Renard Volant de Madagascar

DISTRIBUTION: Found throughout, mainly in forest, although day roost sites are often outside of forest, for example in *Eucalyptus* plantations.
ID: A huge bat with a wingspan of about 1 m (3·3'), looking almost pterodactyl-like in flight. The Madagascar Straw-coloured Fruit Bat is similar but smaller, with a more pointed and less fox-like face, and whitish wings, visible in flight.
VOICE: High-pitched chattering.
BEHAVIOUR: Forms roosts during the day that can contain thousands of individuals. At night, ventures out to feed on fruit, masticating the pulp, then spitting it out after extracting the juice.

VULNERABLE	
Length:	24–27 cm | 9–11"
WS:	1–1·3 m | 3·3–4·1'
Weight:	0·5–0·8 kg | 1·1–1·7 lb

Broad muzzle

WHERE TO SEE: There is a large roost at Berenty. Also not difficult to see on and around Nosy Mangabe, on Masoala, and on Nosy Tanikely near Nosy Be.

1 Dull buffy coloration

2 Bright buffy coloration

① Mauritian Tomb Bat *Taphozous mauritianus*

M Ramanavy
F Taphien de Maurice

DISTRIBUTION: Found throughout much of the Afrotropics and the Malagasy region. Widespread in many habitats, but seemingly absent from the far north.
ID: Bicoloured: grey on the back and white below. Distinctly upright roosting posture, often supporting the body with folded wings.
VOICE: Quiet chatter.

Length:	10–11 cm	4"
Weight:		30g	1·1 oz

WHERE TO SEE: Can usually be found roosting on trees around the headquarters at Ankarafantsika NP.

BEHAVIOUR: During the day, sleeps in small groups on tree trunks, cliffs, and man-made structures. Stays alert, and may fly off if disturbed. Feeds on insects at night.

E ② Commerson's Leaf-nosed Bat
Hipposideros commersoni

M Valo Orona
F Phyllorhine de Commerson

DISTRIBUTION: Occurs widely in forested habitats.
ID: The relatively large size and bizarre 'leaf-nose' are distinctive. Trident bats *Triaenops* spp. and *Paratriaenops* spp. (not illustrated) are similar, but much less frequently seen by casual visitors. Trident bats can be recognized by the three fleshy spikes protruding from the top of the nose.

NEAR THREATENED		
Length:	11–15 cm	4–6"
WS:	48–67 cm	19–22"
Weight:	40–80g	1·4–2·8 oz

WHERE TO SEE: Can occasionally be found during the day or on night walks in Kirindy Forest, Nosy Mangabe, and Ankarana, Ankarafantsika, and Tsingy de Bemaraha NPs.

BEHAVIOUR: Roosts in small groups in caves and hollow trees. At night, hunts insects and perhaps small frogs.

The caves in Ankarana and Tsingy de Bemaraha NPs are good for several bat species, including the **Madagascar Free-tailed Bat** *Otomops madagascariensis* ③.

1 Small nose and rounded ears

1 Grizzled grey back

2 Large nose and large, pointed ears

Tenrecs are among Madagascar's most engaging creatures, but are unfortunately difficult to see. There are 32 described species, the majority of which are shrew tenrecs *Microgale* spp., which are rarely observed by non-specialists. The largest and most frequently encountered tenrecs are covered here.

E **1** ## Greater Hedgehog Tenrec *Setifer setosus*

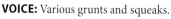

M Sokina
F Grand Tenrec-hérisson

DISTRIBUTION: Throughout Madagascar in most habitats, sometimes even in large towns.

ID: A spiny tenrec that is similar to Lesser Hedgehog Tenrec, but is larger and has a more pointed snout. Smaller than Common Tenrec (*page 76*), and covered in spines rather than coarse fur.

VOICE: Various grunts and squeaks.

BEHAVIOUR: Nocturnal. Forages on the ground for invertebrates and fruit, but can climb into vegetation. When threatened, it rolls into a ball. During the dry season, aestivates in tree hollows. One to four young are born early in the wet season.

| Length: | 16–23 cm | 6–9" |
| Weight: | 0·2–0·3 kg | 0·4–0·7 lb |

WHERE TO SEE: Not uncommon during the wet season, and can be found during night walks in most of the popular protected areas.

E **2** ## Lesser Hedgehog Tenrec *Echinops telfairi*

M Tambotriky
F Petit Tenrec-hérisson

DISTRIBUTION: Southwestern and central-western Madagascsar, in spiny forest and dry forest.

ID: A spiny tenrec that is similar to Greater Hedgehog Tenrec, but is smaller, with a less pointed snout.

BEHAVIOUR: Nocturnal. Found both in trees and on the ground. During the dry season, aestivates in a hollow tree. Feeds on invertebrates and fruit. When threatened, rolls into a ball. One to ten young are born in the wet season.

| Length: | 14–18 cm | 5·5–7" |
| Weight: | 110–230 g | 4–8 oz |

WHERE TO SEE: Night walks during the wet season in Berenty, Kirindy Forest, and around Ifaty.

Hedgehog tenrec defensive posture

1

Smaller than Common Tenrec
(*page 76*), and has spines

2

Snout slightly shorter than that of
Greater Hedgehog Tenrec

❶ ① Lowland Streaked Tenrec
Hemicentetes semispinosus

M Sora
F Tenrec Zébré des Terres Basses

DISTRIBUTION: Eastern Madagascar, in lowland and mid-elevation rainforest, and adjacent human-modified areas.

ID: Covered in spines. Distinctive pattern of black and cream stripes along the body. **Highland Streaked Tenrec** *Hemicentetes nigriceps* (not illustrated) is similar and can be found in Andringitra NP; it has broader and paler stripes, and is less spiny.

VOICE: Makes quiet sounds by vibrating the spines.

BEHAVIOUR: Mainly nocturnal. Roots through leaf-litter to find invertebrates. When threatened, it erects the spines and twitches towards an antagonist. Two to 11 young are born in the wet season.

| Length: | 13–19 cm | 5–8" |
| Weight: | 90–220 g | 3–8 oz |

WHERE TO SEE: Common at night in the villages adjacent the main cluster of lodges on the Masoala Peninsula. Also occasionally found around Andasibe and Ranomafana. Most sightings are in the wet season.

❶ ② Common Tenrec *Tenrec ecaudatus*

M Trandraka
F Hérisson Malgache

DISTRIBUTION: Throughout Madagascar in open grassland, forest, and edge habitat. Introduced to the Comoros, Seychelles, and Mascarenes.

ID: The largest tenrec. Adults have shaggy, uniformly brownish fur. Young have stripes and resemble Lowland Streaked Tenrec, but will usually be with their mother.

BEHAVIOUR: Largely nocturnal and solitary. Roots in leaf-litter and soil to find invertebrates, small vertebrates and fruit. Aestivates during the dry season, and the young are born in December or January.

| Length: | 29–40 cm | 11–16" |
| Weight: | 1–2 kg | 2·2–4·4 lb |

WHERE TO SEE: Scarce due to hunting, but possible in most protected areas, especially at night during the wet season.

2

The Common Tenrec is one of the world's most prolific mammals, with a brood size up to 32! The female has a remarkable 17 pairs of nipples, while the retractable penis of the male is almost as long as its whole body.

1

Lowland Streaked Tenrecs can communicate with an ultrasonic sound produced by quivering a special set of spines on their backs!

2

The largest tenrec

There are 30 species of rodent known from Madagascar. Of these, 27 comprise a subfamily that is endemic to the island, while the other three are introduced species. Most Malagasy rodents are difficult to find; the introduced rodents are seen more often than any indigenous species. Covered here are the rodents that are most likely to be spotted by visiting naturalists.

E 1 Red forest rats Nesomys spp. [3 species]

M Voalavomena
F Rat Rouge Forestier*

DISTRIBUTION: Mainly eastern rainforest: Eastern Red Forest Rat N. rufus **1b** at middle and high elevations and Lowland Red Forest Rat N. audeberti **1c** at lower elevations. The rare Western Red Forest Rat N. lambertoni **1a** is found locally in dry forest in the west.

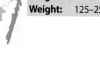

| Length: | 31–41 cm | 12–16" |
| Weight: | 125–250 g | 4·4–8·8 oz |

ID: Always have redder tones to their fur than other rats.
BEHAVIOUR: Diurnal and exclusively terrestrial, feeding on seeds and fruits on the forest floor.

WHERE TO SEE: Eastern Red Forest Rat occurs in Ranomafana, Andasibe-Mantadia and Marojejy NPs. **Lowland Red Forest Rat** can be seen in the lower parts of Ranomafana NP, and in Masoala NP. The uncommon **Western Red Forest Rat** is restricted to Tsingy de Bemaraha NP.

E 2 Tuft-tailed rats Eliurus spp. [12 species]

M Sokitralina, Voalavon'ala
F Rat à Queue Touffue*

DISTRIBUTION: Found in forest throughout. Most species are endemic to eastern rainforest, with a few extending to the north, and two restricted to the west.

| Length: | 22–38 cm | 9–15" |
| Weight: | 20–125 g | 1–4·4 oz |

ID: Long tail (longer than body), with a conspicuous tuft towards the end.
BEHAVIOUR: All species are nocturnal, and most are strictly or mainly arboreal.

WHERE TO SEE: Western Tuft-tailed Rat E. myoxinus **2a** is the species most frequently seen during night walks in Kirindy Forest and Ankarafantsika NP. Tuft-tailed rats are also occasionally seen in eastern rainforest parks. Look for eyeshine in the forest, but much fainter than that of nocturnal lemurs.

E 3 Giant Jumping Rat Hypogeomys antimena

M Vositsy
F Rat Géant Sauteur

DISTRIBUTION: Small area of western dry forest north of Morondava.

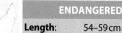

ENDANGERED	
Length:	54–59 cm	21–23"
Weight:	average 1·2 kg	2·6 lb

ID: This large and unmistakable species is the flagship rodent of Madagascar. It is more like a rabbit than a typical rat: grey-brown in colour and with big ears.
BEHAVIOUR: Nocturnal. Walks on forest floor, feeding on plant material. One or two young are born in the wet season.

WHERE TO SEE: Can be found only in Kirindy Forest, often in the camp itself. Becomes active about three hours after sunset, later than most nocturnal mammals.

Western Big-footed Mouse Macrotarsomys bastardi (not illustrated) is an endemic rodent that is occasionally seen in western forests, particularly Ankarafantsika NP and Kirindy Forest. It looks and acts like a gerbil, hopping along the ground in a manner resembling a mini kangaroo.

1a

Dark reddish-brown

1b

The reddest of the three species

1c

Dark brown, with a bushy tail

Introduced Rodents

Black Rat *Rattus rattus* is found throughout, sometimes even in the forest. **Brown** (or Norway) **Rat** *R. norvegicus* (not illustrated) is more local, mainly found in towns. **House Mouse** *Mus musculus* (not illustrated) is found throughout, in association with humans, as well as in marshy areas.

Black Rat

2a

3

Rabbit-like ears

Madagascar is not especially rich in marine mammals, but it is a renowned place to see Humpback Whale, and dolphins are sometimes sighted.

1 Humpback Whale *Megaptera novaeangliae*

M Trozona
F Baleine à Bosse

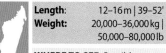

DISTRIBUTION: Found in oceans almost worldwide. One population that spends the summer in cold Antarctic waters migrates thousands of kilometres every year, visiting the Madagascar coast to breed and calve during the austral winter, from May to December. The Bay of Antongil is used in July and August as a major breeding and calving site.

ID: A huge marine mammal with a humped back, short stubby dorsal fin and distinctive long flippers that are mostly white. Sightings of other whales are rare in Malagasy waters.

VOICE: Renowned for its complex, ever-changing undersea song.

BEHAVIOUR: One of the most demonstrative whales due to its frequent breaching, tail and flipper slapping, and bubble-feeding behaviours. Feeds on krill and small fish. The female gives birth to a single calf.

Length:	12–16 m	39–52'
Weight:	20,000–36,000 kg	50,000–80,000 lb

WHERE TO SEE: Possible anywhere around the coast, especially to the east between May and December. St. Marie Island hosts a large whale-watching industry, with July to September being the best time. The Bay of Antongil (bounded by the Masoala Peninsula) is less developed for whale-watching, but sightings are also dependable there.

2 Common / Indo-Pacific Bottlenose Dolphin
Tursiops truncatus / aduncus

M Feso
F Grand Dauphin / Grand Dauphin de L'Océan Indien

DISTRIBUTION: Found in warm and temperate oceans worldwide. Occurs all around Madagascar's coast. These two species were recently split, and the identity of the dolphins in Malagasy waters remains to be determined.

ID: A large, chunky, generally uniformly greyish dolphin with a sturdy, bottle-like beak. This classic, familiar species accounts for the vast majority of dolphin sightings around Madagascar. **Spinner Dolphin** *Stenella longirostris* (not illustrated) is occasionally seen, usually far offshore; it averages smaller and slimmer, with a much longer beak; and often spins when it leaps out of the water.

VOICE: Uses clicks to echolocate prey.

BEHAVIOUR: A social animal that lives in pods, normally containing up to 15 individuals, but sometimes comprising hundreds. Active and playful, and makes spectacular leaps out of the water. Feeds mainly on fish, krill, and squid. Females give birth to a single calf.

Length:	2–4 m	7–13'
Weight:	150–650 kg	330–1,430 lb

WHERE TO SEE: Possible anywhere around the coast, but most frequently seen in the Nosy Be area.

Each individual has distinctive tail markings

Very demonstrative, often breaching or slapping tail or flippers on the surface

Short, stubby dorsal fin

1

2

Dolphins often leap out of the water

Birds

Almost 300 species of bird have been recorded in Madagascar. Of those, about 260 occur regularly, 100 are endemic, and another 30 are Malagasy regional endemics. Four bird families are endemic to Madagascar, and a further two endemic to the Malagasy region.

● Birds have a much greater ability to cross water barriers than groups like reptiles and amphibians. The modern Malagasy avifauna is the result of many 'colonization events', from Africa, Asia and probably even Australasia. Some of these events were ancient, while others were much more recent. Only the recently extinct elephant birds pre-dated the breakup of Gondwanaland; all other bird lineages have colonized the island subsequently.

● Several birds have reached Madagascar with human assistance, namely Feral Pigeon (*page 120*), Common Myna (*page 176*) (unfortunately now the island's most common bird), House Crow *Corvus splendens* (not illustrated: so far restricted to Toamasina) and House Sparrow *Passer domesticus* (not illustrated: still not widespread).

● One of the notable things about Malagasy birds is their relative silence compared to birds elsewhere. Few species have particularly complex or musical songs, and many species simply do not vocalize very often. Lemurs and frogs are usually the predominant voices in Malagasy forest.

● Birds are generally common and conspicuous in Madagascar. Unfortunately, there are vast deforested stretches of the country with only a handful of native species, plus the ever-present introduced Common Myna. Although rainforest birding is always difficult, Madagascar's rainforest birds tend to be more approachable and less shy than rainforest birds elsewhere in the world. To find retiring forest specialties like mesites and ground-rollers, the best strategy is to enlist the services of guides who specialize in birding.

● Some Malagasy birds breed year-round, but most do so during the wet season. As such, they are most vocal between October and December in the rainforest, and slightly later in the dry forest.

● Migration is inconspicuous on Madagascar, even compared to mainland Africa. There are a few species, such as Madagascar Pratincole (*page 114*), Madagascar Cuckoo (*page 126*) and Broad-billed Roller (*page 140*) that breed on the island then migrate to the mainland during Madagascar's dry season. Madagascar also hosts some birds from Europe and Asia, predominantly shorebirds, that migrate south to escape the northern winter.

● Bird identification on Madagascar is generally straightforward, as there is not the diverse range of drab birds found in most of the world's tropics.

Couas, like these Giant Couas, are members of the cuckoo family.

- Shorebirds and terns can be difficult to identify, but their diversity is relatively low in Madagascar, reducing the chances of confusion.

- Among forest birds, the only tricky ones are the warbler-like birds, most of which are best found and identified by song.

- Sadly, Madagascar's biggest and perhaps best birds have already become extinct. There were at least five species of elephant bird, one of which, *Aepyornis maximus*, was the largest bird that the world has ever known. It stood about three metres (ten feet) tall and weighed as much as 400 kg (880 lb). Its enormous eggs were larger even than those of the largest dinosaurs, and the largest single cell known to biology.

- The arrival of humans seems to have doomed the elephant birds, along with all of the larger mammals such as pygmy hippopotamuses and 'gorilla' lemurs, although they probably survived until well after Madagascar's first contact with Europe. Sturdy fragments of elephant bird eggs can still be found on the beaches of the southwest, a sad reminder of Madagascar's lost biological riches.

Endemic bird families: Madagascar

Mesites (*page 102*). Strange, primitive, rail-like, ground-dwelling birds.

Asities (*page 148*). A small family of gem-like birds. Also a primitive group.

Bernierids (*page 162*). A family of cryptic species, the existence of which has only recently been recognized.

Ground-rollers (*pages 142–147*). Colourful birds that can easily be overlooked by those who are not prepared to search for them.

Endemic bird families: Malagasy Region

Cuckoo-roller (*page 146*). One species, found on both Madagascar and the Comoros. It is a strange and enigmatic bird whose loud calls often dominate the rather quiet Malagasy forest.

Vangas (*pages 166–175*). Madagascar's counterpart of Darwin's finches, this family has close ties to some African groups and has evolved to exhibit an incredible diversity on Madagascar.

① Little Grebe *Tachybaptus ruficollis*

M Vivy
F Grèbe Castagneux

Length:	23–29 cm | 9–11"

WHERE TO SEE: Generally uncommon, but can be seen on almost any lake or pond. Even in Tana at Lake Alarobia.

DISTRIBUTION: Europe, Afrotropics, and much of Asia. Fairly common though local throughout Madagascar on freshwater lakes and ponds, and occasionally rivers.
ID: Much smaller than any duck, with a pointed bill. Bright chestnut and dark grey in breeding plumage **1br** and dull brownish at other times **1nb**. The less common but also widespread, although Vulnerable, **Madagascar Grebe** *T. pelzelnii* is smaller, and generally prefers ponds and lakes in more forested environments. In breeding plumage, it has a diagnostic white stripe behind the eye and a pale throat. Very similar to Little Grebe in non-breeding plumage.
VOICE: A loud, rattling trill sometimes reveals its presence on a pond before it is seen.
BEHAVIOUR: Usually in pairs. Dives to catch fish.

Madagascar Grebe has a pale throat and a white stripe behind the eye.

② Red-billed Duck (Teal) *Anas erythrorhyncha*

M Menamolotra
F Canard à Bec Rouge

Length:	43–48 cm | 17–19"

WHERE TO SEE: Fairly common in Tana, especially at Lake Alarobia. Often seen on ponds around Isalo and Anjozorobe.

DISTRIBUTION: Eastern and southern Afrotropics. Locally common throughout Madagascar on freshwater wetlands, especially marshes and shallow lakes. Will use flooded rice paddies, but not as commonly as White-faced Whistling-duck.
ID: Much slimmer than whistling-ducks, with red bill, pale cheeks and dark cap, and a swifter flight.
BEHAVIOUR: Feeds on aquatic plants and invertebrates by dabbling. Forms flocks, especially when not breeding.

③ White-faced Whistling-duck *Dendrocygna viduata*

M Tsiriry
F Dendrocygne Veuf

Length:	44–48 cm | 17–19"

WHERE TO SEE: Common around Tana, especially at Lake Alarobia. Also common in the west, especially Ankarafantsika and Tsingy de Bemaraha NPs, and around Maroantsetra.

DISTRIBUTION: Central and South America and the Afrotropics. Locally common throughout Madagascar on freshwater wetlands, including lakes, ponds and rice paddies. The most common duck in Madagascar.
ID: Mostly rufous and dark brown, with a white face and finely barred flanks The superficially similar **Fulvous Whistling-duck** *Dendrocygna bicolor* (not illustrated) is golden-brown, lacks the white face, and is much less common.
VOICE: Distinctive, insistent, three-part whistle, most often given by birds in flight, sometimes at night.
BEHAVIOUR: Social; frequently in flocks. In some areas, roosts during the day and feeds on rice paddies at night to avoid persecution. Feeds mostly on aquatic plants.

1

1nb

1br

1br

Duck-like, but smaller than any duck

Mostly brown, with a red bill

2

2

3

Colourful, with a white face and dark bill

3

E 1 Madagascar Partridge
Margaroperdix madagarensis

M Tsipoy
F Perdrix Malgache

DISTRIBUTION: Endemic to Madagascar, and introduced to Mascarenes. Widespread but uncommon and local in grassland, scrub and other open habitats.
ID: The beautiful rufous and grey, speckled and spotted male is unmistakable; female much more drab; its larger size and more powerful flight distinguish it from Madagascar Buttonquail.
BEHAVIOUR: Generally shy, although it will occasionally walk onto roads and into other open areas, especially at dawn and dusk. Most often seen when flushed into explosive and startling flight.

Length: 24–26 cm | 9–10"
Where to see: Widespread but never common. Sometimes in the grasslands around Isalo, Anjozorobe and Tsingy de Bemaraha NP. Occasionally even along the runway at the Ivato Airport in Tana.

R 2 Madagascar Buttonquail *Turnix nigricollis*

M Kibobo
F Turnix Malgache

DISTRIBUTION: A regional endemic found on Madagascar and Réunion. Found in most habitats except rainforest interior and wetlands. Most common in grassland, dry scrub, spiny forest and western dry forest.
ID: Tiny size and quail-like shape are distinctive. Male is pale brown, while the female is much more colourful, with a black breast patch and a rufous side to the neck.
VOICE: Quiet, low-pitched, pulsing *"huhuhuhuhu…"*.
BEHAVIOUR: Runs on the ground. Often feeds by rotating and kicking away the leaf-litter, leaving clean circles of bare earth. The male incubates the eggs and cares for young.

Length: 14–16 cm | 6"
WHERE TO SEE: Possible anywhere, but most common in western dry forest (as at Ankarafantsika NP and Kirindy Forest) and spiny forest.

Although they look like quails, buttonquails are in a completely different family whose closest relatives are still not certain. They have recently been considered to be relatives of the cranes, but may actually be most closely related to gulls and sandpipers.

Buttonquail feeding circles

3 Helmeted Guineafowl *Numida meleagris*

M Akanga
F Pintade de Numidie

DISTRIBUTION: Most of the Afrotropics. Thinly distributed throughout Madagascar in a wide variety of habitats, including savannah, scrub, forest edge, forest and marsh. Probably colonized Madagascar without human assistance.
ID: A large, distinctive and familiar bird with a colourful bare head and copious small white spots on the body.
VOICE: A loud series of harsh clucks that speeds up then slows down: a classic sound of the African bush.
BEHAVIOUR: Highly social and usually found in flocks. Roosts in tall trees at night. Feeds on seeds, small fruits and invertebrates.

Length: 55–60 cm | 22–24"
Where to see: Generally uncommon, but can be seen almost anywhere. Frequently sighted around Ankarafantsika and Tsingy de Bemaraha NPs, Berenty, and the lodges on the Masoala Peninsula.

The Malagasy name for guineafowl (Akanga) seems to have come from Kiswahili (Kanga).

1♂ Male colourful

1♀ Female brownish

2♀ Female colourful

2♂ Male brownish

Heavily spotted

3

e 1 Grey Heron *Ardea cinerea firasa*

M Vanokasira
F Héron Cendré

DISTRIBUTION: Most of Europe, Africa and Asia. In Madagascar mostly along the west coast, in a variety of both salt and freshwater wetlands. Uncommon in the interior, sometimes on rice paddies.
ID: Tall, long-necked bird with grey wings and pale head and underparts. Larger and paler than Purple Heron (*page 90*) and slightly smaller and paler than Madagascar Heron.
VOICE: A loud and grumpy *"graaak"* mainly given in flight.
BEHAVIOUR: Usually solitary. Stands motionlessly or slowly stalks prey, which includes fish and almost any other animal.

| Length: | 0·9–1·0 m | 3′ |

WHERE TO SEE: Most easily found in the west, as in wetlands around Morondava and Toliara.

R 2 Madagascar (Humblot's) Heron *Ardea humbloti*

M Vorompasika
F Héron de Humblot

DISTRIBUTION: Rare and local in Madagascar and the Comoros. Mainly coastal, although very rare on most of the east coast. Uses both salt and freshwater wetlands.
ID: Large size, massive bill and dark grey colour. Darker and more uniform than Grey Heron.
VOICE: Similar to Grey Heron.
BEHAVIOUR: Similar to Grey Heron; sometimes shows hostility to that closely related species.

ENDANGERED

| Length: | 1·0–1·1 m | 3·3–3·6′ |

WHERE TO SEE: Most common in the west, such as wetlands in and around Ankarafantsika NP and coastal flats around Toliara. Occasionally seen at Lake Alarobia in Tana.

Madagascar Heron (*left*) with Grey Heron (*right*); on average, Madagascar Heron is slightly larger

1

1

Pale grey and white, with black marks on neck and head

2

2

Dark grey

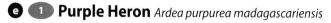

e **1** **Purple Heron** *Ardea purpurea madagascariensis*

M Vanomena
F Héron Pourpré

DISTRIBUTION: Much of Europe, Africa and Asia. Found throughout Madagascar in small numbers, preferring freshwater marshes with dense reedbeds.
ID: Medium-sized heron that is mostly slate grey, with a heavily striped neck. Smaller than Grey and Madagascar Herons (*page 88*).
VOICE: Similar to Grey and Madagascar Herons.
BEHAVIOUR: Mainly solitary, waiting motionlessly before stabbing prey, which comprise a wide range of fish, invertebrates, frogs and lizards.

Length:	78–86 cm | 2·6–2·8'

WHERE TO SEE: More widespread than the previous two herons. Can be seen in small numbers in wetland habitat almost anywhere on the island.

2 **Black Heron** *Egretta ardesiaca*

M Lombokohomana
F Aigrette Ardoisée

DISTRIBUTION: Afrotropics. Locally fairly common throughout Madagascar, mainly in freshwater wetlands. Often feeds in rice paddies.
ID: Small and compact all-black heron with bright yellow feet. Distinguished from dark morph Little Egret (*page 92*) by shorter neck and bill, dark throat, and lack of any white in the wing.
BEHAVIOUR: Fairly social, and often seen in groups, which form tight packs in flight. Sometimes uses an 'umbrella' feeding technique with wings spread over hunched head. This either reduces glare, attracts prey, or both. Preys mainly upon small fish.

Length:	50–60 cm | 1·7–2'

WHERE TO SEE: Fairly common around Tana, and throughout much of the island.

Black Herons adopting the 'umbrella' feeding technique

Complex pattern on head and neck; favours thick vegetation

Rich coloration visible in flight

1

2

Dark and compact

Yellow feet

① Cattle Egret *Bubulcus ibis*

M Vorompotsy
F Héron Garde-boeufs

DISTRIBUTION: Almost worldwide. Common in Madagascar in many habitats including dry fields, cultivated areas and wetland shores. This is the least aquatic of Madagascar's herons and egrets.

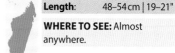

Length:	48–54 cm | 19–21"

WHERE TO SEE: Almost anywhere.

ID: Smaller and more compact than Little Egret, and much more terrestrial. Also identified by yellow bill, unicoloured legs and buff patches on the head and breast of breeding birds.

BEHAVIOUR: Usually in groups, often with livestock. Insects are its main food, so it benefits from the disturbance created by cattle, which flush grasshoppers and other small animals.

② Little Egret *Egretta garzetta dimorpha*

M Vanofotsy
F Aigrette Garzette

DISTRIBUTION: Much of the Old World. Throughout Madagascar in a variety of salt and freshwater wetlands. Most common along the muddy shores of the west coast. Dark morph birds generally predominate along the coast while light morph birds are more common inland.

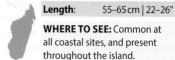

Length:	55–65 cm | 22–26"

WHERE TO SEE: Common at all coastal sites, and present throughout the island.

The race *dimorpha* of Little Egret that ocurs in Madagascar is sometimes split as Dimorphic Egret.

ID: Light and dark morphs are very different. Light morph can be distinguished from Great Egret by its smaller size, dark bill and legs, and yellow feet. Dark morph differentiated from Black Heron (*page 90*) by longer bill and neck, and usually a white throat and white patch in the wing. Slaty-grey intermediate birds look unlike other Malagasy egrets.

BEHAVIOUR: Can be solitary or in groups. Feeds more actively than most egrets and herons, sometimes dashing around frantically. Fish are its primary food.

③ Great Egret *Ardea alba*

M Vanofotsy Be
F Grande Aigrette

DISTRIBUTION: Much of the world. Common throughout Madagascar in fresh and saltwater wetlands, including rice paddies.

Length:	85–95 cm | 2·8–3·1′

WHERE TO SEE: Common around Tana and throughout the island.

ID: The largest white egret, with dark legs and feet. Never shows head plumes. In flight, wingbeats are slow and long legs trail behind.

BEHAVIOUR: Forages alone or in groups, primarily eating fish. Like most egrets and herons, roosts communally with other species.

Facial skin turns bright green when breeding

Size is one of the quickest ways of telling the white egrets apart

intermediate

1

2

2

dark morph

2

light morph

2

dark morph

light morph

3

Dark feet and yellow bill

① **Squacco Heron** *Ardeola ralloides*

M Mpiandrivoditatatra
F Crabier Chevelu

DISTRIBUTION: Europe, Middle East and Africa. Fairly common throughout Madagascar in freshwater wetlands. Sometimes in rice paddies.

ID: Compact shape, bicoloured bill, and mix of brown and white plumage. Streaky in non-breeding plumage. The **Madagascar Pond Heron** *A. idae* ③ is rare and Endangered, but has been recorded throughout most of Madagascar. It is all-white in breeding plumage and dark brown (rather than buff) and white in non-breeding plumage.

BEHAVIOUR: Secretive and usually solitary. Feeds mainly on fish and insects, which it catches by waiting motionlessly, then striking.

Length:	42–46 cm | 17–18"

WHERE TO SEE: Commonly seen in most wetlands. Large breeding colony in Tana at Lake Alarobia.

ⓔ ② **Striated Heron** *Butorides striata rutenbergi*

M Vorompantsika
F Héron Strié

DISTRIBUTION: Old World tropics and South America. Fairly common, though inconspicuous, throughout Madagascar in salt and freshwater wetlands.

ID: Small, compact and dark, with streaks on the breast and a blackish cap.

VOICE: Gives a harsh *"quaak"* call in flight.

BEHAVIOUR: Mainly solitary, standing motionless for long periods, waiting for prey such as fish to come close. Easily missed, as it blends into its surroundings.

Length:	40–44 cm | 16–17"

WHERE TO SEE: Can be found in almost any wetland.

3br

Lake Alarobia in Tana is a good place to see the rare Madagascar Pond Heron.

1nb

Buff and brown plumage

1nb

1br

2

2im

Greenish-grey and brown plumage

2

Black-crowned Night Heron *Nycticorax nycticorax*

M Goaka
F Bihoreau Gris

DISTRIBUTION: Much of the Americas, Europe, Asia, and Africa. Locally fairly common throughout Madagascar in salt and freshwater wetlands. Needs thick marsh or swamp areas for roosting.
ID: Adults are sharply tricoloured: black, grey and white. Brown juveniles could be could be confused with Striated or Squacco Herons (*page 94*), but are larger, with bold spotting on the back.
VOICE: Grumpy "*goak*" given mainly in flight.
BEHAVIOUR: Nocturnal. Away from breeding colonies, usually seen roosting motionlessly in thick vegetation during the day, or flying out to feed at dusk. Diverse diet of small animals.

Length:	54–60 cm	21–24"

WHERE TO SEE: Breeding colony at Lake Alarobia in Tana. Sightings possible in most wetlands.

Although superficially like a heron, the Hamerkop is taxonomically very different, so much so that it is placed in its own family.

Hamerkop *Scopus umbretta tenuirostris*

M Takatra
F Ombrette Africaine

DISTRIBUTION: Afrotropics. Occurs throughout Madagascar in small numbers in shallow wetlands, including rice paddies.
ID: All-brown colour and hammer-headed shape are unmistakable.
BEHAVIOUR: Usually solitary or in pairs. Eats amphibians, small fish, invertebrates, and other small animals. Builds huge nests in trees that rank among the largest in the world, and can resemble a pile of material left by a flood.

Length:	50–58 cm	20–23"

WHERE TO SEE: Possible in rice paddies or other wetlands almost anywhere. Watch especially along the RN7 highway between Fianarantsoa and Antsirabe.

1

1im

1ju

Often seen in flight at dusk and dawn

Hamerkop flies high and sometimes soars

🅔 ① Madagascar Buzzard *Buteo brachypterus*

M Hindry
F Buse Malgache

DISTRIBUTION: Fairly common throughout Madagascar, except in treeless areas. Will feed in open areas as long as there are some trees nearby.

ID: A variable brown-and-white raptor, with narrower wings than those of Madagascar Harrier-hawk. Black Kite (*page 100*) shows a forked tail and less pale coloration.

VOICE: Whiny, slightly descending whistle.

BEHAVIOUR: Frequently soars, and often perches conspicuously. Hunts birds, small mammals, reptiles and amphibians.

| Length: | 48–51 cm | 19–20" |

WHERE TO SEE: Common in many places, although perhaps easiest to find in the west.

🅔 ② Madagascar Harrier-hawk
Polyboroides radiatus

M Fihiaka
F Gymnogène Malgache

DISTRIBUTION: Uncommon throughout the island, except in treeless areas.

ID: Big, long-legged, and broad-winged. The grey-and-black adult is distinctive. When excited, the bare yellow skin on the face turns pink. The brown immature could be confused with Madagascar Buzzard, but can be recognized by its broad wings, long legs, bare facial skin, and pale head.

VOICE: Gives a whistle similar to that of Madagascar Buzzard, but longer and higher-pitched.

BEHAVIOUR: Frequently soars. Unique highly flexible knee joint allows it to insert its legs into crevices and cavities to extract prey. Its varied diet includes eggs, nestling and adult birds, lemurs, rodents, tenrecs, reptiles and amphibians.

| Length: | 68 cm | 2·3' |

WHERE TO SEE: Possible almost anywhere in the proximity of forest, but easiest to see in the west, such as around Morondava, in Ankarafantsika NP, and in the spiny forest around Toliara.

🅔 ③ Madagascar Fish Eagle *Haliaeetus vociferoides*

M Ankoay
F Pygargue Malgache

DISTRIBUTION: Rare and local along the west coast of Madagascar, sometimes up to 100 km (60 miles) inland. Uses both saltwater and freshwater wetlands with adjacent forest (including mangrove and gallery forest).

ID: Large brown eagle with broad wings and a short white tail. Immature is buff and brown, and lacks white tail of the adult. Generally rare, and unlikely to be seen except in a few select locations.

VOICE: Very vocal and has an evocative call more like that of a gull than a raptor. A ringing *"whee weet-weet-weet"*. The male has a higher-pitched voice than the female.

BEHAVIOUR: Usually seen in pairs. Sometimes soars. Feeds almost exclusively on fish, which are caught by swooping down and plucking them from just below the water's surface.

CRITICALLY ENDANGERED

| Length: | 70–80 cm | 2·3–2·7' |

WHERE TO SEE: Lake Ravelobe in Ankarafantsika NP and the Manambolo River in Tsingy de Bemaraha NP. Sightings are also possible at the Tsiribihina River north of Morondava and around Nosy Be.

Madagascar Fish Eagle is Critically Endangered – only about 120 breeding pairs remain.

Brown and white, with feathered face

1

2

3

1

2

3

Madagascar's largest raptor

2im

Long legs and bare facial skin

Black (Yellow-billed) Kite *Milvus migrans*

M Papango
F Milan Noir

DISTRIBUTION: Most of Europe, Asia, Australasia and Africa. Common throughout Madagascar in most habitats except dense forest. Often seen around towns.
ID: Dark brown, medium-sized raptor with a distinctive forked tail.
VOICE: Quavering whistles, often given in flight.
BEHAVIOUR: Usually seen on the wing, often soaring. Feeds mostly by scavenging, but also hunts small animals.

Length:	50–58 cm | 20–23"

WHERE TO SEE: The most common raptor in Madagascar. Visitors will see it many times while travelling around the country.

Frances's Sparrowhawk
Accipiter francesiae francesiae

M Firasamadinika
F Épervier de Frances

DISTRIBUTION: Madagascar and the Comoros. Found throughout the island in almost any habitat with woody vegetation; fairly common but inconspicuous.
ID: Typical sparrowhawk shape: long tail and short, rounded wings. The grey back and pale underparts of the male are distinctive. Female distinguished from uncommon **Banded Kestrel** *Falco zoniventris* (not illustrated) by slim shape, longer legs, and fine barring underneath. **Madagascar Sparrowhawk** *A. madagascariensis* (not illustrated) can be extremely similar, but is rarely seen. **Henst's Goshawk** *A. henstii* (not illustrated) is much larger, and also much less frequently seen.
VOICE: Single raspy *"kreek"* often repeated over and over.
BEHAVIOUR: Fairly shy, secretive and solitary. Often perches inside the forest, where it hunts for reptiles, birds and insects.

Length:	30–35 cm | 12–14"

WHERE TO SEE: Throughout, but most easily found in the more open forest of the west.

Madagascar Kestrel
Falco newtoni newtoni

M Hitsikitsika
F Faucon de Newton, Crécerelle Malgache

DISTRIBUTION: Madagascar and Seychelles (Aldabra). Common in small numbers throughout Madagascar in a variety of open habitats. Often nests on buildings in human settlements.
ID: Quite similar to the world's widespread kestrel species, American *Falco sparverius* and Common Kestrels *F. tinnunculus* (neither illustrated), one of which is likely to be familiar to most visitors. Long tail, pointed wings, and variable buffy colour are distinctive.
VOICE: A quick series of high-pitched and squeaky notes.
BEHAVIOUR: Often perches conspicuously on poles, wires and branches. Capable of quick and powerful flight, and also hovers skilfully. Hunts lizards and insects.

Length:	25–30 cm | 10–12"

WHERE TO SEE: Common throughout the island. Nests on buildings in Tana.

There are other falcons on Madagascar (not illustrated): the rare **Banded Kestrel**, the scarce resident **Peregrine Falcon** *F. peregrinus*; and two migratory species, **Sooty Falcon** *F. concolor* and **Eleonora's Falcon** *F. eleonorae*, the majority of which arrive in December and depart by May, a period during which few tourists visit the island.

Madagascar's most common and widespread raptor

1

2♂

2♀

3♀   pale morph

3   dark morph

In flight, Madagascar Cuckoo (*page 126*) looks very similar to a small sparrowhawk or falcon. However, the cuckoo is slimmer than any raptor, and has more pointed wings than a sparrowhawk.

3♂   pale morph

1

2

3

(E) (1) Madagascar Crested Ibis *Lophotibis cristata*

M **Akohonala**
F **Ibis Huppé Malgache**

DISTRIBUTION: Uncommon and local in extensive patches of rainforest or western dry forest, though most common in eastern rainforest. Prefers wet areas within forest, such as swamps and stream banks.

ID: Difficult to see, but the brown body, white wings, pale crest and red bare facial skin make this bird unmistakable. Often only glimpsed in dense forest as a blur of bright white wings flying away.

VOICE: Very vocal and loud, especially at dusk and sometimes during the night. Gives a variety of yelping and whining notes. Calls often become quite repetitive, emphatic and plaintive, especially when a pair is calling together.

BEHAVIOUR: Very shy. Usually found in pairs. Feeds on invertebrates and small frogs and reptiles on the forest floor. Roosts and nests high in trees.

NEAR THREATENED	
Length:	50 cm | 20"

WHERE TO SEE: Finding this shy bird takes some luck, and usually the help of a skilled local guide. Andasibe-Mantadia, Amber Mountain and Masoala NPs are the best sites.

> Mesites constitute a family that is found only in Madagascar. They are unusual, primitive birds, so different from anything else that they may deserve to be placed in their own order; they are therefore of considerable taxonomic significance.

(E) (2) White-breasted Mesite *Mesitornis variegata*

M **Agolinala**
F **Mésite Variée**

DISTRIBUTION: A rare endemic whose presence has been confirmed in only a few scattered sites, most of which support dry forest habitat.

ID: Strange rail-like bird with spotted underparts and striped face. Unlikely to be seen to be seen unless you are looking for it.

VOICE: Usually found after being heard: a loud, elaborate duet of rasping and piping notes. This duet has a whirling, frantic, up-and-down sound to it. When heard up close, it attracts the attention even of forest visitors who are not looking for birds.

BEHAVIOUR: Pairs and family groups walk on the forest floor with heads bobbing and tails wagging. When severely startled, flies into mid-storey of forest, perches with tail cocked up and head down, and remains motionless until the threat has passed.

VULNERABLE	
Length:	31 cm | 12"

WHERE TO SEE: With the help of a good local guide, usually not difficult to find in Ankarafantsika NP or Kirindy Forest. Also possible but less common in Ankarana NP.

There are two other mesite species (neither illustrated). **Brown Mesite** *Mesitornis unicolor* is found in the eastern rainforest, and can be seen with some effort and the help of a guide in Ranomafana and Masoala NPs. **Subdesert Mesite** *Monias benschi* is restricted to spiny forest, and can be seen near Ifaty.

1

Builds a very large stick nest

White wings

Walks along forest floor

2

White-throated Rail *Dryolimnas cuvieri cuvieri*

M Tsikoza
F Râle de Cuvier

DISTRIBUTION: Madagascar and Seychelles (Aldabra). Fairly common although inconspicuous throughout Madagascar in most wetland habitats, including rice paddies, moist forest and scrub, and mangroves.
ID: Shape, rich brown head and underparts, and white throat are distinctive. The juvenile shows duller coloration, but still has a white throat.

Length:	31 cm | 12"

WHERE TO SEE: Common but shy. Andasibe-Mantadia and Ankarafantsika NPs and Berenty are some of the best sites.

VOICE: A series of loud ascending cries, often given in duet. Also makes deep, grunting calls.
BEHAVIOUR: Usually found in pairs. Fairly shy, but will sometimes walk into the open, often flicking its tail up as it walks. Diet is mainly invertebrates.

② Common Moorhen *Gallinula chloropus*

M Akohondrano
F Gallinule Poule-d'eau

DISTRIBUTION: Found throughout much of the Old World. Locally fairly common across Madagascar, mostly in freshwater marshes.
ID: Grey, rail-like bird with a mostly red bill and yellow legs. Immature browner with a dark bill and legs.

Length:	30–36 cm | 12–14"

WHERE TO SEE: Easily seen at Lake Alarobia in Tana, and in Andasibe-Mantadia and Ankarafantsika NPs.

VOICE: Creaking and hooting calls which are distinctive once you know them.
BEHAVIOUR: Feeds while walking across wetland vegetation, or swimming like a duck. Eats a wide variety of plant and animal matter.

❸ Madagascar Jacana *Actophilornis albinucha*

M Mokimbo
F Jacana Malgache

DISTRIBUTION: Scarce and local, mainly in western Madagascar, in freshwater wetlands with extensive floating vegetation, especially water lilies.
ID: Adults are black, white and chestnut, with a blue bill. Juveniles are pale on the head and underparts and have a grey bill. The structure of jacanas is distinctive, and in laboured flight the huge feet trail behind.

NEAR THREATENED
Length:	30 cm | 12"

WHERE TO SEE: Wetlands in and around Ankarafantsika NP and Morondava.

VOICE: A series of short trills.
BEHAVIOUR: Usually seen singly or in pairs, and occasionally in small groups. Uses its enormous feet to walk across wetland vegetation.

1

Usually walks but can swim like a duck

2

2im

Equally comfortable walking or swimming

3

3ju

Walks on top of marshy vegetation

ⓔ ①Three-banded Plover
Charadrius tricollaris bifrontatus

M Monditra
F Pluvier à Triple Collier

DISTRIBUTION: Afrotropics. Uncommon throughout Madagascar on freshwater mudflats, wetland verges and rice paddies.

ID: The two black bands on the chest, one white band around the head, and red-based bill are diagnostic. If you see a plover in the interior, it is probably this species.

VOICE: High-pitched, three-part *"tsii-tsii-tsii"*.

| Length: | 18 cm \| 7" |

WHERE TO SEE: Perhaps easiest in Ankarafantsika NP, but watch for it on rice paddies and other wetlands throughout the country.

BEHAVIOUR: A typical plover that feeds by alternating stretches of running and stopping, plucking invertebrates from the surface.

Some scientists treat the Madagascar Three-banded Plover as a full species, *C. bifrontatus*, adding yet another avian endemic to the island's impressive tally.

ⓔ ② White-fronted Plover
Charadrius marginatus tenellus

M Fotsihandrina
F Pluvier à Front Blanc

DISTRIBUTION: Sub-Saharan Africa. Fairly common on sandy beaches and mudflats all along the coast of Madagascar. Less common inland, occurring mostly along rivers.

ID: Small and pale. Can be separated from Greater Sand Plover (*page 108*) by its smaller size and pale collar.

VOICE: Quiet *"whiit"*.

| Length: | 16–17 cm \| 6–7" |

WHERE TO SEE: Watch for it on any coastal beach or mudflat.

BEHAVIOUR: Like other plovers, feeds by alternating periods of running and stopping, picking invertebrates from the surface.

2

Often found on sandy beaches frequented by sunbathing tourists

2ju

1

Two bands on the chest and one on the head

2

① Greater Sand Plover *Charadrius leschenaultii*

M Fandiafasikabe
F Gravelot

DISTRIBUTION: Breeds in Asia. Winters on coasts of Africa, Arabia, India, Southeast Asia, and Australia. Found on mudflats and sandy beaches all around the coast of Madagascar. Occurs year-round, but more common from October to April.

Length:	22–25 cm	9–10"

WHERE TO SEE: Common on most tidal flats, including those around Diego-Suarez, Maroantsetra, and Toliara.

ID: In Madagascar, seen mainly in non-breeding plumage, which is nondescript: pale grey-brown on the back, and with white underparts. Compared to White-fronted Plover (*page 106*), larger, longer-legged, bigger-billed, and lacks a pale collar. The very similar but less common **Lesser Sand Plover** *C. mongolus* (not illustrated) has smaller bill and shorter, darker legs, but can be very hard to separate from Greater Sand Plover.

BEHAVIOUR: Like other plovers, feeds by alternating stretches of running and stopping, gleaning invertebrates from the surface.

② Grey (Black-bellied) Plover
Pluvialis squatarola

M Vikivikivolombatolalaka
F Pluvier Argenté

DISTRIBUTION: Circumpolar, breeding in Arctic tundra. Winters along most of the world's coastlines away from the far north. In Madagascar, found on mudflats and in other coastal habitats all around the coast year-round, but most common from October to April.

Length:	27–31 cm	11–12"

WHERE TO SEE: Easily seen in much the same places as Greater Sand Plover.

ID: A large plover with long legs and a heavy bill. In Madagascar, seen mostly in plain grey non-breeding plumage. Black 'wingpits' in flight are distinctive. Larger than Greater Sand Plover, with a checkered pattern on the back.

VOICE: Plaintive, whistled *"peeeowee"*, frequently given in flight.

BEHAVIOUR: Often in loose groups. Like other plovers, feeds with a run-stop action and picks invertebrates from the surface.

2br

2nb

① Common Sandpiper *Actitis hypoleucos*

M Vikiviky
F Chevalier Guignette

Length:	19–21 cm | 7–8"

WHERE TO SEE: Possible in almost any wetland.

DISTRIBUTION: Occurs almost throughout the Old World, either as a breeder, migrant, or wintering bird. Non-breeding birds are fairly common throughout Madagascar, mainly from October to March. Uses a wide variety of salt and freshwater wetlands.

ID: Short-legged, medium-sized shorebird. Constantly bobs its tail, and flies in a distinctive weak and fluttering manner.

VOICE: High-pitched, three-part *"tsii-tsii-tsii"*, very like call of Three-banded Plover (*page 106*).

BEHAVIOUR: Usually solitary. Diet mainly invertebrates.

② Curlew Sandpiper *Calidris ferruginea*

M Vikivikimena
F Bécasseau Cocorli

NEAR THREATENED

Length:	18–23 cm | 7–9"

WHERE TO SEE: Fairly common in coastal areas with mudflats, including Toliara and Maroantsetra.

DISTRIBUTION: Breeds in Arctic tundra, mainly in the Old World. Winters in Africa, south Asia and Australia. In Madagascar, found mainly on mudflats along the west coast, although it can occur anywhere along the coast or inland. Present year-round, but largest numbers occur between September and May.

ID: Mid-sized shorebird with a long, drooping bill. Red underparts of breeding plumage are distinctive, but in Madagascar seen mostly in grey-and-white non-breeding plumage.

BEHAVIOUR: Often found in flocks. Strong, fast flight. Feeds by probing mudflats with its long bill for invertebrates.

③ Sanderling *Calidris alba*

M Agolibe
F Bécasseau Sanderling

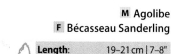

Length:	19–21 cm | 7–8"

WHERE TO SEE: Possible on almost any sandy beach, including popular tourist areas like Nosy Be and St. Marie Island.

DISTRIBUTION: Breeds throughout much of the Arctic tundra, and winters along most of the world's coastlines away from the far north. Found all the way around the coast of Madagascar, on sandy beaches and flats; occurs year-round, but the largest numbers are present between September and April.

ID: Pale, short-billed sandpiper in non-breeding plumage. Brighter breeding plumage rarely seen in Madagascar. Much more likely to be seen along sandy beaches than Curlew Sandpiper.

BEHAVIOUR: Usually feeds and roosts in flocks. Follows the surf, rushing down to forage when a wave retreats, then scurrying back up the beach when the next wave arrives. Feeds mainly on invertebrates.

Shorebirds are often seen in flocks

1

'Flicking' flight with white wing stripe

2nb

Fast flight with white wing stripe and white rump

3nb

3br

Fast flight with white wing stripe and dark rump

① Ruddy Turnstone *Arenaria interpres*

M Viko
F Tournepierre à Collier

Length: 21–25 cm | 8–10"

WHERE TO SEE: Small numbers found in most coastal areas, including Toliara, St. Marie Island, Nosy Be and Diego-Suarez.

DISTRIBUTION: Breeds on the Arctic tundra. Winters along much of the world's coastline, generally at moderate latitudes in the northern hemisphere. Uses a variety of habitats all along the coast of Madagascar, although it prefers rocky shores and reefs. Some remain year-round, but largest numbers occur from August to April.

ID: Distinctive, squat, orange-legged shorebird. In breeding plumage, boldly marked with black, chestnut and white; otherwise more subdued brown and white.

VOICE: Short, low-pitched trills.

BEHAVIOUR: Often in flocks. Searches for invertebrates by turning over small rocks and other debris with its bill, or by probing into the substrate.

② Common Greenshank *Tringa stagnatilis*

M Vikivikipotaka
F Chevalier Aboyeur

Length: 30–34 cm | 12–13"

WHERE TO SEE: Fairly common in most coastal areas, including Diego-Suarez, Mahajanga and Toliara.

DISTRIBUTION: Breeds in northern Eurasia. Winters in southern Eurasia, Africa, and Australia. Found throughout Madagascar in a wide variety of wetlands, although most common on the coast. Some can be found year-round, but largest numbers occur between September and April.

ID: Tall grey-and-white shorebird with a slightly upturned bill.

VOICE: Distinctive three-part *"tew-tew-tew"*, most often given in flight.

BEHAVIOUR: Often in small groups. Feeds actively in shallow water or along water's edge. Eats invertebrates, small fish and tadpoles.

③ Whimbrel *Numenius phaeopus*

M Koikoika
F Courlis Corlieu

Length: 40–43 cm | 16–17"

WHERE TO SEE: Common in most coastal areas, including Diego-Suarez, St. Marie Island, Nosy Be and Toliara.

DISTRIBUTION: Breeds in tundra all around the Arctic. Winters along much of the world's coastline, although in the northern hemisphere only at moderate latitudes. Fairly common in a variety of habitats around the coast of Madagascar. Some remain year-round, but largest numbers occur from August to April.

ID: Big brown shorebird with a long, downcurved bill.

VOICE: Rapid, multi-note call with a bubbly, haunting quality.

BEHAVIOUR: Often in flocks. Like many shorebirds that occur in mangrove areas, perches in mangrove trees at high tide, when the mudflats are covered. Feeds mainly on crabs by both picking them from the surface and probing into the substrate.

A mixed flock of waders: Whimbrel, Common Greenshank, Grey Plover and Little Stint

1nb

1br

2nb

White stripe on back; slightly upcurved bill

3

White stripe on back; downcurved bill

B 1 Madagascar Pratincole *Glareola ocularis*

M **Vorombato**
F **Glaréole Malgache**

VULNERABLE

Length: 25 cm | 10"

DISTRIBUTION: Breeds exclusively in Madagascar, and spends the non-breeding season (May to August) in east Africa. Generally scarce and local, although it uses a variety of different habitats: rocky coast, rivers with exposed rocks and sand banks, and short grassland. Ranges widely when feeding and can be see in flight almost anywhere.

WHERE TO SEE: Common on rocks around the Masoala Peninsula and Nosy Mangabe, plus the Manambolo River in Tsingy de Bemaraha NP.

ID: This elegant brown, buff and white bird looks halfway between a tern and a shorebird when perched. The belly is white, and there are white patches on the rump and behind the eye.

VOICE: Often the first clue to the presence of pratincoles. High-pitched *"vik"* call, often doubled, tripled, or given in excited chorus by a flock of birds. Pratincoles call frequently when perched, and incessantly in flight.

BEHAVIOUR: Often in pairs or flocks. Perches on seaside rock formations, sand banks or rocks in rivers, or on man-made structures such as bridges. Feeds on insects, which are caught on the wing. Its bounding and swooping flight is graceful and powerful. Sometimes flies very high.

2 Crab-plover *Dromas ardeola*

M **Tsakaranta**
F **Drome Ardéole**

Length: 33–38 cm | 13–15"

DISTRIBUTION: Western Indian Ocean and Red Sea coast. Scarce and local non-breeding visitor to Madagascar, although some occur year-round. Uses most coastal habitats, although it prefers sandy beaches and mudflats.

WHERE TO SEE: Often seen in Toliara Harbour, on the island of Nosy Ve (southwest of Toliara) and around Nosy Be.

ID: An unmistakable large, black-and-white shorebird that is so different from other shorebirds that it is placed in its own family.

VOICE: Simple yelps and cries, given mainly in flight.

BEHAVIOUR: Usually seen in flocks, sometimes containing dozens of birds. Feeds much like a typical plover, walking along the shore, pausing frequently, and scanning for food. As the name suggests, eats mainly crabs, but also takes other crustaceans.

Strong black-and-white pattern particularly noticeable in flight

White
rump

Rufous
underwing

Big, unmistakable shorebird

① Greater Crested (Swift) Tern *Thalasseus bergii*

M Trobakamavovava
F Sterne Huppée

DISTRIBUTION: Coast of southern and eastern Africa, Arabia, India, Southeast Asia and Australia. Breeds only locally in Madagascar, but can be seen in small numbers anywhere along the coast.

Length:	46–49 cm | 18–19"

WHERE TO SEE: Possible at most coastal sites, including Toliara, Mahajanga and Nosy Be.

ID: Among Madagascar's common tern species, this is the largest. Can sometimes be identified at long distances simply by its graceful and powerful flight. When seen at close range, its heavier yellow bill and darker grey back separate it from Lesser Crested Tern. The globally widespread **Caspian Tern** *Hydroprogne caspia* (not illustrated) is uncommon in Madagascar, seen mainly along the coast. It is larger, bulkier, shorter-tailed, and has a heavy orange bill.

VOICE: Various low-pitched rasping calls, often given in pairs.

BEHAVIOUR: A typical tern: hunts on the wing, making shallow plunge-dives into the water to catch fish and other small aquatic animals. Flocks roost on sandbars and rocks, often with other species of terns

② Lesser Crested Tern *Thalasseus bengalensis*

M Trobakamadinika
F Sterne Voyageuse

DISTRIBUTION: Similar to Greater Crested Tern, although also present along the coast of northern Africa. Also more migratory and localized as a breeder; not known to breed in Madagascar. Fairly common all around the coast as a non-breeding visitor, mainly from November to June, although some remain year-round.

Length:	35–37 cm | 14–15"

WHERE TO SEE: More common than Greater Crested Tern, and likewise possible at most coastal sites.

ID: Smaller, slimmer and paler than Greater Crested Tern, with a smaller, slimmer, orange bill. Flight is graceful, but not as powerful as Greater Crested Tern.

VOICE: Rasping and piping calls, higher-pitched than those of Greater Crested Tern.

BEHAVIOUR: A typical tern. More likely to be seen far from shore than Greater Crested Tern.

③ Roseate Tern *Sterna dougallii*

M Varevaka
F Sterne de Dougall

DISTRIBUTION: Wide but patchy distribution across the world's oceans. Breeds on islands off the Malagasy coast. Not commonly seen in most places, but possible anywhere, both along the coast and at sea.

Length:	33–38 cm | 13–15"

WHERE TO SEE: Roosting on offshore islets around the Masoala Peninsula.

ID: Much slimmer than Lesser Crested Tern, with a proportionally longer tail. Also lacks crest and has a black tip to the bill. **Common Tern** *S. hirundo* (not illustrated) is a frequent non-breeding visitor to the Malagasy coast. It is less common than Roseate Tern around Masoala, but more common elsewhere. Identification can be difficult, but in all plumages, Common Tern is shorter-tailed, darker grey on the back, and flies with deeper wingbeats than Roseate Tern.

VOICE: Two-part *"skidgit"* call is distinctive. Also gives simpler, lower-pitched calls.

BEHAVIOUR: A typical tern in most respects. Flies with shallow wingbeats, unlike the strong, rowing wingbeats of crested terns. Feeds on small fish, exclusively offshore.

All three of these tern species show a black forehead in breeding plumage, and a white forehead in non-breeding plumage.

① Lesser Frigatebird *Fregata ariel*

M Bomomandry
F Frégate Ariel

Length:	70–82 cm | 28–32"

WHERE TO SEE: Frequent around Nosy Be, especially on Nosy Tanikely.

DISTRIBUTION: Patchily distributed around Pacific, Indian and Atlantic Oceans. Not confirmed as a breeder in Madagascar, but frequently seen along the coast, especially in the north and west.
ID: Big black bird with long wings and a jagged shape. Female has a white band across the chest, and male has an inflatable red throat pouch.
Great Frigatebird *Fregata minor* (not illustrated) also occurs but is less common. From a distance it is very difficult to separate the two species, but with a good view Lesser Frigatebird can be identified by the white 'wingpit' markings which are absent in Great Frigatebird.
VOICE: Silent at sea.
BEHAVIOUR: Spends most of its time on the open sea. Huge wings and long tail allow graceful flight. Feeds mainly on squid and flying fish. Unlike other frigatebirds, it does not regularly pirate food from other birds.

② White-tailed Tropicbird *Phaethon lepturus*

M Kafotsy
F Phaéton à Bec Jaune

Length:	45–50 cm | 18–20"
	(without tail streamers, which are 30–50 cm long)

WHERE TO SEE: Around Nosy Be, especially Nosy Tanikely. Near Diego-Suarez at places often visited on tourist excursions: the 'Three Bays' and Nosy Diego on the Emerald Sea.

DISTRIBUTION: Distributed patchily in tropical seas worldwide. Breeds on rocky coastlines and feeds far out at sea. In Madagascar, it breeds between Nosy Be and Diego-Suarez and is rarely seen elsewhere.
ID: Very white and tern-like (*page 116*) but with longer tail streamers. Tropicbirds fly in a distinctive way: the wings are held straight and the wingbeats are shallow, powering strong and steady flight.
VOICE: Quiet "*chik*", often given in series.
BEHAVIOUR: Usually solitary, or in small loose groups around breeding colonies. Strong and elegant flight, sometimes very high. Feeds by plunge-diving for fish and squid.

③ Red-tailed Tropicbird *Phaethon rubricauda*

M Vorompano
F Phaéton à Brins Rouges

Length:	60–70 cm | 24–28"
	(without tail streamers, which average 40 cm long)

WHERE TO SEE: Likely to be seen only on Nosy Ve, a small island just off Anakao, and southwest of Toliara.

DISTRIBUTION: Warm stretches of Indian and Pacific Oceans. The sole Malagasy breeding colony is on Nosy Ve, off the southwest coast. Occasionally seen from the coast elsewhere.
ID: Larger and heavier than White-tailed Tropicbird, with all-white wings, and thin, red tail streamers.
VOICE: Croaking calls given around breeding colony.
BEHAVIOUR: Flight powerful, but not as elegant as that of White-tailed Tropicbird; somewhat pigeon-like. Feeds mainly on fish, which it catches by diving.

Nosy Ve was only recently colonized by Red-tailed Tropicbirds, probably in the late 1970s. This vulnerable colony has been protected by a local fady (taboo).

1

1♀

Long, jagged wings

Long, forked tail

1♂

2

Yellow bill

Black slashes on upperwing

2

White tail streamers

Red bill

3

Thin red tail streamers

ⓡ ① Madagascar Turtle Dove *Streptopelia picturata*

M Domohina
F Pigeon Malgache

DISTRIBUTION: Throughout the Malagasy region. Fairly common though inconspicuous in all habitats that have some woody vegetation.
ID: A large brown pigeon that is distinctive if not colourful. Obvious white corners to the tail in flight.
VOICE: A low-pitched rising *"hwooo"* or *"ho-hwoooo"*, repeated about every 1·5 seconds. The wings flap noisily at takeoff.

Length:	28 cm | 11"

WHERE TO SEE: Common in most natural and semi-natural habitats, from spiny forest to rainforest. Can even be found in the more vegetated parts of Tana.

BEHAVIOUR: Solitary or in small groups. Shy, and often flushes off roads and paths. Walks along the ground searching for seeds and secondary foods such as fruits, flowers and insects. Fast, powerful flight is generally low, through or just above forest.

℮ ② Namaqua Dove *Oena capensis aliena*

M Katoto
F Tourtelette Masquée

DISTRIBUTION: Sub-Saharan Africa and Arabian Peninsula. Found in most of Madagascar, although most common in the west, south and far north. Prefers open woodland, scrub, cultivated areas and spiny forest. Rarely found in pure grassland.
ID: A tiny-bodied, long-tailed dove. The male has a black face and a red and yellow bill, while the female is more drab.
VOICE: A rising *"hoowooo"*, repeated about every two seconds. Similar to Madagascar Turtle Dove, but much higher-pitched.

Length:	28 cm | 11"

WHERE TO SEE: Easily seen in the dry west and north, as around Toliara, Morondava, and Ankarafantsika and Ankarana NPs.

BEHAVIOUR: Solitary, or in pairs or small groups. Walks on the ground, feeding on seeds.

ⓘ ③ Feral Pigeon (Rock Dove) *Columba livia*

M Voromailala
F Pigeon Biset

DISTRIBUTION: Originally Eurasia and North Africa, but widely introduced and found locally in small numbers throughout Madagascar, in close association with humans.
ID: Extremely variable, ranging from all-white to all-black, but generally grey with green iridescence on the

Length:	32–34 cm | 13"

WHERE TO SEE: Found in most towns.

neck and dark bars across the wings. The variation in plumages often gives flocks a 'patchwork' appearance. Its association with humans is usually sufficient for identification.
VOICE: Low-pitched cooing.
BEHAVIOUR: Usually in flocks. Roosts and nests mainly in man-made structures. Walks on the ground searching for seeds and scraps left by humans.

2♀

Female Namaqua Dove is plainer than the male

White band on end of tail

ℝ ① Madagascar Green Pigeon *Treron australis*

M Voronadabo
F Colombar Maïtsou

DISTRIBUTION: Comoros (Mohéli) and Madagascar. Erratic and perhaps semi-nomadic throughout much of the island, but rarely above 1,000 m (3,300'), and absent from the High Plateau. Uses a variety of woodland and forest, although usually not closed-canopy forest.

ID: A large, mostly green pigeon. Distinctive even in flight, when green body and black wings with white wingbars are evident. Usually flies higher than the similarly sized, all-brown Madagascar Turtle Dove.

VOICE: A rather maniacal, crackling mix of trills, cackles and hoots.

BEHAVIOUR: Often in small groups. Arboreal species that feeds mainly on fruit, especially figs. In the east, sometimes found in fruiting trees alongside Madagascar Blue Pigeons.

Length:	32 cm | 13"

WHERE TO SEE: Easiest to see in the west. Usually common around the headquarters at Ankarafantsika NP. Also frequent around Toliara.

❸ ② Madagascar Blue Pigeon
Alectroenas madagascariensis

M Finengo
F Founingo Bleu

DISTRIBUTION: Uncommon, mainly in rainforest in eastern and northern Madagascar.

ID: Dark blue, with red bare skin around the eyes and a red tail. In flight, looks shorter-tailed and darker than other pigeons and doves.

VOICE: Virtually silent, unusually for a pigeon.

BEHAVIOUR: Often in small flocks. An arboreal species that feeds exclusively on fruits. Perches on snags and tall trees.

Length:	28 cm | 11"

WHERE TO SEE: Forest edges in and around Andasibe-Mantadia NP. Also quite common in Anjozorobe-Angavo forest. Less common but possible in Ranomafana and Amber Mountain NPs.

Tale of two pigeons Madagascar's two native pigeons exemplify the varied origins of its biological riches. Green pigeons are found in both Africa and Asia, but the Madagascar Green Pigeon is closely related to the African Green Pigeon *Treron calvus*, and it seems clear that Madagascar was colonized from nearby Africa in this case. Blue pigeons on the other hand are found only in the Malagasy region. Their closest relative seems to be the Cloven-feathered Dove *Drepanoptila holosericea*, found on the island of New Caledonia, 1,200 km east of Australia in the Pacific Ocean. Despite having managed to arrive from Oceania and thrive on the remote opposite side of the Indian Ocean, blue pigeons never successfully colonized the African mainland.

Vasa parrots have one of the strangest breeding systems among birds. Males are among a small group of birds that develop a phallus and mating takes place over protracted periods – as opposed to the 'blink-and-you-miss-it' copulation typical of most birds. Mating can be highly social, with large and demonstrative groups of birds gathering around a courting and mating pair. The larger females are dominant, and both males and females have multiple partners. One male will bring food to the nests of several females.

R 1 e **Lesser Vasa Parrot** *Coracopsis nigra*

M Bolokikely
F Perroquet Noir

DISTRIBUTION: Comoros and Madagascar. Fairly common in all types of forest throughout the island. Generally more common in eastern rainforest than Greater Vasa Parrot.

Length:	35 cm | 14"

WHERE TO SEE: Generally common, but perhaps most conspicuous in western dry forest, as at Ankarafantsika NP or Berenty.

ID: Vasa parrots are distinctive as a group but separation of the two species is difficult. Lesser Vasa Parrot is 20–25% smaller than Greater Vasa Parrot, but size can be hard to judge. Lesser Vasa Parrot has a smaller head and bill. Details of the bare parts are also useful: Lesser Vasa Parrot has less bare skin around the eye, a crooked line of bare skin at the back of the upper mandible, and a darker bill; Greater Vasa Parrot has extensive bare skin around the eye, a straight line of bare skin at the back of the upper mandible, and a very pale bill.

VOICE: Highly vocal, with a wide repertoire. The most distinctive vocalization is the song, a series of melodic whistles that first descend then ascend. Also gives simpler and rougher calls.
BEHAVIOUR: Often in groups. Nests in cavities. Feeds on fruit.

R 2 **Greater Vasa Parrot** *Coracopsis vasa*

M Bolokibe
F Perroquet Vaza

DISTRIBUTION: Comoros and Madagascar. Found primarily in forest, but more tolerant of human-modified areas than Lesser Vasa Parrot.

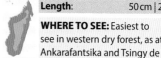

Length:	50 cm | 20"

WHERE TO SEE: Easiest to see in western dry forest, as at Ankarafantsika and Tsingy de Beharaha NPs or Berenty.

ID: See Lesser Vasa Parrot. The female Greater Vasa Parrot becomes completely or partially bald when rearing chicks, so any parrot with a bare head is a Greater Vasa Parrot.
VOICE: Calls generally louder and harsher than those of Lesser Vasa Parrot.
BEHAVIOUR: Similar to Lesser Vasa Parrot.

E 3 **Grey-headed Lovebird** *Agapornis canus*

M Sarivazo
F Inséparable à Tête Grise

DISTRIBUTION: A Madagascar endemic that has been introduced to the Comoros. Common in the north, west, and south in a variety of open habitats, both natural and human-modified. Uncommon in the east in deforested areas. Absent from the High Plateau, but escaped cage birds can be seen anywhere.

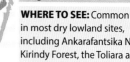

Length:	15 cm | 6"

WHERE TO SEE: Common in most dry lowland sites, including Ankarafantsika NP, Kirindy Forest, the Toliara area and Berenty.

ID: A tiny, short-tailed parrot with bright green plumage.
VOICE: Short, dry *"prrrtt"*, mainly given in flight.
BEHAVIOUR: A highly sociable bird that is always found in pairs or flocks. Flight is very fast and direct. Nests in cavities. Feeds on seeds and is considered a pest in some agricultural areas.

Lesser Vasa Parrot: smaller bill, more 'in front' of head; less bare skin around eye;

bare skin at the back of the upper mandible is jagged;

Greater Vasa Parrot: larger bill, in line with head; more bare skin around eye;

bare skin at the back of the upper mandible is straight;

Can resemble a raptor in flight

1

2

1

Vasa parrots show iridescent highlights in bright light

2

3 Very fast and direct flight

3♂

3♀

3♂

R 1 e Madagascar Coucal *Centropus toulou toulou*

M Toloho
F Coucal Toulou

DISTRIBUTION: Seychelles (Aldabra) and Madagascar. Fairly common although inconspicuous in any habitat with thick cover, including scrub, marsh and forest.
ID: A large, rufous-and-black bird with a heavy bill. Floppy flight with long tail and short wings is distinctive.
VOICE: Liquid, descending series of hoots, often likened to water glugging out of a bottle.

Length:	45–50 cm | 18–20"

WHERE TO SEE: Almost anywhere, even in Tana.

The scientific, Malagasy and French names all reflect the coucal's 'water bottle' call.

BEHAVIOUR: Sometimes perches up, but more often creeps through the undergrowth, almost like a reptile. Eats almost any animal it can catch and swallow.

B 2 Madagascar (Lesser) Cuckoo *Cuculus rochii*

M Taotaonkafa
F Coucou Malgache

DISTRIBUTION: Breeds exclusively on Madagascar, from August to April, when it is often heard, although can be hard to spot. Most migrate to Africa after breeding. Found in all habitats with a woody component.
ID: When perched, grey colour, barred underparts and horizontal posture are distinctive. Strong flight, long tail and pointed wings make it look very like a falcon or sparrowhawk when flying.

Length:	28 cm | 11"

WHERE TO SEE: Widespread and common, but easiest to see in the more open western forest, as at Ankarafantsika NP, Kirindy Forest, and in the spiny forest around Ifaty and Toliara.

VOICE: A whistled, descending, three- or four-note *"hew hew tew tew"*. It sings incessantly day and night from October to January – one of the most frequently heard and distinctive natural sounds of Madagascar.
BEHAVIOUR: Generally shy, but often sings from a prominent perch. A brood parasite that lays its eggs in the nests of many species of smaller birds. Eats insects, mainly caterpillars.

E 3 Crested Coua *Coua cristata*

M Tivoka
F Coua Huppé

DISTRIBUTION: The most widespread coua, found in forest throughout Madagascar. It is most common in dry forest, and tolerates degraded forest.
ID: Floppy crest and arboreal habits usually identify it easily. Mostly grey, with a buff chest, white belly and colourful two-tone bare skin around the eye.

Length:	42 cm | 17"

WHERE TO SEE: Easiest in dry forest – Berenty, around Toliara, Ankarafantsika and Ankarana NPs and Kirindy Forest.

VOICE: Highly vocal, with many different calls. The most common is a doubled, wooden *"touk-touk"*. Also gives a long series of piercing 'laser gun' calls.
BEHAVIOUR: This is the coua most likely to be seen bouncing around high in trees. More sociable than other couas, often in groups. Eats small animals and fruit.

1

Coucals act almost like mammals, creeping through the undergrowth and running along the ground.

1br

1nb

2

3

Colourful bare
facial skin typical
of couas

Couas are members of the cuckoo family. They form a genus, or perhaps even a sub-family of birds that is found only in Madagascar. Their bold patterns of bare facial skin and exuberant tree-bouncing or ground-strutting behaviours make them favourites with many visitors.

❸ ➊ Red-capped Coua *Coua ruficeps*

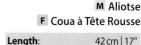

M Aliotse
F Coua à Tête Rousse

DISTRIBUTION: Two distinctive subspecies: one with a red cap, and one with an olive-brown cap. 'Red-capped' is in western Madagascar in dry forest. 'Green-capped' is found in spiny forest and other dry woody habitats in the southwest.

Length: 42 cm | 17"

WHERE TO SEE: Common in Ankarafantsika NP. For the 'Green-capped' subspecies, try the Arboretum d'Antsokay in Toliara.

ID: Tall, slim, long-tailed coua. The red-capped subspecies overlaps in range with Coquerel's Coua, but is separated by its red cap, longer legs and slimmer shape.

VOICE: Vocal, with several different calls. Most distinctive is series of higher rising notes followed by lower pitched notes: *"quee-quee-quee-hm-hm-hm"*. Also makes agitated scratchy calls and a simple low-pitched note.

BEHAVIOUR: Walks along the forest floor feeding on insects. Often calls from higher perches.

❸ ➋ Coquerel's Coua *Coua coquereli*

M Gory
F Coua de Coquerel

DISTRIBUTION: Uncommon to fairly common in western and far northern Madagascar in dry forest; rare and local in the southwest.

Length: 42 cm | 17"

WHERE TO SEE: Fairly common in Kirindy Forest and Ankarafantsika and Zombitse-Vohibasia NPs.

ID: Relatively small, compact, short-legged, brownish coua with a rufous belly and bright blue bare facial skin. Giant Coua is very similar coloration, but is much larger.

VOICE: Song is a single lower note followed by several higher notes: *"chwee-quee-quee-quee"*. Call comprises two notes: the first high and rising, and the second raspy and low-pitched.

BEHAVIOUR: The most terrestrial of the western couas: walks along the forest floor feeding on insects.

❸ ➌ Giant Coua *Coua gigas*

M Lejabe
F Coua Géant

DISTRIBUTION: Uncommon in dry forest in much of the south and west, although absent from the northwest.

Length: 62 cm | 24"

WHERE TO SEE: Easy to see at Berenty and Kirindy Forest. Also present in Zombitse-Vohibasia NP, although more shy.

ID: Well-named, as this is an enormous coua. Like Coquerel's Coua, has brownish coloration, rufous belly and blue facial skin, but is much larger and also shows a pink patch behind the eye.

VOICE: Loud, resonant, ringing calls. Some are similar to the calls of Coquerel's Coua, but are usually lower-pitched and louder.

BEHAVIOUR: Walks on the forest floor and feeds on insects and small vertebrates. Sometimes goes high into trees to roost or call.

1

Often seen on paths, but shies away at the approach of people.

The subspecies in the southwest has an olive cap, and is sometimes split as 'Green-capped Coua' *Coua olivaceiceps*.

2

Blue bare skin on face

3

Similar to Coquerel's Coua, but much larger

Blue and pink bare skin on face

❸ ① Red-fronted Coua *Coua reynaudii*

M Taitoaka
F Coua de Reynaud

DISTRIBUTION: Uncommon to locally fairly common in eastern rainforest.

ID: Dark grey-green coua with a red forehead. Smaller than Red-breasted Coua, with grey rather than dark red underparts.

VOICE: Most frequent and distinctive vocalization is a very long, mechanical rattle, unlike the calls of other couas.

BEHAVIOUR: A shy species, found alone or in pairs. Walks on the ground, sometimes along trails, or creeps through thick tangles, sometimes well above the forest floor. Insects are its main food.

Length: 40 cm | 16"

WHERE TO SEE: With some effort, can usually be found in Ranomafana, Andasibe-Mantadia and Masoala NPs.

❸ ② Red-breasted Coua *Coua serriana*

M Koa
F Coua de Serre

DISTRIBUTION: Uncommon to locally common in the lush rainforests in the northern half of eastern Madagascar.

ID: Dark coua with red underparts.

VOICE: Song is a loud, whistled "*koaaaaa*", often followed by a much quieter, low-pitched grumble. Distinctive call is an abrupt "*chik-wit*".

BEHAVIOUR: Shy species that is found alone or in pairs. Walks on the forest floor, feeding on fruit, insects and small vertebrates.

Length: 42 cm | 17"

WHERE TO SEE: Masoala and Marojejy NPs. Also present in Andasibe-Mantadia NP, but much harder to find.

❸ ③ Blue Coua *Coua caerulea*

M Mariha
F Coua Bleu

DISTRIBUTION: Fairly common in eastern rainforest and in some patches of Sambirano forest in the north.

ID: A large, dark blue coua, one of the most spectacular Malagasy birds when seen in good light.

VOICE: Growls, rasps and explosive short trills. Also gives a more melodic, descending series of notes: "*kwee-kwe-kwe-kwe-kwe...*".

BEHAVIOUR: An arboreal species, usually found singly or in pairs. More likely to make long flights than most couas, gliding on its short wings and steering with its huge tail. Eats fruit, large invertebrates and reptiles.

Length: 50 cm | 20"

WHERE TO SEE: Usually not difficult to find in Ranomafana, Andasibe-Mantadia and Masoala NPs.

Last of the giant couas Giant and Blue Couas are big, but Madagascar used to have even larger couas. There are two huge extinct species known from subfossils, plus the Snail-eating Coua *C. delalandei* that was found on the island of St. Marie until its extinction in the 19th century.

Blue Coua is often found in the canopy, and is seen in flight more often than other couas.

1

Multi-coloured bare facial skin

2

Blue bare facial skin

3

Large and blue

E **1** **White-browed Owl** *Ninox superciliaris*

M Tovotovoka
F Ninoxe à Sourcils Blancs

DISTRIBUTION: Found in forest and woodland throughout much of the island. Prefers clearings, forest edge and scrub. Most common in the southwest and northeast, although still quite local even in those parts of Madagascar.
ID: Medium-sized brown owl with a barred belly. Larger size, dark eyes and barring on the belly separate it from Madagascar Scops Owl. Darker than Barn Owl, and less likely to be found in a village or open grassland.
VOICE: Distinctive vocalizations are given frequently, including during the day: a rising *"hwoooo"* and a series of yelps.
BEHAVIOUR: Pairs often roost together in a dense tangle of vegetation. Hunts at night, watching from a perch, then swooping down on insects and small vertebrates.

Length: 30 cm | 12"

WHERE TO SEE: Local guides at Berenty and Zombitse-Vohibasia NP often know the location of a day roost. Fairly common in Masoala and Kirindy Forest; may be heard at night from the lodges at those sites.

2 **Barn Owl** *Tyto alba*

M Tararaka
F Effraie des Clochers

DISTRIBUTION: Found throughout most of the world, including all of Madagascar. More common in towns, farms and deforested areas than in natural habitats.
ID: Medium-sized, grey, buff and white owl with a heart-shaped face.
VOICE: Unnerving raspy shriek, probably the reason that many Malagasy people consider this owl to be a bad omen.
BEHAVIOUR: Hunts small animals, especially mammals. In some cities and villages, subsists mainly on introduced rats and mice. Nests in cavities in rocks, trees and man-made structures.

Length: 30–35 cm | 12–14"

WHERE TO SEE: Nests in many Malagasy villages, and even in central Tana. Sometimes seen at a day roost at Tsimbazaza Zoo.

E **3** **Madagascar Scops Owl** *Otus rutilus*

M Torotoroka
F Petit-duc Malgache

DISTRIBUTION: Fairly common throughout Madagascar in most wooded habitats, from primary forest to heavily disturbed scrub. Two subspecies are recognized: 'western' *O. r. madagascariensis* (west, south and central) and 'eastern' *O. r. rutilus* (east). 'Eastern' has a red **3a** and a grey-brown morph **3b**, 'western' a grey **3c** and grey-brown morph **3d**. These are sometimes split as full species: Torotoroka Scops Owl in the west and Malagasy (or Rainforest) Scops Owl in the east.
ID: Madagascar's only small owl, which sports distinctive ear-tufts.
VOICE: A plaintive series of several hoots that become first louder then softer. In the east, the notes tend to be very pure, while in the west they are slightly trilled.
BEHAVIOUR: Roosts in dense tangles of vegetation, often in pairs. Hunts insects at night.

Length: 22–24 cm | 9"

Often seen roosting in tree cavities and dense tangles during the day

WHERE TO SEE: Local guides in Berenty, Kirindy Forest, and Zombitse, Ankarafantsika and Andasibe-Mantadia NPs often know the location of a day roost. At night, can be found in almost any forest.

1

Often found roosting during the day

2 Heart-shaped face

3c

3b

3a

® ① Madagascar Nightjar
Caprimulgus madagascariensis madagascariensis

M Matoriandro
F Engoulevent Malgache

DISTRIBUTION: Madagascar and Seychelles (Aldabra). Common throughout Madagascar in most habitats except closed-canopy forest and treeless grassland.

ID: The only nightjar likely to be seen in most of Madagascar, usually in graceful, bounding flight, when its long-tailed, crooked-winged shape is distinctive. Shows white in the wings and tail, and is not found inside thick forest, unlike Collared Nightjar.

VOICE: A highly distinctive call that is one of the most evocative sounds of Madagascar: a single introductory note followed by an accelerating trill: *"tuk t-r-r-r-r-r-r-r-r-r-r"*. Most vocal at dusk.

BEHAVIOUR: Roosts on the ground during the day, and becomes active at dusk. Feeds on the wing, swooping across open areas and catching flying insects.

Length:	21 cm | 8"

WHERE TO SEE: Very common and familiar bird that can be heard and seen almost anywhere on the island at dusk, even on buildings in central Tana. Guides at Arboretum d'Antsokay in Toliara can sometimes point out roosting birds.

The Malagasy name for Madagascar Nightjar (Matoriandro) means 'day sleeper'.

ⓔ ② Collared Nightjar *Gactornis enarratus*

M Tataroala
F Engoulevent à Nuque Rousse

DISTRIBUTION: Rare and local in undisturbed eastern rainforest.

ID: Unlikely to be seen except by those who are particularly looking for it. If there is any doubt, the scaly back and rufous collar should clinch the identification. Madagascar Nightjar does not roost on the floor of thick rainforest. In flight, Collared Nightjar lacks white in the wings and tail.

VOICE: Unusually among nightjars, the song is unknown.

BEHAVIOUR: Single birds or pairs roost on or near the forest floor during the day. They are active at night, when they hunt for insects on the wing, inside the forest. Nests in a small palm or fern, up to two metres above the ground.

Length:	24 cm | 9"

WHERE TO SEE: Andasibe-Mantadia NP. Among the feats regularly performed by Madagascar's amazing local guides, the ability consistently to find this cryptic species on the forest floor during the day is particularly impressive.

The Collared Nightjar is an unusual and mysterious bird, seemingly more primitive than most other nightjars. Its atypical behaviours include feeding inside the forest and nesting in small trees. The fact that its voice is still unknown is quite amazing.

1

Nightjars have bristles around their bill which serve to funnel insects into their mouth when they are feeding aerially at night.

Nightjars often sit in open areas, such as on roads, at night.

Shows white in the wings

Cryptic, but sometimes spotted roosting on the ground during the day.

2

Often roosts in pairs

ⓔ ① African Palm Swift *Cypsiurus parvus gracilis*

M Manaviandro
F Martinet des Palmes

DISTRIBUTION: Most of Afrotropics. Fairly common in open habitats below 1,100 m (3,600') in much of Madagascar, often in association with palms, especially Bismarck Palm *Bismarckia nobilis*, Coconut Palm *Cocos nucifera* and *Hyphaene* spp. Absent from the High Plateau.

ID: Spindly, long-tailed swift with agile but weak flight. Smaller, slimmer, and paler grey than African Black Swift.

VOICE: Weak, rattling trills given in flight.

BEHAVIOUR: Like all swifts, normally seen only in flight. It eats, drinks and mates on the wing, and perches only near the nests, inside palm trees.

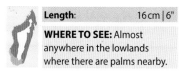

Length:	16 cm	6"

WHERE TO SEE: Almost anywhere in the lowlands where there are palms nearby.

ⓔ ② African Black Swift *Apus barbatus balstoni*

M Sidintsidinamainty
F Martinet du Cap

DISTRIBUTION: Scattered areas of sub-Saharan Africa. The two subspecies in the Malagasy region may prove to be full species. Occurs throughout Madagascar, though erratically; perhaps semi-migratory. Often feeds over wet areas like rice paddies, lakes and the ocean.

ID: Big, dark, powerful swift. Much stronger flier than African Palm Swift, and tends to fly higher.

VOICE: High-pitched trill given in flight.

BEHAVIOUR: As is typical for swifts, usually seen only on the wing, often in flocks, and even seems capable of sleeping in flight! Eats flying insects.

Length:	16–18 cm	6–7"

WHERE TO SEE: Ranges widely and can be seen almost anywhere. Can usually be spotted in the skies over Tana.

Ⓡ ③ Mascarene Martin *Phedina borbonica*

M Sidintsidina
F Hirondelle des Mascareignes

DISTRIBUTION: Breeds on Madagascar, Réunion and Mauritius. Common in Madagascar year-round, but some regularly reach mainland Africa, suggesting migratory behaviour. Widespread in many habitats, although gathers especially over wetlands. Readily nests on man-made structures, and can be seen in towns.

Length:	14 cm	5.5"

WHERE TO SEE: When in Madagascar, look up! Very common.

ID: This is the default swallow in Madagascar. Although superficially similar to swifts, swallows are not in a closely related family. Flight more relaxed than a swift. Wings are more crooked, and less sickle-shaped. Unlike swifts, martins are often seen perched. Brown back and pale, dark-streaked underparts are unlike those of any swift. The **Brown-throated Martin** *Riparia paludicola* (not illustrated) is uncommon, mainly in the highlands: it is smaller than Mascarene Martin, has plain underparts, and is a much weaker flier.

VOICE: Short sizzling call given mainly in flight.

BEHAVIOUR: Often in small flocks. Insect prey is caught in flight.

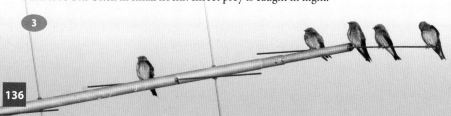

③

1

Long, thin tail

2

Much heavier than African Palm Swift, with much stronger flight

Malagasy subspecies are sometimes split as a full species: Madagascar Black Swift *A. balstoni*

3

Broader wings and more squared off tail than swifts

Madagascar Malachite Kingfisher
Corythornis vintsioides vintsioides

M Vintsirano
F Martin-pêcheur Vintsi

DISTRIBUTION: Comoros and Madagascar. Fairly common in small numbers throughout Madagascar in almost any kind of wetland habitat, including marshes, rivers, lakes, rice paddies, mangroves and seashore.
ID: Colour, shape and habits all distinctive: a chunky little bird with a brilliant blue back and rufous underparts.
VOICE: High-pitched *"tsip"*.
BEHAVIOUR: Perches motionlessly, watching for prey, which it swoops down to snatch. Eats a wide variety of small animals including fish, insects and crustaceans.

Length: 15 cm | 6"

WHERE TO SEE: Can be seen almost anywhere, even on rice paddies. Present in Tana, such as at Lake Alarobia.

Madagascar Pygmy Kingfisher
Corythornis madagascariensis

M Vintsiala
F Martin-pêcheur Malgache

DISTRIBUTION: Rainforest and dry forest below 1,200 m (4,000'). Absent from most of centre and southwest. Most common in eastern rainforest, probably due to a higher abundance of prey, particularly frogs.
ID: Unmistakable jewel of a bird with an orange bill and back, and white underparts. Despite its bright colour, can be surprisingly hard to spot in the gloomy forest interior.
VOICE: Single note that is similar to that of Madagascar Malachite Kingfisher, but slightly lower-pitched, stronger, and more penetrating.
BEHAVIOUR: This is a forest kingfisher, unlike the aquatic Madagascar Malachite Kingfisher. Like the Madagascar Malachite Kingfisher, it hunts from a perch. Eats insects and small vertebrates, especially frogs and small reptiles. Digs a nest cavity into an embankment, which can be along a dry streambed or beside a road.

Length: 14 cm | 5·5"

WHERE TO SEE: Present at most forest sites, but most common at Ranomafana and Andasibe-Mantadia NPs.

---

3 Olive (Madagascar) Bee-eater
Merops superciliosus

M Kiriokirioke
F Guêpier Malgache

DISTRIBUTION: Eastern and southern Africa, Comoros and Madagascar. Common throughout the island in virtually all types of habitat. Nests in colonies in earthen banks, often along rivers and streams.
ID: Green colour and elongated central tail feathers are distinctive, even in flight.
VOICE: A short rolling trill, often given in flight: *"k-r-r-r-ree"* which gives the bird its Malagasy name.
BEHAVIOUR: Perches conspicuously on branches, snags or wires, often in small groups. Catches insect prey in flight.

Length: 23–31 cm | 9–12"

WHERE TO SEE: Almost anywhere, in open habitat.

Always near water

Always in forest, sometimes near water

Colourful and conspicuous

1 Broad-billed Roller *Eurystomus glaucurus*

M Vorombaratra
F Rolle Violet

DISTRIBUTION: Breeds throughout Madagascar in open forest, forest edge, woodland and savannah. Not usually found in closed-canopy forest or in treeless areas. Present mainly between October and March, migrating to Africa during the dry season.

Length:	32 cm | 12·5"

WHERE TO SEE: Generally common and conspicuous, but especially prominent around the Ankarafantsika NP headquarters and Isalo.

ID: A large, colourful bird with a yellow bill, although can look dull and dark at a distance. Flies powerfully and can easily be mistaken for a falcon, although the roller has a yellow bill, light blue tail, and less smooth, more jerky flight action.

VOICE: Loud series of complaining *"kachak-kachak-kachak"* notes that can be short or long and frequently repeated. Often sounds quite agitated, especially when a pair is calling together.

BEHAVIOUR: Single birds or pairs spend long periods sitting high on prominent perches. Also flies around for extended periods, especially at dawn and dusk. Feeds mainly on insects, caught on the wing.

E 2 Madagascar Hoopoe *Upupa marginata*

M Takodara
F Huppe Malgache

DISTRIBUTION: Fairly common throughout much of Madagascar, although scarce or absent in the east. Uses natural woodland and forest, as well as human-modified habitats.

Length:	32 cm | 12·5"

WHERE TO SEE: Western dry forest, as around Berenty, Kirindy Forest, and Ankarafantsika and Ankarana NPs.

ID: Hoopoes are among the most unusual-looking and distinctive of all birds, and are readily identified by their peachy head and breast, prominent crest, and broad, black-and-white wings that makes them look like huge butterflies in flight.

VOICE: Low trill, very different from that of the world's other hoopoes.

BEHAVIOUR: Usually seen alone or in pairs. Walks along the ground with a bobbing gait, feeding on insects. Uses trees for perching (especially when singing), and nests in cavities.

One of countless surprising things about Madagascar is that it lacks woodpeckers, despite being close to the African mainland, where woodpeckers are common. Madagascar Hoopoe, Nuthatch Vanga (*page 170*) and some tetrakas (*page 162*) are among the birds that extract invertebrates from dead wood and bark, filling the woodpecker niche on Madagascar.

1

2

Boldly marked black-and-white wings and tail.

Ground-rollers form a family of birds found only on Madagascar. They are among the most beautiful and remarkable of the island's birds. Most species that are elusive and local have not been covered in this book. However, an exception was made with ground-rollers, due to the attractive and unique nature of the group, and in the hope that including them will inspire more visitors to seek them out. The best way to find ground-rollers is to enlist the help of guides who specialize in birds. Ground-rollers are burrow nesters. When they fly through the rainforest, they seem surprisingly large, an impression that is enhanced by their noisy wingbeats.

E **1** Pitta-like Ground-roller *Atelornis pittoides*

M Tsakoaka
F Brachyptérolle Pittoïde

DISTRIBUTION: Eastern rainforest. This is the most adaptable ground-roller, found in different kinds of forest from low elevation up to 2,000 m (6,500').

ID: Distinctive bird with a dazzling array of colours: white, rufous, green and blue. Do not miss the spangles behind the eyes.

VOICE: Like all the rainforest ground-rollers, gives a *"boop"* song that can easily be imitated by humans. This vocalization is quiet but penetrating, and repeated at intervals of several seconds.

BEHAVIOUR: A shy and elusive bird, usually seen singly. Walks on the ground, sometimes on paths, dashing and jumping acrobatically to catch its prey, including insects, chameleons and frogs. Often wags its long tail. Will ascend to the mid-storey of the forest, especially to call.

Length:	27 cm | 11"

WHERE TO SEE: This is the ground-roller most likely to be seen without expressly searching for it. Fairly common in Ranomafana and Andasibe-Mantadia NPs. Possible but less common in Amber Mountain NP. Like all the ground-rollers, best searched for when vocal, from late September to early January.

E **2** Rufous-headed Ground-roller
Atelornis crossleyi

M Voromboka
F Brachyptérolle de Crossley

DISTRIBUTION: Uncommon in middle- and high-elevation rainforest in eastern Madagascar. Prefers very moist forest with lots of bamboo, moss and fallen trees.

ID: Smallest ground-roller. Shape and back colour similar to Pitta-like Ground-roller, but the rufous head and underparts are diagnostic. If flushed, the tail is uniformly coloured, unlike the brown-and-blue, two-toned tail of Pitta-like Ground-roller. Both species show a white blaze in the wing, both on the ground and in flight.

VOICE: Gives a *"boop"* similar to that of Pitta-like Ground-roller, but slightly lower-pitched and more disyllabic.

BEHAVIOUR: Similar to Pitta-like Ground-roller. Less likely to call from a high perch; generally remains low to the ground.

NEAR THREATENED	
Length:	25 cm | 10"

WHERE TO SEE: The Vohiparara Trail in Ranomafana NP. But even here, seeing this bird is difficult and likely to take some time. Other places that hold this bird include the higher sections of Andasibe-Mantadia NP and the Anjozorobe-Angavo forest.

1 The most widespread and frequently encountered ground-roller

2 Shy and difficult to see

E ① Short-legged Ground-roller
Brachypteracias leptosomus

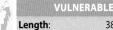

M Fandikalalana
F Brachyptérolle Leptosome

DISTRIBUTION: Locally uncommon to rare in eastern rainforest, in the most moist microhabitats. Prefers low and middle elevations.

ID: The largest ground-roller, with a heavy chest and big square head. White tips to the tail feathers are diagnostic in flight.

VOICE: Typical ground-roller *"boop"*, higher-pitched than that of Pitta-like or Rufous-headed Ground-rollers (*page 142*). Sometimes gives a quick rolling series of notes without pausing.

BEHAVIOUR: Unusual among ground-rollers in terms of behaviour, as it spends most of its time in trees. Nests in trees, either in a natural cavity or a burrow excavated into the roots of a big epiphyte. Forages for insects, crabs, frogs, chameleons, geckos and other reptiles. Often found in pairs.

VULNERABLE	
Length:	38 cm | 15"

WHERE TO SEE: In Masoala NP, this species is common enough that it may be encountered by chance. It can also be found in Andasibe-Mantadia NP with a dedicated search and the help of a guide. Occasionally found in Ranomafana NP.

E ② Scaly Ground-roller
Geobiastes squamiger

M Fangadiovy
F Brachyptérolle Écaillé

DISTRIBUTION: Locally uncommon to rare in rainforest of eastern Madagascar. Found in lower and middle elevations, especially in damp valleys, often along streams.

ID: One of the most spectacular of all Malagasy birds, with rufous, green and blue highlights, and fine scaly markings. Pale blue tips to the tail feathers are distinctive in flight, although not as striking as the white tail tips of Short-legged Ground-roller.

VOICE: Song is a series of *"boop"* notes like other ground-rollers, but the individual notes are lower-pitched and longer than those of other species. Seems to be less vocal than other rainforest ground-rollers.

BEHAVIOUR: Similar to Rufous-headed Ground-roller (*page 142*). Often leaves forest floor to call from a low perch. Feeds mainly on invertebrates, plus some small vertebrates.

VULNERABLE	
Length:	30–32 cm | 12"

WHERE TO SEE: Easiest to find in Masoala and Marojejy NPs. It can also be found in the Mantadia sector of Andasibe-Mantadia NP with a dedicated search and the help of a guide. Occasionally found in Ranomafana NP.

Like New World antpittas and Old World pittas, ground-rollers are sometimes seen on forest trails.

1

Purple highlights on the back
of the head

The most arboreal
ground-roller

2

Complex and beautiful
patterning

Long-tailed Ground-roller
Uratelornis chimaera

VULNERABLE	
Length:	47–52 cm | 19–20"

WHERE TO SEE: Not found anywhere on the circuit of sites frequently visited by general naturalists. Birders who are keen to find this, and other spiny forest specialties, visit the small private forest reserves near Ifaty, north of Toliara. There, skilled local guides assist in locating this shy species.

DISTRIBUTION: A small portion of the spiny forest along the southwest coast, north of Toliara.
ID: One of Madagascar's most distinctive birds, with a long tail, powder blue wing patch and boldly marked head.
VOICE: Less vocal than rainforest ground-rollers. Gives a variable series of *"toop"* calls which are delivered faster than in the other ground-rollers.
BEHAVIOUR: Secretive and elusive despite the open nature of its spiny forest habitat. Behaves much like a roadrunner (distinctive New World birds), running on its strong legs, and cocking up its long tail. Eats insects.

Cuckoo-roller is another of Madagascar's odd avian treasures, and one of the world's most enigmatic birds. It is so different from other birds that it is placed in its own family, which, in turn, may even deserve to be considered a distinct order. What this means is that it has been evolving independently for a long time.

  Cuckoo-roller *Leptosomus discolor*

Length:	50 cm | 20"

WHERE TO SEE: Widespread but easiest to see in the western dry forest, as in Ankarafantsika, Zombitse and Tsingy de Bemaraha NPs, and Kirindy Forest.

DISTRIBUTION: Comoros and Madagascar. Found throughout Madagascar in all forest types. Sometimes found in heavily degraded habitats that still contain trees. Less common in the spiny forest than in other forest types, and most common in eastern rainforest.
ID: A large, distinctive bird with an oddly reptilian aspect when seen up close. Very different male and female plumages. Brown female could be mistaken for a raptor when perched, but has a hook-less bill and a different pattern from any raptor. The male has a dark wings with iridescent highlights and blue-grey underparts; it is unlike any other bird. Could also be mistaken for a raptor in flight, but can usually be recognized by its incessant call.
VOICE: One of the most obvious and distinctive Malagasy natural sounds: an incessantly-given, three-part, whistled, descending *"pheeeew teeeew teeew"*. This may be the only bird sound to be heard on a hot afternoon in the forest. This song is given both when perched, and more often in flight. Male makes an elaborate flight display that includes calls, gliding, flapping and rolling.
BEHAVIOUR: Perches motionlessly in the canopy for long periods. Frequently flies over the forest, alternating periods of flapping and soaring. Nests in cavities. Eats a range of small animals, although especially fond of chameleons.

Most often seen in flight; soars like a raptor

Off-centre positioning of the eye gives the Cuckoo-roller an oddly reptilian appearance.

Asities are yet another family of birds found only in Madagascar, the closest relatives to which are the broadbills of Asia. Breeding males sport caruncles, bizarre patches of bright blue and/or green skin on their face. These caruncles grow at the start of the breeding season but fade away during the non-breeding season. Asities have a unique method of constructing their hanging nests. They first weave an orb then poke a hole into it to create an entrance, rather than building the entrance into the nest.

E **1** ## Velvet Asity *Philepitta castanea*

M Asity
F Philépitte Veloutée

DISTRIBUTION: Uncommon in eastern rainforest, especially at middle elevations.
ID: The black male with green caruncles when breeding or yellow fringes when not breeding **1a** is unmistakable. The female is a drab bird, but can be identified by its round shape and short tail.
VOICE: Most common call consists of very high-pitched notes, almost like a rusty hinge.
BEHAVIOUR: Lives mainly in forest mid-storey. Perches motionlessly for long periods and often allows close approach. Feeds on fruit. Unusual breeding system in which males have leks where they compete to attract the attention of females. Display behaviours include opening the wings, displaying the bright caruncle, and sometimes even performing somersaults.

Length:	16 cm | 6"

WHERE TO SEE: Andasibe-Mantadia and Ranomafana NPs.

E **2** ## Schlegel's Asity *Philepitta schlegeli*

M Soisoy
F Philépitte de Schlegel

DISTRIBUTION: Rare and local, mainly in western dry forest, but also in Sambirano forest in the north.
ID: Breeding males' multi-coloured caruncles render them unmistakable. Non-breeding males, females and immature birds are fairly drab, but within their range can be identified by their round shape and short tail.
VOICE: Extremely high-pitched *"sit"* notes usually delivered in series.
BEHAVIOUR: Similar to Velvet Asity, although more shy, and more often found in canopy. Also leks, but has a different display from Velvet Asity; lekking behaviour may involve drooping the wings, fluffing up the breast feathers, cocking the tail and singing.

NEAR THREATENED

Length:	13 cm | 5"

WHERE TO SEE: Ankarafantsika and Tsingy de Bemaraha NPs.

E **3** ## Common Sunbird Asity *Neodrepanis coruscans*

M Zafindrasity
F Philépitte Souimanga

DISTRIBUTION: Fairly common, although hard to see, in middle- and high-elevation eastern rainforest.
ID: One of Madagascar's smallest birds. Although the breeding male is distinctive, having a blue caruncle, the female and non-breeding male could be confused with a sunbird (*page 164*), but are smaller, shorter-tailed and have a more curved bill.
VOICE: Short series of extremely high-pitched *"seep"* notes.
BEHAVIOUR: Usually seen singly. Generally stays in the canopy, but will descend to lower flowering trees. Feeds mainly on nectar.

Length:	11 cm | 4"

WHERE TO SEE: Not rare, but mostly confined to the high canopy – so be prepared to get a stiff neck when searching for it! Best looked for in Ranomafana and Andasibe-Mantadia NPs.

In breeding plumage, male asities develop colourful caruncles

E **1** # Madagascar Lark *Mirafra hova*

M Sorohitra
F Alouette Malgache

DISTRIBUTION: One of the most common and widespread Malagasy birds, found throughout in open habitat.
ID: A small, short-tailed, streaky bird with a pale bill. Larks can be confusing, but this is the only small terrestrial brown bird in Madagascar. Madagascar Cisticola (*page 158*) is somewhat similar but smaller, and only occasionally walks on the ground.
VOICE: Mixture of drawn-out and musical notes, and shorter, chatty notes. Sings in flight.
BEHAVIOUR: Walks on the ground, feeding on seeds and insects.

Length: 13 cm | 5"

WHERE TO SEE: Common throughout most of Madagascar. This is one of few native birds that manages to thrive in completely deforested places, like the desolate grasslands of the High Plateau.

E **2** # Madagascar Wagtail *Motacilla flaviventris*

M Triotrio
F Bergeronnette Malgache

DISTRIBUTION: Throughout the island in open habitats, often near water. Especially common on the High Plateau, often in towns.
ID: A small, long-tailed bird with a grey back, yellow belly and a black 'necklace' across the chest.
VOICE: Normal call is a two-part *"trio-trio"*. The song includes more musical, whistled notes.
BEHAVIOUR: Continually walks around and wags its tail. Feeds on invertebrates.

Length: 19 cm | 7.5"

WHERE TO SEE: Common in Tana and throughout most of the island.

Some English common names and even scientific names of birds are 'onomatopoeic', created in imitation of a call made by the bird. But a much higher proportion of Malagasy names are delightfully onomatopoeic. The wagtail is a good example: 'Triotrio' in imitation of the wagtail's scratchy two-part call.

3 # Pied Crow *Corvus albus*

M Goaika
F Corbeau Pie

DISTRIBUTION: Sub-Saharan Africa. Common in small numbers throughout Madagascar in almost any open habitat. Generally less common on the High Plateau.
ID: Large black-and-white bird. Can soar and look raptor-like at a distance, but no raptor has its pied patterning.
VOICE: Rough *"crrrraw"*, similar to that given by most crows.
BEHAVIOUR: Often in pairs or small groups. Frequently seen flying, often quite high. Highly adaptable, and feeds on almost anything; will eat many plant materials, prey on small animals, and scavenge.

Length: 46–50 cm | 18–20"

WHERE TO SEE: Conspicuous and numerous, especially in dry, open habitat in the west.

3

Often mobbed by smaller birds like Crested Drongo (*page 176*)

1

Sings while performing a display flight

2

Usually seen on the ground or perched on man-made structures

3

Looks raptor-like in flight, but is strikingly black-and-white

ℝ ① Madagascar Bulbul *Hypsipetes madagascariensis*

M Horovana
F Bulbul Malgache

DISTRIBUTION: Seychelles (Aldabra), Glorieuses, Comoros and Madagascar. Found throughout Madagascar in almost any habitat with woody vegetation.
ID: Slim, medium-sized brown-black bird. Separated from all other species by its orange bill.
VOICE: A complex series of rattling calls. Also gives a cat-like whining.
BEHAVIOUR: Often in pairs or groups, which are active and conspicuous. Feeds on fruit and insects.

Length:	24 cm | 9.5"

WHERE TO SEE: Almost anywhere, including Tana.

The Madagascar Bulbul belongs to a genus that is found in Asia and the Malagasy region, but not on mainland Africa, a clear example of a Malagasy species with Asian origins.

ℝ ② Madagascar Paradise Flycatcher
e *Terpsiphone mutata mutata*

M Tsingitry
F Gobe-Mouche de Paradis de Madagascar

DISTRIBUTION: Comoros and Madagascar. Fairly common throughout Madagascar in woodland and forest habitat, including areas heavily modified by humans.
ID: Long-tailed males are easy to recognize, and occur as white or rufous morphs. The shorter-tailed all-rufous female is slightly less obvious, but still distinctive. All birds show blue bare skin around the eye.
VOICE: The call is a short, rough *"shree-shreet"*. The song is an exuberant and bubbling series of pure whistles.
BEHAVIOUR: Usually seen singly or in pairs, moving restlessly through the middle storey. Feeds mainly on insects.

Length:	18 cm | 7" (long–tailed males up to 30 cm | 12")

WHERE TO SEE: Common at all forest sites, although perhaps easiest to see in western dry forest.

𝔼 ③ Madagascar Mannikin *Lonchura nana*

M Tsiporitika
F Capucin Malgache

DISTRIBUTION: Fairly common although inconspicuous throughout Madagascar in almost any open habitat.
ID: Tiny brown bird with a black bib.
VOICE: Short whistled *"tsweet"*, most frequently given in flight and often in chorus by a flock.
BEHAVIOUR: Highly social, and usually in active flocks of up to 20. Feeds exclusively on seeds, especially those of grasses.

Length:	9 cm | 3.5"

WHERE TO SEE: Common at most sites, but can be inconspicuous and is easily overlooked.

3

Almost always found in flocks

1

2♂

Male white morph. Can show a white or black back

2♀

Orange bill

Tiny, social birds

3

2♂

Immature male rufous morph. Tail is elongated, but shorter than full adult plumage, which takes 3–5 years to attain

E **1** Madagascar Magpie-robin
Copsychus albospecularis

M Fitatrala
F Shama Malgache

DISTRIBUTION: Fairly common throughout Madagascar in all types of forest. Although absent from completely deforested areas, it is found in forest edge and secondary habitats.

ID: Black-and-white male is distinctive. Brown-and-white female is less obvious, but can still be identified by white wing patch. The males in the northeastern rainforest have a black belly.

VOICE: The song is a complex, variable series of thin whistles and lower notes, sometimes incorporating mimicry of other birds.

BEHAVIOUR: Usually seen singly or in pairs, on the ground or in the understorey. Hops rather than walks along the ground. Feeds mainly on insects and spiders.

Length: 18 cm | 7"

WHERE TO SEE: Common in all forest sites, although most easily seen in dry forest. Look for black-bellied males in Masoala and Marojejy NPs.

E **2** Forest Rock Thrush *Monticola sharpei*

M Androbaka
F Monticole de Forêt

DISTRIBUTION: Patchily distributed and generally uncommon in eastern rainforest and in rocky areas of the west. There is also an isolated population in the rainforest of Amber Mountain.

ID: Rufous-and-grey male is distinctive. Brown female lacks the white patch in the wing of Madagascar Magpie-robin, and is larger than female African Stonechat. Western populations are paler than eastern and northern ones, and were formerly split as **Benson's Rock Thrush** *M. bensoni* **2a**.

VOICE: Astoundingly variable series of mournful-sounding whistles. Often mimics other birds within its song.

BEHAVIOUR: Eastern and northern birds are found in the understorey of forest, often adjacent to rocky areas. Western birds live on exposed rocks. Eats insects and fruit.

WHERE TO SEE: The Isalo area, including the vicinity of some of the lodges. Also often seen along the main highway through Ranomafana NP, and in Tsingy de Bemaraha and Amber Mountain NPs.

Length: 16 cm | 6"

Beachgoers who visit Anakao, south of Toliara, should see the **Littoral Rock Thrush** *M. imerinus*, a localized bird of the southwest coast.

e **3** African Stonechat *Saxicola torquatus*

M Fitatra
F Tarier d'Afrique

DISTRIBUTION: Sub-Saharan Africa, Comoros, and Madagascar. Occurs widely in brushy habitat and marshes. One of the few birds that occurs on top of the highest mountains.

ID: The distinctive male is black-and-white, with a rufous chest patch. The brown female is less obvious, but is the only brown robin-like bird likely to be seen perching in open country.

VOICE: Harsh *"chak"* calls and complex, musical song.

BEHAVIOUR: Single birds and pairs perch conspicuously on exposed twigs. Often flicks wings and tail. Eats insects and spiders.

Length: 14 cm | 5.5"

WHERE TO SEE: Widespread and common. Can be seen on the deforested High Plateau.

1♂

1♂

1♀

1

Males have black belly and tail in the northeast. Birds away from the east have a big white patch in the wing and white in the tail.

2a♂

2♀

2♂

The isolated subspecies of Forest Rock Thrush on Amber Mountain (*M. s. erythronotus*) is distinctive, and was long considered a full species, Amber Mountain Rock Thrush. Males have a rufous-brown, rather than grey, back.

3♂

3ju

Brownish juvenile and female are similar

1 Madagascar Brush Warbler *Nesillas typica*

M Poretaka
F Nésille Malgache

DISTRIBUTION: Comoros and Madagascar. Common in forest undergrowth and brushy habitats in most of Madagascar except the southwest, where it is replaced by the similar but paler Subdesert Brush Warbler.

ID: Surprisingly large, long-tailed grey-brown bird. Its size and skulking habits usually serve to identify it, even when it is not seen well. See Subdesert Brush Warbler and Madagascar Swamp Warbler (*page 158*) for separation from those similar species.

VOICE: Dry 'ticking' call, like playing with the tines of a comb.

BEHAVIOUR: Stays low in thick undergrowth. Usually alone or in pairs. Eats small insects and spiders.

Length:	17–18 cm | 7"

WHERE TO SEE: Common in many places, including around Andasibe and Ranomafana, although its skulking habits can make it difficult to see.

2 Subdesert Brush Warbler *Nesillas lantzii*

M Poratakatanoravolo
F Nésille de Lantz

DISTRIBUTION: Common throughout the southwest in a variety of dry, brushy habitats, from spiny forest to village gardens.

ID: Like a bleached-out Madagascar Brush Warbler. There is little overlap between these two species, so they can normally be identified by range.

VOICE: Similar to Madagascar Brush Warbler, but the 'ticking' call is higher-pitched and drier.

BEHAVIOUR: Like Madagascar Brush Warbler.

Length:	17 cm | 7"

WHERE TO SEE: Common in the southwest, including Berenty and the Toliara area.

1

Long bill and tail, and rather drab colours

2

Shape like a Madagascar Brush Warbler, but much paler

(R) (1) Madagascar Cisticola *Cisticola cherina*

M Tsintsina
F Cisticole Malgache

Length:	12 cm	5"

WHERE TO SEE: Almost anywhere except thick forest.

DISTRIBUTION: Glorieuses, Seychelles, and Madagascar. Common throughout Madagascar in open habitats like grasslands, marshes, and cultivated areas.
ID: The only small, brown, warbler-like bird to be found in open habitats. In flight, the white tips to the tail are distinctive.
VOICE: Dry *"tsip"*, usually repeated several times, given in a display flight.
BEHAVIOUR: Often perches up conspicuously on grass and shrubs, but can be skulking. Eats insects and spiders.

(E) (2) Madagascar Swamp Warbler
Acrocephalus newtoni

M Vorombararata
F Rousserolle de Newton

Length:	18 cm	7"

WHERE TO SEE: Almost any wetland, including Lake Alarobia in Tana.

DISTRIBUTION: Locally fairly common throughout Madagascar in thickly vegetated wetlands, including papyrus and mangrove swamps.
ID: Similar to Madagascar Brush Warbler (*page 156*). A large warbler in a soggy marsh is probably a Madagascar Swamp Warbler, but the two species overlap in wet scrub. Madagascar Swamp Warbler can be distinguished by its striped throat, greyer colour, thicker bill and very different voice.
VOICE: Complex, musical, chortling song. Harsh *"chak"* calls.
BEHAVIOUR: Lone birds and pairs hop about in marsh vegetation. Sometimes perches in the open to sing.

Sometimes looks quite grey

1

Sings in flight

Pale tips and black band on tail

2

Long bill and tail, striped throat and breast, and dull plumage

ⓔ ① Common Jery *Neomixis tenella*

M Jijikely
F Petite Éroesse

DISTRIBUTION: Fairly common throughout Madagascar wherever there are trees or brush.

ID: Greenish colour and thin, pointed bill typical of jeries. Very similar to Stripe-throated Jery, but distinguished by grey back of the head, pale bill and smaller size.

VOICE: Bouncy, accelerating series of several buzzy notes.

BEHAVIOUR: Active little bird that often sings from the top of the tallest available vegetation, whether bushes, tall trees, or dead snags. Joins flocks with other jeries, white-eyes, and vangas. Eats mainly insects.

Length:	10cm|4"

WHERE TO SEE: Common everywhere, but especially easy to see in the spiny forest of the southwest, where they perch conspicuously and sing.

ⓔ ② Stripe-throated Jery *Neomixis striatigula*

M Kimitsy
F Grande Éroesse

DISTRIBUTION: Found in all types of forest, though strangely absent from the northwest and most of the centre and far north. Fairly common in much of the east and southwest

ID: See Common Jery for separation from that species.

VOICE: Accelerating series of notes: more musical, structured and longer than the song of Common Jery.

BEHAVIOUR: Canopy species that often often joins mixed flocks. Like Common Jery, sings from prominent perch. Eats insects.

Length:	12cm|5"

WHERE TO SEE: Consistently perched up and singing around the Ranomafana NP headquarters. Also easy to see at Andasibe-Mantadia NP and in the spiny forest.

The behaviour of some of the cryptic brown-and-green Malagasy warblers is among the strangest natural phenomena on an island that is famous for the unusual. The **Stripe-throated Jery** (*right*) and the **Rand's Warbler** (*left*) belong to different bird families, but sing almost the same song, and take turns singing side-by-side on the same tall trees and snags during the breeding season. Both species must benefit from this 'double coverage' of their territory's auditory space.

ⓔ ③ Rand's Warbler *Randia pseudozosterops*

M Biritsy
F Randie Malgache

DISTRIBUTION: Uncommon to fairly common in eastern rainforest.

ID: Separated from Stripe-throated Jery by broad eyebrow, greyer colour, and less pointed bill.

VOICE: Very similar to Stripe-throated Jery, but less varied. A musical, accelerating trill.

BEHAVIOUR: A canopy species that is most often seen when perched up on a snag or tall tree to sing. Feeds by creeping along branches and checking on the underside.

Length:	12cm|5"

WHERE TO SEE: Reliable at Ranomafana NP, including at the headquarters alongside Stripe-throated Jery. Also fairly common in Andasibe-Mantadia NP.

Rand's Warbler is a member of the Bernieridae family (see *page 162*), which was recognized only in 2010, and is endemic to Madagascar. Despite their profound genetic distinctiveness, and despite being described, the members of this family were overlooked by taxonomists for many years, due to their superficial similarity to birds within other families.

1
Eastern birds are darkest and dullest

Southwestern birds are pale below

Western and northern birds are brightest

2
Strong, dark bill; prominent stripe over the eye

Southwestern birds are paler

3
Grey back and pale underparts; broad stripe over the eye

Creeps along branches

This guide covers the most widespread and easily seen warbler-like birds of Madagascar. However there are others, including **Green Jery** *Neomixis viridis*, **Madagascar Yellowbrow** (or Yellow-browed Oxylabes) *Crossleyia xanthophrys* and **Grey-crowned Tetraka** (or Grey-crowned Greenbul) *Bernieria cinereiceps*. Although these are not Madagascar's most colourful birds, they do have interesting behaviours, and provide some evidence of the course of evolution on this isolated island.

E **1** Long-billed Tetraka *Bernieria madagascariensis*

M Tretraka
F Tétraka à Bec Long

Length:	18–20 cm | 7–8"

WHERE TO SEE: Fairly common in all forested sites except in the southwest.

DISTRIBUTION: Found throughout most of Madagascar in all types of forest. Generally absent from spiny forest, although it occurs locally in this habitat north of Toliara.

ID: A relatively large, long-tailed, olive-green bird with a large bill. Male is bigger overall than female, and has a very long bill. Female is smaller-billed, and can look similar to Spectacled Tetraka, but is larger and has a weaker eye ring.

VOICE: Call is a short, rough *"brrrt"*. Song is a series of musical whistles.

BEHAVIOUR: An active understorey and mid-storey species that often flocks with other species. Probes for arthropods, sometimes creeping along tree trunks and limbs like a woodpecker.

Madagascar's tetrakas were formerly known as 'greenbuls' before their true status as an endemic family was recognized.

Feeds by creeping along trunks, sometimes even vertical ones

E **2** Spectacled Tetraka *Xanthomixis zosterops*

M Farifotramavo
F Tétraka à Bec Court

Length:	16 cm | 6"

WHERE TO SEE: One of the most common forest birds in Ranomafana, Andasibe-Mantadia, and Masoala NPs.

DISTRIBUTION: Fairly common in eastern rainforest, plus some patches of northern Sambirano forest, and the isolated rainforest on Amber Mountain.

ID: See Long-billed Tetraka for separation from that somewhat similar species. The Spectacled Tetrakas in the northeast, such as at Masoala and Marojejy, are quite dark, while those on Amber Mountain are pale and greyish.

VOICE: Piercing, high-pitched *"tsit"* calls, which sometimes run into a short series: very different from any call of Long-billed Tetraka.

BEHAVIOUR: Active and social bird of the understorey and mid-storey, where it is a core member of mixed flocks. Primarily eats insects.

E **3** White-throated Oxylabes
Oxylabes madagascariensis

M Farifotra Mena
F Oxylabe à Gorge Blanche

Length:	17 cm | 7"

WHERE TO SEE: Ranomafana and Andasibe-Mantadia NPs.

DISTRIBUTION: Uncommon to fairly common in eastern rainforest, plus some patches of northern Sambirano forest, and the isolated rainforest on Amber Mountain.

ID: Distinctive, unlike most other Bernierids, having a brown back, rufous cap and underparts, and bright white throat.

VOICE: Call is a sizzling, descending trill. Song is a musical, oscillating series of cheerful notes.

BEHAVIOUR: Pairs and small groups found on or near the ground. Hops on the ground and readily climbs low branches, especially when vocalizing. Feeds on insects and spiders.

1♂
Male has a very large bill

1♀

2
Broken yellow eye-ring

3
An understorey skulker

Bright white throat

® ① Souimanga Sunbird *Cinnyris souimanga*

M Soimangakely
F Souimanga Malgache

DISTRIBUTION: Seychelles (Aldabra), Glorieuses, and Madagascar. Fairly common throughout Madagascar in virtually all habitats with some woody vegetation.

Length:	10 cm	4"
WHERE TO SEE: Almost anywhere, including Tana.	

ID: Breeding male is distinctive, with a green head and back, yellow belly and multi-coloured breast. Female and non-breeding male distinguished from Madagascar Green Sunbird by smaller bill and lack of strong streaks on underparts. Female could also be confused with female Common Sunbird Asity (*page 148*), but is longer-tailed and has a longer straighter bill.

VOICE: One of the most commonly heard bird songs on the island, a joyous jumble of notes. Call is a short, high-pitched whine.

BEHAVIOUR: Pugnacious bird that is constantly active. Uses its long bill to extract nectar from flowers, and to catch small insects and spiders.

® ② Madagascar Green Sunbird *Cinnyris notatus*

M Soimangabe
F Souimanga Angaladian

DISTRIBUTION: Comoros and Madagascar. Found throughout the island in most habitats with a woody component. Generally less common than Souimanga Sunbird.

Length:	14 cm	5.5"
WHERE TO SEE: Fairly common throughout, including Tana. Perhaps most easily found in western forest, as at Ankarafantsika NP.	

ID: Male looks all-black in poor light, although in good light it shows a green head and back with purple highlights. Female distinguished from Souimanga Sunbird by its thicker bill and heavily streaked underparts.

VOICE: Most common vocalization is a sparrow-like *"cheep"*.

BEHAVIOUR: Similar to Souimanga Sunbird, but its larger bill allows it to extract nectar from bigger flowers.

® ③ Madagascar White-eye *Zosterops maderaspatanus*

M Fotsy Maso
F Zostérops Malgache

DISTRIBUTION: Seychelles, Comoros, Glorieuses, Europa, and Madagascar. Found throughout Madagascar in habitats with some woody vegetation.

Length:	12 cm	5"
WHERE TO SEE: Quite common at most sites.	

ID: Somewhat like a jery (*page 160*), but has bright yellow throat and undertail, and a white ring around the eye.

VOICE: Extremely vocal. The song is a warbling chatter. Calls a variety of simple notes and phrases.

BEHAVIOUR: A hyperactive bird that is usually found in flocks, which often contain jeries, newtonias, and sunbirds.

3

1♂ transitioning to breeding plumage

1♂

1♀

2♂

Heavy bill

2♀

3 Bold white ring around the eye

Vangas comprise another bird family that is endemic to the Malagasy region. They are the Malagasy counterpart to the Darwin's finches of Galápagos, both astounding examples of groups of birds that colonized new parts of the world, then evolved to fill a wide variety of previously vacant niches. There are warbler-like vangas, shrike-like vangas, babbler-like vangas and even a nuthatch vanga! This single family of 21 species contains almost the same range of diversity of body sizes, bill shapes and feeding feeding strategies of the whole world's songbird radiation, containing more than 5,000 species. Vangas are closely related to the helmetshrikes of Africa, and some authorities now place them in the same family.

E **1** Common Newtonia *Newtonia brunneicauda*

M Tretreka
F Newtonie Commune

DISTRIBUTION: Fairly common in all types of forest, including heavily disturbed and secondary forest, throughout Madagascar.

Length:	12 cm	5"

WHERE TO SEE: Easily seen at any site with forest.

ID: Small, thin-billed dull greyish vanga. Angry-looking pale eye separates it from all potential confusion species like jeries and female Red-tailed Vanga. Vocalizations also distinctively different from similar species.

VOICE: Jerky, syncopated series of harsh calls. Often sounds like *"gidyup-gidyup-gidyup"*.

BEHAVIOUR: Highly active and feisty bird. Joins flocks with many other species of birds including other vangas, jeries, Madagascar Paradise Flycatcher, and Souimanga Sunbird.

Dark Newtonia *Newtonia amphichroa* (not illustrated) is a species of eastern rainforest, with an isolated population on Amber Mountain; it is darker than Common Newtonia and has a dark eye.

E **2** Red-tailed Vanga *Calicalicus madagascariensis*

M Totokarasoka
F Calicalic Malgache

DISTRIBUTION: Uncommon to fairly common throughout in all types of forest.

Length:	13–14 cm	5"

WHERE TO SEE: Fairly common in all forested sites.

ID: Red, grey, and black male is distinctive. Grey-brown female can be confused with Common Newtonia, but is larger, with a bigger bill, and a dark eye.

VOICE: Loud 'wolf whistle' with some regional variation. Also gives various calls, including a harsh *"krrrrrit"*.

BEHAVIOUR: Similar to the chickadees or tits which are familiar to most visitors from the northern hemisphere. Active, pugnacious birds that often form the core of forest bird flocks, and whose calls lead the group. Eats invertebrates.

E **3** Chabert Vanga *Leptopterus chabert*

M Patsatsatra
F Artamie Chabert

DISTRIBUTION: Fairly common throughout Madagascar in all forest types, mainly below 1,300 m (4,300'). This is also the only vanga likely to be found in heavily modified habitats like plantations and artificial savannah.

Length:	14 cm	5·5"

WHERE TO SEE: Present throughout, but especially easy to see in the west, such as around Toliara and Morondava, and Ankarafantsika NP.

ID: Blue-black and white, with bright blue eye ring.

VOICE: Harsh repeated *"chak"* call mainly given in flight.

BEHAVIOUR: Acts more like a finch than a vanga; usually seen in small, active flocks, which fly high. Feeds on insects both in trees and on the wing.

Pale eye and thin bill

Dark eye and red tail

White patches in tail

The three species shown here are perhaps the most 'average' of the vangas in terms of size and shape.

R **1** Blue Vanga
e
Cyanolanius madagascarinus madagascarinus

M Patsatsatrala
F Artamie Azure

Length:	16 cm | 6"

WHERE TO SEE: Found in all forest sites, although perhaps easiest to see in dry forest, such as at Kirindy Forest and Ankarana and Ankarafantsika NPs.

DISTRIBUTION: Uncommon to fairly common throughout most of Madagascar in all types of forest, although largely absent from spiny forest.

ID: Blue back and pale underparts are diagnostic. The female is duller. Has the same overall pattern as Chabert Vanga (*page 166*), but with blue, rather than blue-black, on the back.

VOICE: Harsh rolling *"trrrt-trrrt-trrrt"*.

BEHAVIOUR: Often in flocks with vangas and other birds. Usually in the upper-storey of the forest. Feeds on invertebrates and fruit.

E **2** White-headed Vanga *Artamella viridis*

M Voromasiaka
F Artamie à Tête Blanche

Length:	20 cm | 8"

WHERE TO SEE: Found in all forest sites, although perhaps easiest to see in dry forest, such as at Ankarana and Ankarafantsika NPs.

DISTRIBUTION: Uncommon throughout Madagascar in all types of forest, including edge habitat and secondary forest.

ID: Shares pied plumage with Sickle-billed (*page 172*) and Chabert (*page 166*) Vangas, but is much smaller and shorter-billed than Sickle-billed, and larger, and paler-headed than Chabert Vanga.

VOICE: The calls are harsh, grating notes. The song comprises various low, penetrating whistles.

BEHAVIOUR: Often joins mixed flocks. Usually in the upper-storey of the forest. Feeds on invertebrates.

In the west, large numbers of White-headed and Sickle-billed Vangas sometimes roost together, and even nest together; it is as if the smaller, stubby-billed White-headed Vangas feel safe with their bruising 'older brothers'!

E **3** Rufous Vanga *Schetba rufa*

M Vangamena
F Artamie Rousse

Length:	20 cm | 8"

WHERE TO SEE: Most easily found in the western dry forest, as at Kirindy Forest, and Zombitse and Ankarafantsika NPs.

DISTRIBUTION: Found in both eastern rainforest and western dry forest, although more common in western forest. Absent from most of the spiny forest and from the far north.

ID: Bright rufous back, black head, and white underparts are distinctive. Male shows black onto the breast, while female has a pale breast.

VOICE: Most common and distinctive vocalization is a long, melodic, descending trill. Also gives a clear, three-part *"whit-whit-tew"*, which pairs sometimes combine with the descending trill for a beautiful duet.

BEHAVIOUR: Found mainly in the forest mid-storey. Often sits motionlessly for long periods. Joins flocks less frequently than most other vangas. Eats invertebrates.

1♀ Usually seen in the canopy

1♂

2♀

2♂

Female has dusky markings on head and underparts

3♀

3♂

Rufous back

E **1** **Ward's Vanga** *Pseudobias wardi*

M Serikalambo
F Vanga de Ward

DISTRIBUTION: Fairly common in eastern rainforest, mainly at middle elevations. Particularly favours forest edge.

ID: An odd and unique little bird with black-and-white plumage and blue bare skin around the eye. Much more likely to be taken for a flycatcher than a vanga. Some male Madagascar Paradise Flycatchers (*page 152*) are black-and-white, but they are much larger, longer-tailed, and lack the black chest band of Ward's Vanga.

VOICE: Short, dry trill.

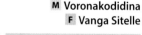

Length:	15 cm │ 6"

WHERE TO SEE: Ranomafana and Andasibe areas. Look especially along the main road through Ranomafana, and behind the Feon'ny Ala Hotel near Andasibe.

BEHAVIOUR: Found singly or in pairs in the upper-storey of the forest. Sometimes in flocks with other species. Feeds by catching insects on the wing, much like a flycatcher.

E **2** **Nuthatch Vanga** *Hypositta corallirostris*

M Voronakodidina
F Vanga Sitelle

DISTRIBUTION: Rare and local in eastern rainforest below 1,000 m (3,300').

ID: The blue plumage, coral-red bill and behaviour are distinctive. Male is brighter than the female.

VOICE: Short, very high-pitched trill. Very easy to overlook if you are not specifically listening for it.

Length:	13 cm │ 5"

WHERE TO SEE: Most readily found in vanga flocks in Andasibe-Mantadia NP. Also possible in Masoala NP.

BEHAVIOUR: Usually found in flocks of vangas and other birds. This unusual little vanga seems to have evolved to fill the niche of birds like nuthatches and woodpeckers, which are absent from Madagascar. It creeps up tree trunks in search of insects.

E **3** **Crossley's Vanga** *Mystacornis crossleyi*

M Talapiotanty
F Vanga de Crossley

DISTRIBUTION: Uncommon in eastern rainforest, mainly below 1,300 m (4,300').

ID: Behaviour and bold black, grey and white facial markings identify this bird. Very different from other vangas.

VOICE: Piercing, high-pitched whistle, which is often repeated several times.

Length:	16 cm │ 6"

WHERE TO SEE: Ranomafana and Andasibe-Mantadia NPs. Also present although uncommon in Masoala NP.

BEHAVIOUR: Walks around on forest floor in singles or pairs. Pairs display by circling each other with tails cocked up. Feeds on insects and spiders.

Crossley's Vanga was formerly known as 'Crossley's Babbler', while Ward's Vanga was known as 'Ward's Flycatcher'. It was only recently that genetic analysis revealed that these babbler- and flycatcher-like species are actually vangas.

1 Blue eye ring like a paradise flycatcher; canopy-dwelling

2♀ / **2♂** Surprisingly woodpecker-like in behaviour

3♀ / **3♂** A shy bird of the forest floor

E **1** Hook-billed Vanga *Vanga curvirostris*

M Vangasoratra
F Vanga Écorcheur

DISTRIBUTION: Fairly common in small numbers throughout the island in all forest types. Tolerates secondary forest and degraded habitat not used by many other vanga species.
ID: Big, black-and-white, shrike-like vanga.
VOICE: Drawn-out, hollow whistle.

Length:	25–29 cm | 10–11"

WHERE TO SEE: Easiest to find in western dry forest, as at Berenty, Kirindy Forest, and Ankarafantsika NP.

BEHAVIOUR: Slowly moves through the mid-storey of forest. Usually seen alone or in pairs, and rarely in mixed species flocks. This large vanga is a major predator both of invertebrates and a range of vertebrates, including reptiles, amphibians, small birds, and even baby mouse lemurs.

E **3** Helmet Vanga *Euryceros prevostii*

M Siketribe
F Eurycère de Prévost

DISTRIBUTION: Rare and local in rainforest in northeast Madagascar.
ID: The huge blue bill alone identifies this bird.
VOICE: A quiet bird that sometimes gives a soft, musical, descending trill.
BEHAVIOUR: Ranges mainly in mid-storey of forest, sometimes perching motionlessly for long periods. Often joins flocks of other large vangas. Feeds on invertebrates and small vertebrates like geckos and frogs.

VULNERABLE	
Length:	29 cm | 11.5"

WHERE TO SEE: Masoala is the most accessible site. Easiest to find September–December, when local guides have often located nests. Marojejy NP is also excellent, for those willing to hike. Does occur in the Andasibe area, though rarely in areas that are easily accessible.

E **2** Sickle-billed Vanga *Falculea palliata*

M Voronjaza
F Faculie Mantelée

DISTRIBUTION: Fairly common and conspicuous in all types of dry forest and woodland in northern, western, and southwestern Madagascar, including secondary forest and savannah. Especially fond of areas with baobabs.
ID: Large, black-and-white, curve-billed bird. Floppy flight on broad wings is distinctive.
VOICE: Arresting combinations of cackles, rasps, and mournful wails.

Length:	32 cm | 12.5"

WHERE TO SEE: Fairly common and quite conspicuous at Ankarana and Ankarafantsika NPs, Kirindy Forest, and Berenty.

BEHAVIOUR: Social bird that is usually found in groups. Adept at probing for invertebrates with its huge bill.

Some of the vocalizations of Sickle-billed Vanga are uncannily like the wails of a child, giving rise to its Malagasy name, which means 'baby bird'.

1

2

3

Hook-billed and Helmet Vangas have hefty bills, and are serious predators in the Malagasy forest.

One of Madagascar's most sought-after birds

Floppy flight

🇪 ① Tylas Vanga *Tylas eduardi*

M Mokazavona
F Vanga Tylas

DISTRIBUTION: Recorded throughout Madagascar in all forest types. Fairly common in eastern rainforest, but very rare elsewhere.
ID: Rather similar to Pollen's Vanga but with a much smaller bill. Also reminiscent of Madagascar Cuckoo-shrike, but has rufous underparts.
VOICE: Distinctive song is a three-part whistle: "*whit-wer-whiit*".
BEHAVIOUR: Singles or pairs often join mixed feeding flocks. Generally found in the upper-storey of the forest. Feeds on invertebrates.

| **Length:** | 21 cm | 8" |

WHERE TO SEE: Ranomafana and Andasibe-Mantadia NPs.

Tylas Vanga has been placed in other families, including the oriole family, but recent genetic studies show that it should be placed firmly within the vangas.

🇪 ② Pollen's Vanga *Xenopirostris polleni*

M Vangamaintiloha
F Vanga de Pollen

DISTRIBUTION: Uncommon and local in eastern rainforest, although seemingly absent from the north, such as Masoala and Marojejy NPs.
ID: Underparts white in male and buffy in female; can look similar to Tylas Vanga, but is always bigger, chunkier, and with a much larger bill.
VOICE: Single, penetrating 'laser gun' whistle.
BEHAVIOUR: Slow-moving species that sometimes joins mixed flocks. Feeds on invertebrates.

NEAR THREATENED

| **Length:** | 24 cm | 9.5" |

WHERE TO SEE: Ranomafana NP, especially the Vohiparara Trail.

Female Lafresnaye's Vanga

Two other vangas in Madagascar are similar to Pollen's Vanga, although their ranges do not overlap. The Endangered **Van Dam's Vanga** *Xenopirostris damii* (not illustrated) is found in western dry forest, mainly within Ankarafantsika NP. The more common **Lafresnaye's Vanga** *X. xenopirostris* ②a is endemic to the southwestern spiny forest and can be seen around Toliara, especially at Ifaty.

🇷 🇪 ③ Madagascar Cuckoo-shrike *Coracina cinerea*

M Vorondavenona
F Échenilleur Malgache

DISTRIBUTION: Comoros and Madagascar. Fairly common throughout Madagascar in all types of forest, although unobtrusive.
ID: Although in a completely different family, Madagascar Cuckoo-shrike is somewhat similar to the two dark-headed vangas above. The grey (rather than white or rufous) underparts separate it from both, while its much smaller bill also distinguishes it from Pollen's Vanga.
VOICE: A quiet and easily overlooked series of soft notes. Also a short, explosive call.
BEHAVIOUR: Often joins feeding flocks, especially with larger vangas. Like those species, moves slowly through the upper-storey of the forest. Feeds mainly on invertebrates.

| **Length:** | 24 cm | 9.5" |

WHERE TO SEE: Fairly common in almost all forested sites, including Ranomafana, Andasibe-Mantadia, Ankarana, and Tsingy de Bemaraha NPs.

Buffy
underparts

Can be very
white below

Grey
underparts

R **1** **Crested Drongo** *Dicrurus forficatus forficatus*

M Railovy
F Drongo Malgache

DISTRIBUTION: Comoros (Anjouan) and Madagascar. Common throughout most of Madagascar in almost any habitat with woody vegetation, from open savannah to gardens to dense forest.
ID: Glossy black bird with a towering crest. Impossible to mistake for anything else.
VOICE: Wide variety of whistles, rasps, clicks, and other kinds of notes, including mimicry. Often delivered in long, flowing series.
BEHAVIOUR: A bold, aggressive bird that does not hesitate to harass Pied Crows, raptors, and other large birds. Often perches in the open. Frequent member of mixed flocks. Eats invertebrates, many of which are insects taken on the wing.

Length:	26 cm | 10"

WHERE TO SEE: Very common bird that can be seen at all forest sites, and even around hotels on Nosy Be or St. Marie Island.

E **2** **Madagascar Starling** *Saroglossa aurata*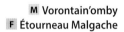

M Vorontain'omby
F Étourneau Malgache

DISTRIBUTION: Most of Madagascar, although largely absent from the southwest. Most common in eastern rainforest, although also found in western dry forest, plus a variety of more open and edge habitats.
ID: Nondescript slim brownish bird. Could be confused with Madagascar Bulbul (*page 152*), but has a shorter tail and lacks that species' orange bill. Big white patches in the wing and tail are distinctive in flight.
VOICE: Quiet, simple, liquid calls that are easily missed.
BEHAVIOUR: Usually in the forest canopy, often on exposed branches and snags, although will descend to the ground to feed. A social species, often found in flocks, although rarely joins mixed flocks. Diverse diet includes fruit, invertebrates, and seeds.

Length:	20 cm | 8"

WHERE TO SEE: Ranomafana, Andasibe-Mantadia, and Ankarana NPs are good places to look, especially on snags adjacent to the main roads through these parks. Sometimes common and at other times scarce.

I **3** **Common Myna** *Acridotheres tristis*

M Maritaina
F Martin Triste

DISTRIBUTION: Native to much of southern Asia, and widely introduced elsewhere, including Madagascar. Abundant throughout the island, usually close to human activity and in disturbed habitat.
ID: A large, dark bird with conspicuous yellow bare skin behind the eye. Shows large white wing patches and a white tip to the tail in flight.
VOICE: Very noisy, with varied and rather unpleasant vocalizations that usually have an aggressive tone.
BEHAVIOUR: A bold, conspicuous bird that perches on man-made structures and feeds mainly on the ground, striding along and snatching up a wide range of animals and plants. Often in flocks.

Length:	25 cm | 10"

WHERE TO SEE: Virtually omnipresent in human-modified areas. One of the most common and conspicuous birds on the High Plateau.

Common Myna is an aggressive non-native species that probably has a negative effect on cavity-nesting native species by out-competing them for nest sites.

1

Perches conspicuously in the open

2♂

2♀

3

This introduced species may now be Madagascar's most common bird. It if often seen on man-made structures.

E ① Nelicourvi Weaver *Ploceus nelicourvi*

M Fodisaina
F Tisserin Nelicourvi

Length:	15 cm | 6"

WHERE TO SEE: Ranomafana and Andasibe areas. Often nests near the restaurant at the Feon'ny Ala Hotel near Andasibe.

DISTRIBUTION: Fairly common in eastern rainforest, some northern Sambirano forest, and the isolated rainforest on Amber Mountain.
ID: The combination of yellow on head and brick-red undertail is distinctive. Male has a mostly black head.
VOICE: Buzzy "*tzz-chhh-chhh-chhh*".
BEHAVIOUR: Unlike most weavers, nests solitarily, rather than in colonies. Its beautiful and distinctive nest is a hanging sack with a long entrance tunnel, and is often built over a stream. Frequently joins mixed flocks that include tetrakas. Feeds mainly on insects.

E ② Sakalava Weaver *Ploceus sakalava*

M Fodisahy
F Tisserin Sakalava

Length:	15 cm | 6"

WHERE TO SEE: A conspicuous resident in the dry lowlands, such as around Toliara, Morondava, and Ankarafantsika and Ankarana NPs.

DISTRIBUTION: Common in dry western, southern, and northern Madagascar. Found in western dry forest, spiny forest, and various open habitats, including those heavily modified by humans.
ID: Yellow-headed male is distinctive. Female is very similar to a female or non-breeding male fody, but is larger, with a larger bill, tan-striped face, and a reddish eye ring.
VOICE: Chirpy and swizzling notes, often delivered in an exuberant chorus by many birds at a colony.
BEHAVIOUR: Nests socially in bustling colonies, unlike Nelicourvi Weaver. The nest is similar to that of Nelicourvi Weaver, though is usually more loosely woven. Often feeds on the ground, searching for seeds and insects. When not breeding, forms large flocks that often include Madagascar Fody.

The Sakalavas are the people who populate most of western Madagascar, and are found in much the same places as their namesake weaver. In some places, it is considered a good omen if weavers nest over or near the house of the village mayor.

R ③ Madagascar Fody *Foudia madagascariensis*

M Fody
F Foudi Rouge

Length:	13 cm | 5"

WHERE TO SEE: Common almost everywhere, including downtown Tana.

DISTRIBUTION: Probably originally endemic to Madagascar, but has been introduced to almost every island of the Malagasy region. Found in almost any habitat except closed-canopy forest.
ID: The bright red plumage of breeding male is distinctive. Female and non-breeding male are quite drab (see Sakalava Weaver). The rarer **Forest Fody** *F. omissa* (not illustrated) is bigger than Madagascar Fody but breeding male has a dark green belly (though beware that male Madagascar Fody coming into breeding plumage can match this pattern). Females of the two species are extremely similar. Forest Fody is found in the interior of eastern rainforest.
VOICE: High-pitched "*tsit*" given singly, or in a quick series.
BEHAVIOUR: Male is bold and conspicuous when breeding. Non-breeding birds form flocks. Eats seeds, which are either gathered on the ground or directly from plants.

1♀

1♂

1 Solitary nester

2 Colonial nester

2♀

2♂

3♀ Females and non-breeeding males look very similar

3♂ In October and November, most males transition into breeding plumage

3♂

Reptiles

- Almost 400 species of reptile have been described from Madagascar, of which more than 90% are endemic.

- There are four orders of reptiles in the world: crocodiles, tuatara, lizards and snakes, and turtles. All of these except New Zealand's tuatara are found in Madagascar. Thirteen families are represented.

- The majority of Malagasy reptiles are diurnal, but about 85 species are nocturnal, including most geckos and many snakes. Some reptiles can be active both night and day, and even some strongly nocturnal species can occasionally be active by day. Nocturnal reptiles generally have vertical 'slit' pupils while diurnal ones have round pupils, although there are exceptions.

- Reptiles are remarkably common and conspicuous in Madagascar, one of the easiest places on Earth for a visiting naturalist to amass an impressive reptile list. Many species can be seen on exposed rocks or tree trunks. Chameleons can be hard to spot during the day, but sleep on low-hanging branches, making them easier to find at night. Plated lizards and skinks often reveal themselves by the noise of their movement through the leaf-litter. Poking around dead wood and taking night walks will increase your chances of finding more secretive and nocturnal reptiles.

- Many reptiles can be seen year-round in Madagascar, but the wet season is the best time, particularly for snakes and chameleons. During the dry season, you might spot only a few snakes, and fail to see any leaf chameleons.

- Most Malagasy reptiles lay eggs, although a few give birth to live young. The eggs are buried in the ground or hidden in crevices. Most hatch after 1–3 months, but the eggs of certain species, like Parson's Chameleon hatch only after more than a year.

- The identification of many reptiles in Madagascar is not difficult. The first thing to consider is range: similar species often do not overlap geographically. Secondly, basic colours and patterns distinguish most species. Colour can be misleading or non-diagnostic for chameleons, where structure is more useful. For herpetologists, characteristics of the scales provide the most definitive means of identifying most species.

- This guide covers about 30% of Madagascar's reptiles, including most of the species likely to be seen in frequently visited sites. Refer to *Amphibians and Reptiles of Madagascar* by Glaw and Vences for thorough coverage (see Further reading (*page 327*) for details).

- In many Malagasy reptiles, males and females are similar. When there is a difference, as in 'typical' chameleons and day geckos, males tend to be larger and more colourful. In the case of chameleons, males also have more elaborate structures on their head. Leaf chameleons form an exception to the rule: females are larger than males.

- There is no up-to-date standardization of common names for reptiles. Common names novel to this book are marked with asterisks. Herpetologists and most local guides use scientific names exclusively.

- In some lizards, total length (TL) is the most useful measurement. In others, the tail length is highly variable, or the tail is often curled up (as in typical chameleons), making the length from the tip of the snout to the vent (SVL) a more useful measurement. For turtles, the carapace length (CL) is given.

Panther Chameleon (*page 192*)

Gold-dust Day Gecko (*page 222*)

Madagacasar tree boa (*page 238*)

Radiated Tortoise (*page 182*)

Madagascar supports several species of terrestrial tortoise and aquatic terrapin, in three different families. Many are rare, local, and in danger of following the island's two giant tortoises into extinction. Included here are the species most likely to be seen by visitors. The standard measurement for tortoises, terrapins, and turtles is carapace length (CL), the length of the curved line that traces the top of the carapace.

E **1** Radiated Tortoise *Astrochelys radiata*

M Sokatra, Sokake
F Tortue Rayonnée

DISTRIBUTION: Dry spiny forest of southwest.

ID: The 'radiated' pattern on the carapace of the adults is variable but distinctive, though it may be absent on older individuals. This is Madagascar's most frequently seen tortoise.

BEHAVIOUR: Remains hidden much of the time. Sometimes located by its tracks in the sand. Can live well over 100 years.

CRITICALLY ENDANGERED	
Length:	CL < 40 cm	16"

WHERE TO SEE: Captive specimens can be seen at many hotels and parks. Sightings in the wild are increasingly rare, but possible around Ifaty (north of Toliara), at Berenty, and elsewhere in the spiny forest.

E **2** Spider Tortoise *Pyxis arachnoides*

M Tsakafy
F Tortue-Araignée

DISTRIBUTION: Spiny forest of the southwest, close to the coast.

ID: Much smaller than full-grown Radiated Tortoise. 'Spider' pattern is quite different from the 'radiated' pattern of that species.

BEHAVIOUR: Similar to Radiated Tortoise.

CRITICALLY ENDANGERED	
Length:	CL 12 cm	5"

WHERE TO SEE: Lucky visitors might find it in the spiny forest, as around Ifaty and Berenty.

The Critically Endangered **Flat-tailed Tortoise** *P. planicauda* **2a** is very similar to Spider Tortoise, but has a different range, occurring only in the central west. Look for it in Kirindy Forest, mainly during the wet season.

3 Terrapins [2 families; 3 genera; 4 species]

M Kapidrano
F Tortue d'Eau Douce

DISTRIBUTION: One species, **Madagascan Big-headed Turtle** *Erymnochelys madagascariensis* **3a**, is endemic, while three (**Yellowbelly Mud Turtle** *Pelusios castanoides* (not illustrated); **East African Black Mud Turtle** *Pelusios subniger* **3b** and **Marsh Terrapin** *Pelomedusa subrufa* **3c**) are also found in Africa. Three species are mainly found in the west, one (*P. subniger*) is in the east, and all are rare or absent from the centre of Madagascar.

ID: These aquatic animals have a different structure from the tortoises: they are more flattened, and also lack the distinctive markings normally shown by tortoises.

BEHAVIOUR: Sometimes seen sunbathing, or just as a head emerging from the water. Occasionally found walking across dry ground, including roads.

Length:	CL < 41 cm	16"
	(Madagascan Big-headed Turtle)
	CL < 25 cm	10"
	(other species)

WHERE TO SEE: At least one species can be found around most wetlands, but seeing any Malagasy terrapin takes a lot of luck. Sightings are most likely in the west during the wet season.

Five of the world's eight species of sea turtles are found along Madagascar's coast. Only the two covered below are seen frequently.

1 Green Sea Turtle *Chelonia mydas*

M Fanozaty
F Tortue Verte

DISTRIBUTION: Tropical and subtropical seas worldwide. Found all around Madagascar's coast.
ID: A huge oceanic turtle. Similar to Hawksbill Sea Turtle, but larger, lacks hooked snout, and adults lack serrations along the edges of the shell.
BEHAVIOUR: Mainly ocean-dwelling, coming onshore only to lay eggs. Unlike other ocean turtles, adults are predominantly vegetarian. Frequently hunted and eaten by humans.

ENDANGERED	
Length:	CL 1–1·5 m	3–5'
Weight:	< 300 kg	660 lb

WHERE TO SEE: Most often seen around Nosy Be, sometimes from the ferry between the mainland and the island. Also frequent at the 'Three Bays' near Diego-Suarez.

2 Hawksbill Sea Turtle *Eretmochelys imbricata*

M Fanohara
F Tortue Imbriquée

DISTRIBUTION: Found in tropical seas worldwide. In Madagascar, occurs along most of the coastline.
ID: Smaller than Green Sea Turtle, with a hooked snout, and strong serrations along the edges of the shell.
BEHAVIOUR: Similar to Green Sea Turtle, but feeds mainly on marine invertebrates and algae. If when snorkelling you observe a turtle eating coral, it is very likely to be this species.

CRITICALLY ENDANGERED	
Length:	CL ·6–1 m	2–3·3'
Weight:	< 140 kg	300 lb

WHERE TO SEE: Often seen around Nosy Be, especially in the coral reefs of the Nosy Tanikely marine reserve.

3 Nile Crocodile *Crocodylus niloticus*

M Voay
F Crocodile du Nil

DISTRIBUTION: Throughout sub-Saharan Africa. In Madagascar, most common in the west. The Malagasy population is estimated at 30,000.
ID: Aquatic habits, streamlined shape, and armoured skin identify even small juveniles. The large adults are unmistakable by size alone; they dwarf all other Malagasy reptiles.
BEHAVIOUR: Feeds on a wide variety of animals, from fish to zebu cattle. Often leaves the water to bask. Courtship is elaborate, and the parents are quite attentive to their eggs and young.

Length:	TL < 4 m	13'
Weight:	< 1,000 kg	1 tonne

WHERE TO SEE: Generally uncommon, but usually easy to see in Ankarafantsika NP. Can occasionally be spotted from major road bridges that cross less-disturbed western rivers.

Crocodilians are the last living non-avian members of the archosaurs, the group of reptiles that includes the dinosaurs, and which dominated the earth before mammals rose to prominence. They have changed little in the last 65 million years. Amazingly, 'crocs' are actually more closely related to birds than to other reptiles.

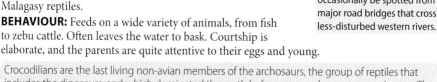

1 Rounded snout

Adults have a smooth edge to the shell

2 Sharp bill

Points along edge of shell

3

Some of world's smallest reptiles belong to the endemic genus *Brookesia*; the smallest less than 3 cm long. There are at least 30 species of leaf chameleon, although new species are still being described. The Elongate Ancient Leaf Chameleon (*page 188*) has been moved into a new genus: *Palleon*. Although only nine species are covered here, these are the ones that most visitors are likely to see, especially away from the far north.

Leaf chameleons are generally small and brownish. They spend the day walking slowly through the leaf-litter, then climb up into the understorey vegetation to sleep at night. Sightings are much more common in the wet season, especially in the dry western forest. These primitive chameleons lack significant capacity to change colour. Their tails are fairly short and not usually rolled up in classic chameleon fashion. Females are larger than males.

E Minute Leaf Chameleon *Brookesia minima*   **M** Rakolaka Kely

DISTRIBUTION: Small distribution in the Sambirano rainforest of the northwest.

ID: Tiny size makes it unmistakable within its range. Among the world's smallest reptiles. Beige above and dark brown below, with fairly smooth skin.

BEHAVIOUR: When threatened by a predator, this species, and most other small leaf chameleons, tuck in their legs and roll to the ground, remaining motionless to 'disappear' into the leaf-litter.

ENDANGERED	
Length:	3 cm | 1"

WHERE TO SEE: Wet season in Lokobe NP, on Nosy Be.

E Montagne d'Ambre Leaf Chameleon   **M** Rakolaka Madinika
Brookesia tuberculata

DISTRIBUTION: Rainforest on Amber Mountain.

ID: Uniformly brown or beige in colour. The legs are sturdier than those of other small leaf chameleons. Tiny size identifies it within Amber Mountain NP. This is another of the world's smallest reptiles.

Northern Madagascar holds the highest diversity of leaf chameleons, with at least five species occurring on Amber Mountain.

VULNERABLE	
Length:	3 cm | 1"

WHERE TO SEE: Endemic to Amber Mountain. Usually easy to find there, and very common during the wet season. Often found around the main picnic area and campsite.

E Antongil Leaf Chameleon *Brookesia peyrierasi*   **M** Rakolak'i Nosy Mangabe

DISTRIBUTION: Small distribution in the rainforest of the northeast, in the Masoala area.

ID: Brown or mottled grey and brown. Tiny size makes it unmistakable within its small range.

ENDANGERED	
Length:	3–4 cm | 1–1.5"

WHERE TO SEE: Wet season on the island of Nosy Mangabe, between Maroantsetra and Masoala.

Male leaf chameleons generally have a longer tail than the female, although females are larger overall.

3♂

3♀

1

Minute Leaf Chameleon was long thought to be Madagascar's smallest reptile. But in 2012, a new, even smaller species of leaf chameleon (*B. micra*) was discovered on the island of Nosy Hara near Madagascar's northern tip, highlighting that much still remains to be discovered about Malagasy reptiles.

Often shows beige above and dark brown below

2♂

Small spikes along sides of spine. Knobby spikes above the eye

3♀

Small spikes along sides of spine

In 2013 the ancient leaf chameleons were removed from the genus *Brookesia* and placed in the new genus *Palleon*, an addition to Madagascar's traditional list of three chameleon genera: *Brookesia*, *Calumma* and *Furcifer*.

E **1** Plated Leaf Chameleon *Brookesia stumpffi* **M** Rakolaka Bory Tandroka

DISTRIBUTION: Widespread in both rainforest and dry forest across the west and north.

ID: Fairly large and uniformly pale brown dwarf Chameleon. Could be confused with Brygoo's Leaf Chameleon in Ankarafantsika NP, but Plated Leaf Chameleon is larger and has much smaller spiny plates along its back.

| Length: | 8–9 cm | 3–3.5" |

WHERE TO SEE: Common in Ankarana NP, especially during the wet season. May also be found in Amber Mountain and Ankarafantsika NPs and on Nosy Be.

E **2** Brygoo's Leaf Chameleon *Brookesia brygooi* **M** Rakolaka Tandrefana

DISTRIBUTION: Dry forests of the west.

ID: Usually pale brown above and dark brown below. Similar to Plated Leaf Chameleon (which has a more northern range although the two overlap at Ankarafantsika NP), but is smaller, darker, less uniform in coloration, and has larger spiny plates along its back. **Decary's Leaf Chameleon** *B. decaryi* (not illustrated) is endemic to Ankarafantsika NP. It is very similar to Brygoo's Leaf Chameleon, but has a fatter body, shorter tail, and less prominent bumps above its eyes. The recently described **Bruno's Leaf Chameleon** *B. brunoi* (not illustrated) is similar to Brygoo's Leaf Chameleon, but has a discrete range, being found exclusively in Parc Anja, where is it sometimes located by local guides.

| Length: | 7–8 cm | 3" |

WHERE TO SEE: During the wet season in Ankarafantsika and Tsingy de Bemaraha NPs and Kirindy Forest. Most often encountered at night, sleeping on low branches.

E **3** Brown Leaf Chameleon *Brookesia superciliaris* **M** Rakolaka Tatsinanana

DISTRIBUTION: Widespread in eastern rainforest.

ID: Large, variably marked with brown and beige, and with large, triangular projections above the eyes. This is the most common, or only, leaf chameleon in much of the eastern rainforest.

| Length: | 6–9 cm | 2–3.5" |

WHERE TO SEE: Found most frequently around Andasibe, but also possible at Ranomafana and in other eastern rainforest sites.

E **4** Elongate Ancient Leaf Chameleon **M** Rakolaka Fisa-batana
Palleon (Brookesia) nasus

DISTRIBUTION: Rainforest of the southeast.

ID: Distinctively pointed nose. Lacks the big triangular projections above the eye of Brown Leaf Chameleon.

| VULNERABLE |
| Length: | <9 cm | 3.5" |

WHERE TO SEE: Ranomafana is the best site, although it is still uncommon there. Best searched for on the Vohiparara Trail.

1

2 Usually pale above and dark below

Pale brown

3 Large cones above the eyes

Small spikes on chin

Small bump on the tip of the snout

4

Most of Madagascar's chameleons are in two genera of 'typical chameleons': *Furcifer* and *Calumma*. There is no simple way to separate them, although *Calumma* are generally found in rainforest in the north and east, while *Furcifer* are more widespread and better able to adapt to degraded habitat. They vary from being small (similar in size to large leaf chameleons) up to 70 cm (2'), the largest chameleons on earth. These are the classic chameleons, often colourful, and with the astonishing ability to rapidly change colour. The males of many species sport impressive structures on their head, while the females are more modest. All typical chameleons are arboreal and active during the day, although they are sometimes found walking on the ground to cross open areas. They are frequently spotted sleeping on low branches at night.

E 1 Oustalet's Chameleon *Furcifer oustaleti*

M Tarondro
F Caméléon d'Oustalet

DISTRIBUTION: Occurs throughout the island. Found inside western dry forest, but largely avoids the interior of eastern rainforest. Common in degraded areas, even in towns and gardens.

ID: Big rounded casque (rounded helmet-like projection) on the back of the head of the male. No horns on the nose. More than 45 fairly large spikes along the spine. Variable, but

| Length: | SVL < 28 cm | 11" |

WHERE TO SEE: One of the most common Malagasy chameleons; possible almost anywhere, although most common in the west.

usually not colourful: grey, brown, or dull green. Warty Chameleon (*page 206*) can be extremely similar to Oustalet's Chameleon and some females cannot be separated. Jewelled Chameleon (*page 192*) is also widespread and common in many habitats. It averages much smaller, has a less prominent casque, lacks spikes along the spine, and females are always colourful (although highly variable). See Panther Chameleon (*page 192*) for separation from that species. *Furcifer nicosiai* (not illustrated) resembles Oustalet's Chameleon, but is smaller. It can be found in Tsingy de Bemaraha NP and Kirindy Forest.

E 2 Parson's Chameleon *Calumma parsonii*

M Tarondro Maitso Be
F Caméléon de Parson

DISTRIBUTION: In the eastern rainforest zone, but not usually inside of thick forest. Prefers forest edges, roadsides, and sometimes even degraded areas.

ID: Large, with a big, triangular head. The female is green, while the male can be green, turquoise, or yellow. Both usually show several diagonal dark slashes along the sides. The male has twin horns on its nose. See O'Shaughnessy's Chameleon (*page 198*) for distinction from that species.

NEAR THREATENED

| Length: | SVL ♂ < 30 cm | 12" |
| | ♀ < 20 cm | 8" |

WHERE TO SEE: Andasibe and Ranomafana areas.

2ju

2♀

Female lacks a nose horn

1♂

Male grey or brown

Female can be bright green, but is usually duller than the male

Male Oustalet's Chameleons can be up to 70 cm (28") long (including the tail), and females up to 40 cm (16")

2♂

Male has a large, triangular head and a prominent nose horn

Along with Oustalet's Chameleon (*page 194*) and Warty Chameleon (*page 206*), these are the species most likely to be seen away from prime forest habitats.

❸ ① Panther Chameleon *Furcifer pardalis*

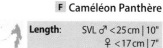

M Sakorikita
F Caméléon Panthère

DISTRIBUTION: Found in a variety of habitats, mainly in the northern third of Madagascar. It does occur inside forest, especially western dry forest, but is more often in degraded areas.

ID: Males have highly variable coloration, both individually and geographically. Colourful individuals can show a rainbow of colours, and are among the most beautiful of chameleons. Male shows a bump on the tip of the nose and a small casque, which separate even a dull male from Oustalet's Chameleon. Female Oustalet's Chameleon can be very similar, although Panther Chameleon usually has more grey-and-orange or grey-and-pinkish (rather than brown or green) coloration, and shows a small bump on the top front of the nose; Oustalet's Chameleon has a smooth nose.

Length: SVL ♂ <25 cm | 10"
♀ <17 cm | 7"

WHERE TO SEE: Common in the north and northeast. Watch for it around Diego-Suarez, Ankarana NP, Nosy Be, and Maroantsetra. Frequently seen crossing the road, even the main northern artery, the RN6.

Diego-Suarez

Nosy Be

Ankarana NP

❸ ② Jewelled Chameleon *Furcifer lateralis*

M Tanalahy

DISTRIBUTION: Found in a wide variety of habitats in the southern two-thirds of Madagascar.

ID: Medium-sized chameleon with a moderate casque. Male usually green, females are a variety of colours. Both usually show a pale line and three dark circles along the sides. Oustalet's Chameleon is larger and lacks these flank markings. Panther Chameleon can be similar, but their ranges do not overlap. Very similar to several scarce chameleon species, but full coverage of these is beyond the scope of this guide.

Length: SVL ♂ <14 cm | 5·5"
♀ <11 cm | 4·5"

WHERE TO SEE: Common in many places. This is the most frequently encountered chameleon in the central highlands, including cities like Tana and Antsirabe.

A host of Malagasy beliefs and traditions surround chameleons. In some places, chameleons are revered as reincarnations of the ancestors, and it is forbidden to point at them, except with a curled finger. Many people fear these creatures, and the sight of a vazaha (foreigner) touching or approaching them can be shocking. Some people believe that you will be cursed if you touch a chameleon, and will die a death as slow as the chameleon's gait.

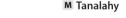

Female is variable in colour

1♀

1♂

1♂
Marojejy NP

1♂
Ambanja

1♂
Amber Mountain NP

Male shows a small nose horn and casque
Female usually shows some orangish or pinkish coloration

OPPOSITE AND ABOVE: Male Panther Chameleons are highly variable, both individually and geographically

2♂
Males are drab, often green, but note the pale stripe and three ovals on the side

2♀

E **1** **Perinet** (Band-bellied) **Chameleon**
Calumma gastrotaenia

M Tana Maitso Kely
Tatsinanana

DISTRIBUTION: Common in rainforest from central to southern Madagascar.

ID: A small, mainly green chameleon without any outstanding structural features. Male shows a bold white line along the sides; female is more muted. See similar Glaw's Chameleon.

Length:	SVL < 7 cm	3"

WHERE TO SEE: Often abundant on night walks along the main road through Ranomafana NP. Also occurs around Andasibe.

E **2** **Glaw's Chameleon** *Calumma glawi*

M Tana Maitso Kelin'i Ranomafana

DISTRIBUTION: Small range in mid-elevation rainforest in the southeast.

ID: Small green chameleon that is very similar to Perinet Chameleon. Traits which may be present, and which can identify Glaw's Chameleon, include pale blue spots on the body; black on the casque of the males; and a larger flap (occipital lobe) at the back of the head, especially on males.

Length:	SVL < 7 cm	3"

WHERE TO SEE: Uncommon around Ranomafana NP. Mainly found on night walks.

E **3** **Canopy Chameleon** *Furcifer willsii*

M Sakorkita misy Tandroka Roa

DISTRIBUTION: Patchy distribution in eastern rainforest.

ID: The male has two large horns protruding from its nose, but female lacks horns. Both show only a small casque. Usually green, with some markings overlaid. Often shows pale, yellowish diagonal stripes along the sides. When present, these serve to separate female Canopy Chameleon from the similar Perinet Chameleon.

Length:	SVL < 8 cm	3"

WHERE TO SEE: Uncommon in Andasibe and Ranomafana.

E **4** **Big Nose Chameleon** *Calumma nasutum*

M Tana Kely misy Orona

DISTRIBUTION: Widespread in eastern rainforest and forest edge. Also occurs in some places in the Sambirano rainforest of the north.

ID: A small chameleon with a warty horn on the nose. Coloration variable but usually dull. Similar to several other less frequently seen species, but full coverage of their separation is beyond the scope of this guide.

Length:	SVL < 5 cm	2"

WHERE TO SEE: Fairly common in most eastern rainforest sites, including Andasibe and Ranomafana.

4 Sometimes called Nose-horned Chameleon

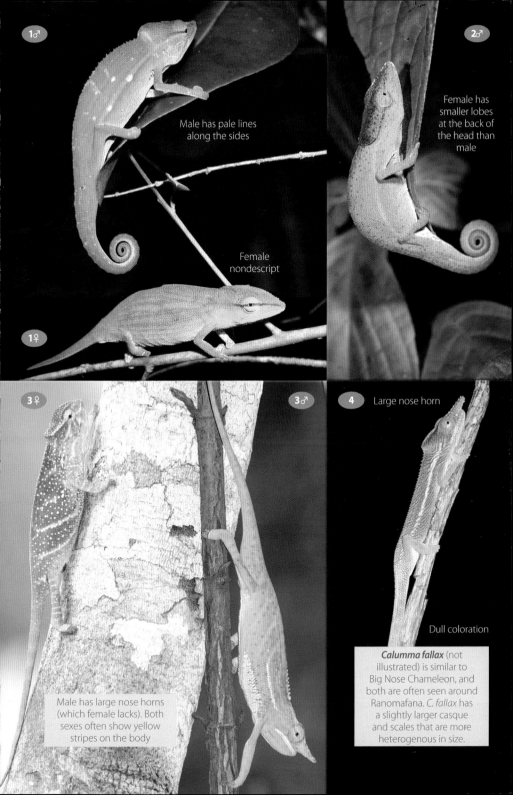

1♂

Male has pale lines along the sides

2♂

Female has smaller lobes at the back of the head than male

Female nondescript

1♀

3♀

3♂

Male has large nose horns (which female lacks). Both sexes often show yellow stripes on the body

4   Large nose horn

Dull coloration

Calumma fallax (not illustrated) is similar to Big Nose Chameleon, and both are often seen around Ranomafana. *C. fallax* has a slightly larger casque and scales that are more heterogenous in size.

🄴 ① Cryptic (Blue-legged) Chameleon
Calumma crypticum

Ⓜ Tarondro Pentina
Manga

DISTRIBUTION: Middle- and high-elevation rainforest, mainly in the east.
ID: Large flaps (occipital lobes) at the back of the head. Male has a single modest nose horn. Often colourful, marked with blue, green, and rich brown. Often has blue markings on its legs, hence its alternate common name. Short-horned Chameleon is very similar: the male Cryptic Chameleon has a slightly longer nose, but females may be inseparable.

Length: SVL < 12 cm | 5"
WHERE TO SEE: Fairly common in Ranomafana NP. Sleeping individuals are often located at night along the main road.

🄴 ② Short-horned Chameleon
Calumma brevicorne

Ⓜ Tarondro Be Sofina

DISTRIBUTION: Patchy distribution in middle-elevation rainforest of the east.
ID: Structure very similar to Cryptic Chameleon. Male Short-horned Chameleon shows a slightly longer brick-red nose horn. Both sexes are generally less colourful than Cryptic Chameleon, more brown-and-grey, though females may be inseparable.

Length: SVL 11–17 cm | 4·5–7"
WHERE TO SEE: Fairly common around Andasibe.

Chameleons are famous for changing colour to match their environment. However, camouflage is just one of the ways they use this ability, since they also make colour changes as a visual display of their mood, or in response to cues like changing light level or temperature.

2♀

Females of both of these species have only a small bump on the nose

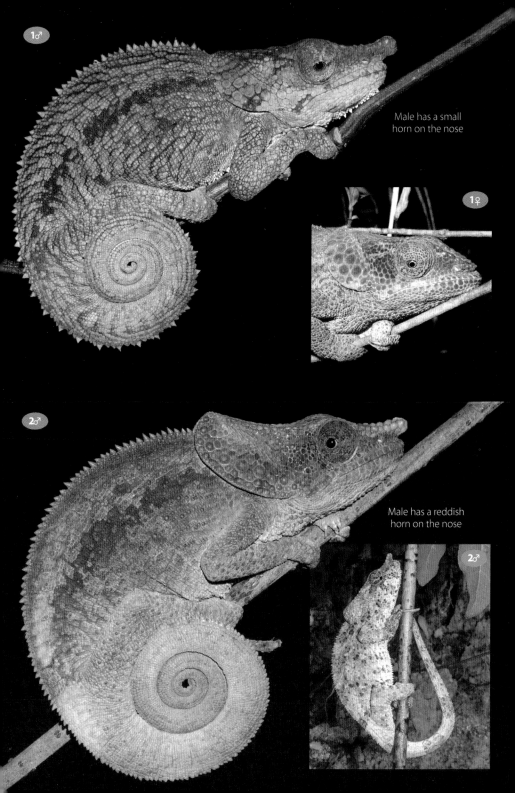

1♂

1♀

Male has a small
horn on the nose

2♂

2♂

Male has a reddish
horn on the nose

E **1** **Two-banded** (Belted) **Chameleon**
Furcifer balteatus

M Tanakely Mitsipibatana

DISTRIBUTION: Middle-elevation rainforest and degraded habitat in the southeast.
ID: Large, usually bright green chameleon. Male shows twin horns on the nose. Can almost always be identified by the long, pale slash that runs along the side, from behind the top of the head down to the hind legs.

ENDANGERED	
Length:	SVL ♂ < 18 cm | 7"
	♀ < 15 cm | 6"

WHERE TO SEE: Ranomafana area. Most common in the degraded areas around the village of Ranomafana.

E **2** **O'Shaughnessy's Chameleon**
Calumma oshaughnessyi

M Tarondro Maitso Be misy Sofina

DISTRIBUTION: Eastern rainforest of the southeast.
ID: Large green chameleon. Can be similar to smaller individuals of Parson's Chameleon (*page 190*). Both species have triangular heads, but O'Shaughnessy's Chameleon has flaps of skin at the back of the head (occipital lobes) that are absent in Parson's Chameleon. O'Shaughnessy's Chameleon also shows heterogeneous scales along its sides, with a regular pattern of much larger scales interspersed among smaller ones, whereas Parson's Chameleon has scales all of roughly the same size.

VULNERABLE	
Length:	SVL < 18 cm | 7"

WHERE TO SEE: Ranomafana NP. Frequently found at night along the main road, often sleeping quite high in the forest.

2♀

The scales on the sides vary significantly in size

1♂ Male has twin horns on the nose; female lacks prominent nose horns

2♂ Male has a large triangular head and prominent twin horns on the nose

E 1 Amber Mountain Chameleon *Calumma amber*   M Tarondro Marevaka

DISTRIBUTION: Endemic to the rainforest of Amber Mountain.

ID: Within its range, the big 'elephant ears' at the back of the head are distinctive. Arthur's Chameleon is larger, usually green, and has a large, triangular head. Similar to Short-horned and Cryptic Chameleons (*page 196*), but does not overlap in range.

NEAR THREATENED	
Length:	SVL 7–11 cm | 3–4·5"

WHERE TO SEE: Can usually be located during the day along the trails in Amber Mountain NP.

E 2 Arthur's Chameleon* *Calumma ambreense*   M Tarondro Marevaka

DISTRIBUTION: Found in mid-elevation rainforest in the north, on Amber Mountain and perhaps elsewhere.

ID: Very similar to the closely related O'Shaughnessy's Chameleon (*page 198*), but found in the far north instead of the southeast. Big triangular head distinctive within its small range.

NEAR THREATENED	
Length:	SVL < ~18 cm | 7"

WHERE TO SEE: Fairly easy to find in Amber Mountain NP during the wet season; more difficult in the dry season.

2♀

2♀

Female lacks nose horn, and can show yellowish coloration

Male has a small nose horn; female lacks a nose horn, and is usually green

Male has a smaller nose horn than does the closely related O'Shaughnessy's Chameleon, which only occurs in the southeast; the ranges of the two species do not overlap

Ⓔ① Petter's Chameleon *Furcifer petteri* complex

M Tanakelin'ny
Avaratra Andrefana

DISTRIBUTION: Forest and adjacent human-modified habitats in the north. Probably a complex that contains multiple undescribed species.

ID: Male shows two large horns on the nose, but female lacks horns. Overall colour green or yellow-green, and often has white lips. Male has a pale line along the side, while female shows two pale spots.

VULNERABLE	
Length:	SVL ♂ <9cm | 3·5"
	♀ <7cm | 3"

WHERE TO SEE: Ankarana and Amber Mountain NPs and the surrounding areas. Often found in scrubby habitat in the town of Joffreville.

Ⓔ② Northern Blue-nosed / Boettger's Chameleon *Calumma linotum / boettgeri* complex

M Tana Kely Mitsingoloka

DISTRIBUTION: Rainforest and secondary habitats in the north and northeast. *C. linotum* is apparently found only on Amber Mountain, while the *C. boettgeri* complex (containing multiple undescribed species) is more widespread.

Length:	SVL <6cm | 2·5"

WHERE TO SEE: *C. linotum* is fairly common in and around Amber Mountain NP. *C. boettgeri* is possible around Nosy Be and Marojejy NP, often in secondary habitat.

ID: Small chameleon with a small casque, but a big horn on the nose of both sexes. Variable in colour, but usually shows bands on the tail. *C. linotum* usually has a bright blue nose horn.
Big Nose Chameleon (*page 194*) overlaps in range, and is very similar, but lacks the small flap at the back of the head (occipital lobe) shown by Boettger's Chameleon.

2♂

Both sexes have a small casque and a big nose horn

Female lacks a
nose horn

E **1** White-lined (Antimena) **Chameleon**
Furcifer antimena

M Tarondro Ben'ny Atsimo Andrefana

DISTRIBUTION: A small area of spiny forest in the southwest.
ID: Green and brown, with male brighter than female. Usually shows a white line and three dark circles on the side. Within its range, identified by the large warty nose horn of the male, and the much smaller one of the female.

VULNERABLE

Length:	SVL ♂ < 17 cm | 7"
	♀ < 10 cm | 4"

WHERE TO SEE: Spiny forest around Toliara and Ifaty, especially during the wet season.

E **2** Rhinoceros Chameleon
Furcifer rhinoceratus

M Sakorikita Malemy Orona

DISTRIBUTION: Restricted to a small area of dry forest in the northwest.
ID: Coloration variable but usually dull. Within its range, identified by the huge warty horn on the nose of the male, and the much smaller one on the female.

VULNERABLE

Length:	SVL ♂ < 14 cm | 5·5"
	♀ < 7 cm | 3"

WHERE TO SEE: Uncommon in Ankarafantsika NP, seen mainly during the wet season.

2♂

Male has a chainsaw-like projection on the nose

Male has a large casque, spikes along the spine and a nose horn; these are less well developed in the female

ⓔ ① Warty Chameleon *Furcifer verrucosus*

M Sakorikita Be
F Caméléon Verruqueux

DISTRIBUTION: Widespread in dry forest and disturbed habitat across most of western and southwestern Madagascar. Present, but less common, in parts of the central highlands.

ID: Large and generally dull-coloured chameleon that can easily be mistaken for Oustalet's Chameleon (*page 190*). Male Warty Chameleon has larger spikes on the throat and along the spine; it has fewer than 40 spikes on the spine, whereas Oustalet's Chameleon has more than 45. Female generally lacks spikes along the spine, unlike female Oustalet's Chameleon which has prominent spikes, although some may be indistinguishable.

Length:	SVL ♂ <27 cm | 11"
	♀ <10 cm | 4"

WHERE TO SEE: Common in much of the west and southwest. Often in towns and gardens. One reliable spot is the Arboretum d'Antsokay near Toliara. Also occurs in Parc Anja, alongside Oustalet's Chameleon.

ⓔ ② Labord's Chameleon *Furcifer labordi*

M Tarondro Tsara Tarehy

DISTRIBUTION: Wide but patchy distribution in western dry forest.

ID: Structure similar to White-lined Chameleon (*page 204*), but does not overlap in range. Male has white lips and white lines along the sides. Female has green bars along the sides, and some show blue spotting.

VULNERABLE

Length:	SVL ♂ <14 cm | 5·5"
	♀ <8 cm | 3"

WHERE TO SEE: Kirindy Forest, mainly during the wet season.

Uniquely among reptiles, all adult Labord's Chameleons die at the end of the wet season, after they have bred. The breeding population the following year is comprised entirely of individuals that have hatched out of the previous generation's eggs – a breeding cycle analogous to that of an annual plant!

2♀

2♂

Female Warty Chameleon can be indistinguishable from Oustalet's Chameleon

Male Warty Chameleons can be up to 57 cm (22") long; not quite as large as the largest Oustalet's Chameleons, but still impressive

Warty Chameleon is the most common chameleon in the arid southwest

Madagascar's (reptilian) swifts are something of a mystery, as they are closely related to iguanids, found only in the Americas, and on some Pacific islands. They probably originate from the ancient time when Madagascar was connected to South America via Antarctica. Unlike the iguanids, Madagascar's swifts are found only in dry habitats, not in rainforest. It was only recently recognized that Madagascar's seven swift species constitute their own regionally endemic family, the Opluridae: previously they were considered part of the Igaunidae.

'Swifts' is a common name shared by two very different groups: iguana-like lizards from Madagascar and a widespread family of birds (see *page 136*).

E **1** Three-eyed Lizard *Chalarodon madagascariensis*   **M** Dangalia

DISTRIBUTION: Found on the ground in spiny forest, dry forest, and degraded habitat across the west and southwest.

ID: Variable, but usually boldly marked. Boasts a 'third eye', a dark spot on the top of the head which contains photoreceptors.

BEHAVIOUR: Generally stands motionlessly, but is capable of dashing with great speed.

| Length: | Average TL ~20 cm | 8" |

WHERE TO SEE: Common in spiny forest in the southwest. Also found in some western dry forest sites including Kirindy Forest and Zombitse-Vohibasia NP.

E **2** Merrem's Madagascar Swift *Oplurus cyclurus*   **M** Androngovato misy Sanga

DISTRIBUTION: Found mainly on tree trunks in dry forest of the southwest and west. Most common in the southwest.

ID: The extremely spiny tail separates it from Dumeril's Madagascar Swift and Grandidier's Madagascar Swift (both *page 210*). In some places occurs alongside Cuvier's Madagascar Swift, although that species generally prefers moister habitats. Merrem's can be separated by its narrow (rather than broad) black collar, often bordered in white. A close look at the tail also reveals that there are no small rows of scales between the big spiny scales, unlike in Cuvier's Madagascar Swift.

| Length: | TL <25 cm | 10" |

WHERE TO SEE: Fairly common in the spiny forest of the southwest, for example around Toliara and Ifaty.

R **3** Cuvier's Madagascar Swift *Oplurus cuvieri*   **M** Androngon-kazo

DISTRIBUTION: Madagascar and Grande Comore. Found on tree trunks and on the ground in western dry forest and degraded habitat.

ID: Similar to Merrem's Madagascar Swift, but usually larger, with a much broader black collar, and has small scales between the large spines on its tail.

| Length: | TL <37 cm | 14·5" |

WHERE TO SEE: Very common and conspicuous in Ankarafantsika NP, including around the park headquarters. Also common in Tsingy de Bemaraha NP and Kirindy Forest.

The '3rd eye' on the back of the head actually contains photoreceptors!

1

2 Narrow black 'collar'

3

3 **2**

These two species can be separated by a careful look at their tails. There are small rows of scales between the big spiny scales on Cuvier's **3**, but no such scales on Merrem's **2**.

Broad black 'collar'

E **1** Dumeril's Madagascar Swift
Oplurus quadrimaculatus

M Androngovato Atsimo Atsinanana

DISTRIBUTION: Classic habitat is rocky, arid areas of the southwest, but occurs in a variety of habitat from sea level up to 2,000 m (6,500′) in southwest and south-central Madagascar.

ID: A large lizard that lacks the enlarged tail spines of Merrem's Madagascar and Cuvier's Madagascar Swifts (*page 208*). Very similar to Grandidier's Madagascar Swift, but that species usually shows a single pale line along the middle of its back, whereas Dumeril's Madagascar Swift shows either an unlined back, or two pale lines along the sides (rather than the centre) of the back. In the far south, such as around Fort Dauphin and Berenty, confusion is possible with the very similar **Marked Madagascar Swift** *O. saxicola* **1a**, but that species never shows stripes on the sides of the back.

BEHAVIOUR: Often sits on rocks. Can be surprisingly tame.

Length: TL < 39 cm | 15″

WHERE TO SEE: Common and conspicuous around Isalo, including the tourist lodges. Also common in Parc Anja.

Marked Madagascar Swift
Oplurus saxicola

E **2** Grandidier's Madagascar Swift
Oplurus grandidieri

M Androngovato Be

DISTRIBUTION: Found in south-central Madagascar. Lives on rocks, often within extensive grassland areas.

ID: Similar to Dumeril's Madagascar Swift, but usually shows a pale line along the middle of the back, rather than thin stripes along the sides of the back or no stripes at all. The tail is very fat at its base, then quickly tapers.

BEHAVIOUR: Like other rock-dwelling Madagascar swifts.

Length: TL < 35 cm | 14″

WHERE TO SEE: Parc Anja, where it is common alongside Dumeril's Madagascar Swift.

1

Pale stripes along the sides of the back

Pale stripe along the centre of the back

2

Plated lizards comprise a family that is found across Africa and Madagascar. Of the 19 Malagasy species, the eight that are most frequently seen by visitors are covered. These large lizards are diurnal and conspicuous. Except for the rarely seen green species (see box below), all are ground-dwelling, and can often be located by their noisy movements in the leaf-litter.

🅔 ➊ Tsingy Plated Lizard *Zonosaurus tsingy* M Androngovaton' ny Tsingy

DISTRIBUTION: Dry forest with tsingy rock formations in a small area of the far north.

ID: Base colour is variable, but often includes attractive shades of blue, orange and yellow. There are small pale speckles across the body. Always lacks strong stripes along the back. *Zonosaurus subunicolor* (not illustrated) is similar but occurs farther south, such as on Nosy Be and in Marojejy NP.

BEHAVIOUR: Often sits on tsingy rock formations.

| Length: | SVL < 8·5 cm | 3.5" |

WHERE TO SEE: Fairly common in Ankarana NP.

Breeding males can be colourful

🅔 ➋ Red-legged Plated Lizard *Zonosaurus rufipes* M Androngon'i Lokobe

DISTRIBUTION: Rainforest in a small area of the north.

ID: Mostly brown, with reddish legs, and lots of pale speckles. Unlike most other plated lizards, has stripes on the throat. Lines along the sides of the back are either weak or absent.

NEAR THREATENED

| Length: | SVL < 9 cm | 3.5" |

WHERE TO SEE: Common in Lokobe NP. Also possible in other forests on Nosy Be, and in Marojejy NP.

🅔 ➌ Brygoo's Plated Lizard *Zonosaurus brygooi* M Androngo Vato Fotsy Hatoka

DISTRIBUTION: Lowland rainforest along the northern part of the east coast.

ID: Base colour is brown, with pale and dark speckles. There are lines along the sides of the back, but they are much weaker than those on Madagascar Plated Lizard (see *page 214*).

| Length: | SVL < 8 cm | 3" |

WHERE TO SEE: Not uncommon on the Masoala Peninsula. Also possible on Nosy Mangabe.

Herpetological Holy Grail Some of Madagascar's most sought-after but hardest-to-see reptiles are the green plated lizards. They were first described in the late 19th century, then 'disappeared' for 100 years before being seen again by scientists. There are two species: *Zonosaurus boettgeri*, known from a handful of sites including Lokobe and Masoala NPs in the north; and *Z. maramaintso*, known from Tsingy de Bemaraha NP. Unlike other plated lizards, these green species live in trees, often high in the canopy. Count yourself extremely lucky if you manage to spot one!

Plated Lizards *versus* Skinks Plated lizards resemble skinks (*pages 216–219*), and are often mistaken for them, even by knowledgeable guides. Plated lizards are generally larger; have bodies that are more squared-off rather than rounded; have slightly larger and squarer scales; and diagnostically, have a sharp furrow all along the bottom of the side of their body (a 'lateral longitudinal fold') whereas skinks have such a line only between their head and front legs.

1 Usually dark grey-brown with light spots

2 Reddish legs and flanks; distinctive stripes on throat

3 Weak lines along edges of back

R **1** # Madagascar Plated Lizard
e *Zonosaurus madagascariensis*

M Bekaratsaka
F Zonosaure de Madagascar

DISTRIBUTION: Found in many habitats including heavily human-modified ones, throughout most of eastern and northern Madagascar, with an isolated population in the central west. Mostly absent from rainforest interior.
ID: For separation from the similar Western Plated Lizard, see that species account. On Amber Mountain, Madagascar

Length: Average SVL 13 cm | 5"

WHERE TO SEE: Common throughout much of the east and north.

Plated Lizard is replaced by the similar **Meier's Plated Lizard** *Zonosaurus haraldmeieri* (not illustrated), while the two species hybridize in Ankarana NP. The similar **Bronze Plated Lizard** *Z. aeneus* (not illustrated) overlaps in the central and southern parts of the east. It averages smaller, with a dot-and-dash pattern rather than continuous stripes along the sides of the back.

E **2** # Ornate Plated Lizard *Zonosaurus ornatus*

M Marabe

DISTRIBUTION: Forest edge and open montane habitat in central and central-eastern Madagascar.
ID: A beautiful and distinctive species with five stripes along the back.

Length: SVL < 13 cm | 5"

WHERE TO SEE: Forest edges around Ranomafana NP and Anjozorobe. Also in the high mountains of Andringitra NP.

E **3** # Western Plated Lizard *Zonosaurus laticaudatus*

M Androngoben'i Fiherenana

DISTRIBUTION: Found in dry forest, plantations, and degraded habitats, mainly in the west, although also in the Ambanja region of the north, and around Fort Dauphin in the far south.
ID: Very similar to Madagascar Plated Lizard, but there is little overlap in range. Where they do occur together,

Length: Average SVL 14 cm | 5.5"

WHERE TO SEE: Common around the headquarters of Ankarafantsika NP and in Kirindy Forest.

around Ambanja, Western Plated Lizard can be recognized by the fact that the pale stripes along the sides of its back are very broad just behind the head, then quickly taper.

E **4** # Karsten's Plated Lizard *Zonosaurus karsteni*

M Androngon'i Fiherenana

DISTRIBUTION: Patchy distribution in western dry forest and secondary habitats.
ID: Has fine black markings on the head, unlike the similar Western Plated Lizard, which averages larger and has more tapering pale stripes on the sides of the back.

Length: Average SVL 13 cm | 5"

WHERE TO SEE: Fairly common in Kirindy Forest and around Tsingy de Bemaraha.

E **5** # Madagascar Keeled Plated Lizard
Tracheloptychus madagascariensis

M Sitry

DISTRIBUTION: Dry forest in the southwest.
ID: Pattern of three pale stripes along the back is distinctive. At Berenty, the somewhat similar Three-lined Plated Lizard *Zonosaurus trilineatus* (not illustrated) also occurs. It is more boldly marked, with stripes that extend onto the head.

Length: SVL < 7 cm | 3"

WHERE TO SEE: Fairly common in forest throughout much of the southwest. One good place is the Arboretum d'Antsokay near Toliara.

1 Stripes along sides of back fade towards back legs

1 Can show orange or red below, especially on throat

2 Distinctive pattern of stripes and spots on the side

3 Stripes along sides of back start broad, then narrow but stay strong

3 Throat sometimes red

4 Large spots on sides. Narrow stripes along sides of back

5 Scales along back have 'keels' unlike normal plated lizards

Complex pattern

Skinks are a family of lizards that occurs almost throughout the world. Although over 70 species are found in Madagascar, most live in leaf-litter or burrows, and are seldom seen. Many have reduced limbs and elongated bodies, and are snake-like. The *Trachylepis* skinks (which were formerly placed in the genus *Mabuya*) are familiar lizards that are diurnal and conspicuous, found on the ground, on rocks and on dead tree trunks.

E 1 Gravenhorst's Skink *Trachylepis gravenhorstii*   M Androngo Matetika

DISTRIBUTION: Found throughout most of the island. Seems to be more common than Elegant Skink in montane and rainforest-edge habitats.
ID: Bold striped pattern. Can be very similar to Elegant Skink.

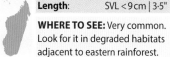

Length: SVL <9cm | 3·5"

WHERE TO SEE: Very common. Look for it in degraded habitats adjacent to eastern rainforest.

R 2 Elegant Skink *Trachylepis elegans*   M Androngo Mena Hatoka

DISTRIBUTION: Most of the island in open habitats. Never inside true forest.
ID: Definitive identification may be impossible, but classic features for Elegant Skink are an orange or red spot on the side of the neck a complex pattern of spots and stripes. Very similar to Gravenhorst's Skink; the true relationship between these two species has yet to be resolved.

Length: SVL <6cm | 2·5"

WHERE TO SEE: Common. Fond of hot, dry places such as Diego-Suarez, Morondava, and Toliara.

E 3 Tandrefana Skink* *Trachylepis tandrefana*   M Katsatsaka Tandrefana

DISTRIBUTION: Western dry forest.
ID: Highly variable. Some individuals similar to Gold-spotted, Elegant, or Gravenhorst's Skinks, but rarely as boldly marked. Definitive identification may require a detailed analysis of the scales.

Length: SVL 5–6cm | 2–2·5"

WHERE TO SEE: Tsingy de Bemaraha NP and Kirindy Forest.

1 Simpler back pattern. Small or no white spots on sides

2 Complex pattern on back. White spots on sides. Orange neck marking.

3 Lacks bold stripes. Highly variable - some much darker than this individual

Gold-spotted Skink *Trachylepis aureopunctata* M Katsatsaka Pentina Fotsy

DISTRIBUTION: Forested and rocky areas of the west and southwest.

ID: Distinctive pale spots on the front half of the body.

BEHAVIOUR: More secretive than the other *Trachylepis* skinks included in this book. Often hides in the crevices of dead trees.

Length: SVL <8 cm | 3"

WHERE TO SEE: Kirindy Forest and the spiny forest around Toliara and Ifaty.

Comoro Skink *Trachylepis comorensis* M Katsatsaka Kaomoriana

DISTRIBUTION: Mainly a species of the Comoros; in Madagascar found only on Nosy Tanikely, where it is very common.

ID: A large brown skink with pale speckles. Madagascar Plated Lizard (*page 214*) is also common on Nosy Tanikely, but it shows bold white stripes along the side of the back. Also see *Plated Lizards versus Skinks* on *page 212* for structural differences between skinks and plated lizards.

Length: SVL 10–11 cm | 4–4.5"

WHERE TO SEE: The small island of Nosy Tanikely, a popular snorkeling destination adjacent Nosy Be.

Secretive skinks several genera [~ 60 species]

DISTRIBUTION: Found in all the island's habitats. The eastern rainforest holds the highest diversity.

ID: Very variable in size, but snout to vent length (SVL) for most is 3–10 cm (1·2–4"). All have relatively smaller limbs and more elongated bodies than the *Trachylepis* skinks, giving them a snake-like appearance. Some lack limbs altogether, but differ from snakes in having eyelids, ear openings and being able to shed their tail as a defence mechanism.

BEHAVIOUR: Most live in leaf-litter, although some of the more snake-like species burrow into the ground.

Length: SVL 2–23 cm | 0·8–9"

WHERE TO SEE: It takes luck or some digging in the leaf-litter to find any of these skinks. Common Madagascar Skink *Madascincus melanopleura* (not illustrated) is sometimes seen at Nosy Mangabe; Ranomafana NP is good for a couple of *Amphiglossus* species.

Voeltzkowia rubrocaudata is one of the snake-like skinks

1

Conspicuous spotting

Gold-spotted Skink has distinctive pale spots on the front half of the body, usually forming seven or eight rows. *Trachylepis vato* (not illustrated) is very similar but has nine rows of white spots on the front half of the body; it is found mainly in the central part of the southern half of Madagascar but overlaps with Gold-spotted Skink in the far south.

2

Only on Nosy Tanikely

3

Amphiglossus frontoparietalis is typical of the secretive skinks that have long bodies and small limbs, but retain basic lizard structure.

This delightful group of geckos is brightly coloured and diurnal. They are restricted to the Indian Ocean region, with the majority endemic to Madagascar. Most species inhabit trees and man-made structures: the walls of your hotel may be the best place to seek out the local species of day gecko. Other favoured haunts include banana trees and Traveller's Palm (*page 316*). Males are larger and more colourful than females.

E **1** ## Giant Day Gecko *Phelsuma grandis*   **M** Fingoko Be*

DISTRIBUTION: Endemic to Madagascar, but introduced to the Mascarene Islands. Found from the northern tip of Madagascar, south to Marojejy and Ambanja. Uses many habitats, from rainforest to heavily human-modified areas.
ID: The largest day gecko, with bright green coloration, and often red spots on the head and/or back. There is always a red stripe between the nostril and the eye, but this stripe ends at the eye rather than continuing onto the neck as in the closely related **Madagascar Day Gecko** *Phelsuma madagascariensis* (not illustrated). These two species also have little overlap in range: Giant Day Gecko is in the north, south to Masoala, while Madagascar Day Gecko is in the east, south of Masoala.

Length: TL 22–30 cm | 9–12"

WHERE TO SEE: Quite common in the north, including in towns and villages.

Giant, Koch's and Madagascar Day Geckos are all similar and closely related, and were considered to be a single species until recently. For the most part, they have discrete ranges. **Giant Day Gecko** is common and frequently seen in the north. **Koch's Day Gecko** is fairly common in much of the west. **Madagascar Day Gecko** is less frequently seen but occasionally spotted around Andasibe and St. Marie Island.

E **2** ## Koch's Day Gecko *Phelsuma kochi*   **M** Fingoko Tandrefana*

DISTRIBUTION: Found throughout most of the west, both in forest and human-modified habitat.
ID: Similar to Giant Day Gecko, but duller-green, and averages smaller. Little or no overlap in range.

Length: TL 22–31 cm | 9–12"

WHERE TO SEE: Check the buildings at headquarters in Ankarafantsika NP. Also found in Tsingy de Bemaraha NP and Kirindy Forest.

E **3** ## Lined Day Gecko *Phelsuma lineata*   **M** Atsatsatra Maitso

DISTRIBUTION: Very widespread in many different habitats, but absent from the southwest and most of the west.
ID: Mostly green, with a black line along the side. The very similar *Phelsuma dorsivittata* (not illustrated) is found in the north, mainly on Amber Mountain. Small Lined Day Gecko (*page 222*) is similar, but smaller.

Length: TL 11–15 cm | 4–6"

WHERE TO SEE: Common in and around most eastern protected areas, including Andasibe and Ranomafana. Also on the High Plateau, and can be found in Tana.

E **4** ## Peacock Day Gecko *Phelsuma quadriocellata*   **M** Atsatsam-bakoana

DISTRIBUTION: Forest and human-modified habitats in the east and far northwest.
ID: Green, with a blue-edged black spot behind the front legs. Lined Day Gecko can show a similar black spot, but it is never edged in blue.

Length: TL 13 cm | 5"

WHERE TO SEE: Fairly common in and around most eastern protected areas, *e.g.* Andasibe and Ranomafana. The 'Belle Vue' viewpoint in Ranomafana NP is a reliable locality.

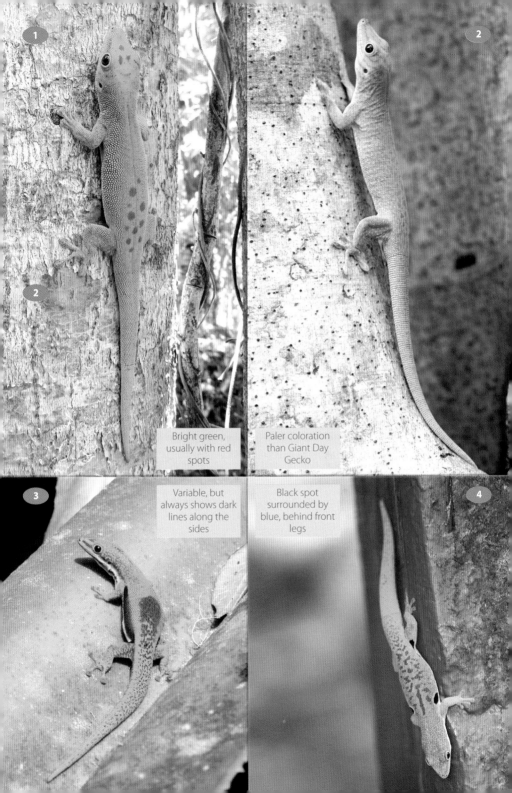

Bright green, usually with red spots

Paler coloration than Giant Day Gecko

Variable, but always shows dark lines along the sides

Black spot surrounded by blue, behind front legs

ⓡ ① Gold-dust Day Gecko *Phelsuma laticauda* M Atsatsa-maitso Tavaratra

DISTRIBUTION: Madagascar, and some other Indian Ocean islands, to which it may have been introduced, as it has been to Hawaii and Florida. In Madagascar, common in rainforest openings, plantations, and villages in the far northwest and northeast.

Length:	TL < 13 cm | 5"

WHERE TO SEE: Common in much of the far north including Nosy Be and Sambava.

ID: A beautiful gecko with blue rings around the eyes and a sprinkle of gold across the back. Three red bars on the head, and three on the back. Lacks the strong line along the side shown by Lined (*page 220*) and Small Lined Day Geckos.

ⓔ ② Speckled Day Gecko *Phelsuma guttata* M Atsatsa-maitso Tatsinanana

DISTRIBUTION: Rainforest and forest edge in the northeast. Usually in sun-lit places, often on Pandanus and Traveller's Palm (*page 316*).

Length:	TL < 13 cm | 5"

WHERE TO SEE: Not hard to find on Nosy Mangabe. Also in Marojejy NP.

ID: Three dark 'V'-shaped marks on the throat are distinctive. Madagascar and Giant Day Geckos (*page 220*) can be similar, but are larger.

ⓡ ③ Aldabra Day Gecko *Phelsuma abbotti* M Atsatsatra
ⓔ

DISTRIBUTION: The Seychelles, and northern and western Madagascar. Found in villages, plantations, and other human-modified habitats. Favours sun-lit tree trunks.

Length:	TL 13–15 cm | 5–6"

WHERE TO SEE: Nosy Be, around Ambanja, and in Tsingy de Bemaraha NP.

ID: A relatively plain green or bluish species. Similar to Speckled Day Gecko, but has minimal overlap in range. If in doubt, can be identified by the dark line along the spine, a maximum of one or two 'V'-shaped markings on the throat (three in Speckled), and the lack of the bold red dots on the back that are usually shown by Speckled Day Gecko.

ⓔ ④ Small Lined Day Gecko* *Phelsuma pusilla* M Atsatsatra Maitsom-bakoana

DISTRIBUTION: Hot east coast lowlands, often in and around towns and villages. Fond of banana and palm trees.

Length:	TL < 8·5 cm | 3·5"

WHERE TO SEE: Toamasina, St. Marie Island, and Maroantsetra.

ID: Similar pattern to Lined Day Gecko (*page 220*), but smaller.

Broad tail. Three red bars on head and back. Fine gold spots

Three dark Vs on throat and sides of neck. Usually red spots on back

Dark stripe through eye and along centre of back; often shows one or two 'V'-shaped marks on throat and sides of neck

Like a miniature Lined Day Gecko

ⓔ ① Modest Day Gecko *Phelsuma modesta*

M Atsatsa-maitso Tandrefana

DISTRIBUTION: Dry forest, scrub and man-made structures, mainly in the southwest.
ID: Pale greenish base colour, often with twin red lines on the back and faded-looking dark stripes along the sides. Looks washed-out and dull compared to many other day geckos. Thicktail Day Gecko can also be pale, but it never shows any red on the back or a darker stripe along the sides.

Length:	TL < 12 cm | 5"

WHERE TO SEE: Fairly common in southwestern towns and villages including Ifaty and Toliara.

ⓔ ② Thicktail Day Gecko *Phelsuma mutabilis*

M Atsatsatra Fotsikibo

DISTRIBUTION: Found in forest, scrub, and on man-made structures in the dry and hot west and southwest.
ID: Capable of remarkable changes in colour, from brown to very pale grey. The tail can be pale blue **2a**, green **2b**, brown or pale grey **2c**. Although highly variable and changeable, all of its colour combinations are different from those of most other day geckos in its range. Very similar to **Bora's Day Gecko** *Phelsuma borai* (not illustrated), which is endemic to Tsingy de Bemaraha NP, and **Gould's Day Gecko** *P. gouldi* (not illustrated), which is known only from Parc Anja, and differs from both of these species in fine details of the scales.

Length:	TL < 10 cm | 4"

WHERE TO SEE: Around Berenty, Toliara, and Zombitse-Vohibasia NP.

ⓔ ③ Standing's Day Gecko *Phelsuma standingi*

M Atsatsabe
F Gecko Diurne de Standing

DISTRIBUTION: Small area of spiny forest and dry forest in the southwest. Frequently seen on baobabs (*pages 320–323*).
ID: Large, beautiful, and distinctive species with green, blue, and greyish base colour overlaid with complex dark markings.

VULNERABLE	
Length:	TL 21–28 cm | 8–11"

WHERE TO SEE: Often pointed out by guides in Zombitse-Vohibasia NP. Also in spiny forest around Ifaty.

ⓔ ④ Barbour's Day Gecko *Phelsuma barbouri*

M Atsatsam-bato

DISTRIBUTION: Found on the ground and on rocks in the central and southern mountains. This is the most terrestrial day gecko.
ID: Variable coloration, with pale green or brownish base colour and darker brown stripes on the head and back. Other day geckos are absent from its habitat.

Length:	TL < 15 cm | 6"

WHERE TO SEE: The mountains of Andringitra NP. Also present in less-disturbed rocky areas along the RN7 highway between Tana and Antsirabe.

1 Modest Day Gecko is a variable species: males are brightest; some females very dull

2a

Often shows blue tail

3

Typically looks 'washed-out'

1

2b

2c

Can be greenish

Some are very dull

Beautiful, complex, pattern

Terrestrial, highland species

4

This large group of small geckos is found mainly in Africa and Madagascar. Dwarf geckos are diurnal and, although cryptic, can often be spotted on rocks, on tree trunks and elsewhere in the forest, and sometimes on man-made structures. They are capable of changing colour, although they generally maintain sombre shades of grey, brown and olive-green. As with chameleons, sleeping dwarf geckos can sometimes be found at night, on low vegetation within the forest.

1 Dwarf geckos *Lygodactylus* spp. [22+ species]

M Antsiantsy

DISTRIBUTION: Found throughout Madagascar in most habitats, including spiny forest, rainforest, western dry forest, tsingy, and rocky high-elevation grassland. Some species readily use man-made structures.
ID: Diurnal habits and small size usually identify them. Pattern variable, but never colourful, always with a base colour of grey or brown.
BEHAVIOUR: Diurnal.

Length: SVL 1·5–4 cm | 0·5–1·5"

WHERE TO SEE: Ankarafantsika, Zombitse, and Lokobe NPs and the town of Antsirabe are among the easier places to spot a dwarf gecko. Although they are common in many places, it takes sharp eyes to spot these small, cryptic geckos.

Definitive identification of dwarf geckos is difficult and requires detailed analysis of the scales. Furthermore, the classification of the Malagasy dwarf geckos is incomplete, and many species remain to be described. As such, this genus is covered without reference to individual species, except for tentative identifications in the photo captions.

Spiny Forest Dwarf Gecko
Lygodactylus tuberosus
Parc Mosa, Ifaty

1

Madagascar Dwarf Gecko
Lygodactylus madagascariensis
Lokobe NP

Robust Dwarf Gecko
Lygodactylus pictus
Lalatsara Forest

Grandidier's Dwarf Gecko
Lygodactylus tolampyae
Zombitse-Vohibasia NP
Variable, but can be boldly marked

Rainforest Dwarf Gecko
Lygodactylus miops
Mitsinjo Reserve, Andasibe
Cryptic: rainforest species; can show greenish tones

1 House geckos *Hemidactylus* spp. [3 species]

M Atsatsaka an-Trano*
F Gecko de Maison

DISTRIBUTION: Introduced widely by humans, and found throughout the warmer parts of the world. Probably at least one species occurred on Madagascar before people arrived. Found mainly in and around man-made structures, although sometimes also in scrub and secondary forest away from human habitation.

ID: Generally small to medium-sized. The upper range of the length measurements applies only to **Flathead House Gecko** *H. platycephalus*, which is restricted to the north. House Geckos are highly variable in colour, from extremely pale to dark grey with strong black markings. Vertical pupils and many bumps (tubercules) on the body and tail.

VOICE: The voice of **Common House Gecko** *H. frenatus* is a familiar sound of human civilization. Its most frequent call is a quick, fading series of 5–10 "*tok*" calls.

BEHAVIOUR: Generally nocturnal, although sometimes active during the day in shaded areas. Often hunt insects around lights at night.

Length: TL 7–19 cm | 3–7.5"

WHERE TO SEE: Can be found on almost any human structure. Especially abundant in hotter, lower-lying areas.

Grey's House Gecko *H. mercatorius* **1c** is the most widespread and common species.
Common House Gecko *H. frenatus* **1b** is found mainly in the north, west, and southwest.
Flathead House Gecko *H. platycephalus* **1a** occurs in the north.

R **2** Fish-scale geckos *Geckolepis* spp. [~ 3 species]

M Matahotrandro misy Kiran-Trondro*

DISTRIBUTION: Endemic to Madagascar and the Comoros. Found throughout most of Madagascar in forest, secondary habitat and plantations. Sometimes on man-made structures.

ID: Among Madagascar's most bizarre creatures. The fish-like scales are unique, but even more remarkable is these geckos' ability to shed almost their entire skin as an escape mechanism if grasped by a predator, regenerating it within a few weeks. Given current knowledge, distinction of the three Malagasy species – **Peters' Spotted Fish-scale Gecko** *G. maculata* **2a** , **Many-scaled Fish-scale Gecko** *G. polylepis* (not illustrated) and **Grandidier's Fish-scale Gecko** *G. typica* (not illustrated) – is difficult.

BEHAVIOUR: Nocturnal, hiding during the day in nooks and crannies in dead trees, roots and Traveller's Palm (*page 316*) trees.

Length: TL 11–14 cm | 4–5.5"

WHERE TO SEE: Possible in and around almost any forest, but hard to find. Seemingly more common in the north, as around Nosy Be and Ankarana and Ankarafantsika NPs.

R **3** Madagascar Clawless Gecko *Ebenavia inunguis*

M Matahotrandro Matrokila

DISTRIBUTION: Comoros, Mauritius, and Madagascar, where it is found in primary and secondary rainforest in the east and north. Found only occasionally on man-made structures.

ID: Somewhat like a house gecko, but has a more pointed nose and a thinner and more elongated body. Also much less likely to be seen on man-made structures.

BEHAVIOUR: Mainly nocturnal, though sometimes active during the day.

Length: TL 8 cm | 3"

WHERE TO SEE: Scarce but possible on night walks in almost any rainforest.

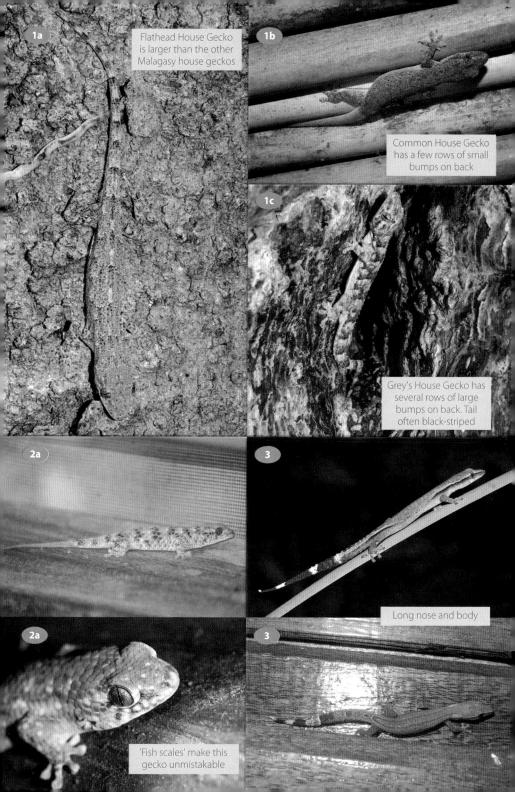

1a Flathead House Gecko is larger than the other Malagasy house geckos

1b Common House Gecko has a few rows of small bumps on back

1c Grey's House Gecko has several rows of large bumps on back. Tail often black-striped

2a

3

2a 'Fish scales' make this gecko unmistakable

3 Long nose and body

There are at least 15 species of ground gecko in Madagascar, but many are rare and local. The three most commonly seen species are covered here.

E **1** Madagascar Ground Gecko *Paroedura picta*   **M** Matahotrandro Mandady

DISTRIBUTION: Lives mostly on the ground in spiny forest and dry western dry forest.

ID: All ground geckos have huge eyes with a vertical pupil. Madagascar Ground Gecko has a beautiful pattern of oblique slashes along the sides. Bumps (tubercules) are scattered across the body.

BEHAVIOUR: Nocturnal.

| Length: | TL < 24 cm | 9·5" |

WHERE TO SEE: Widespread and fairly common in the west and south. Can be abundant at night in Kirindy Forest. Also possible on night walks around Ifaty and Berenty.

E **3** Mocquard's Ground Gecko *Paroedura bastardi*   **M** Matahotrandro Telo Tsipika

DISTRIBUTION: On the ground and in the understorey of spiny forest and dry western dry forest. Sometimes found on man-made structures.

ID: Variable, and probably a complex of species that will be split in the future. Never shows the oblique slashes of Madagascar Ground Gecko. Large bumps (tubercules) on the body are arranged into rows.

BEHAVIOUR: Nocturnal.

| Length: | TL < 23 cm | 9" |

WHERE TO SEE: Uncommon in Kirindy Forest; sometimes in the camp bungalows. Also possible during night walks around Ifaty and Berenty.

E **4** Graceful Big-headed Gecko   **M** Matahotrandro Maintibe
Paroedura gracilis

DISTRIBUTION: Rainforest in central and northern Madagascar. Found on the ground and in forest understorey.

ID: Variable blotchy pattern. The only ground gecko in most of the eastern rainforest.

BEHAVIOUR: Nocturnal.

| Length: | TL < 12 cm | 5" |

WHERE TO SEE: Uncommon but possible at night around Andasibe, Masoala, and Amber Mountain.

Vertical pupil typical of nocturnal Malagasy reptiles

Slashes along the sides. Smaller bumps on body, not in rows.

Large bumps on body, arranged into rows

White tail tip

E ① **Madagascar velvet geckos** *Blaesodactylus* spp. [4 species] **M** Atsatsaka

DISTRIBUTION: Found mainly in dry forest in the west and north, although also occurs in northeastern rainforest. Occasionally on man-made structures.

ID: Usually large; can be impressively huge. Colour variable but often similar to house geckos (*page 228*). Madagascar velvet geckos are larger, with a wider head and thicker body.

BEHAVIOUR: Nocturnal. During the day, hides in deep cracks and crevices.

| Length: | TL <30cm \| 12" |

WHERE TO SEE: Easiest at Ankarana NP, Kirindy Forest and Ifaty, although widespread. See table below.

WHICH MADAGASCAR VELVET GECKO AM I LOOKING AT? The most frequently visited sites in Madagascar that support a species of Madagascar velvet gecko:

Ankarana NP	1c	Northern Madagascar Velvet Gecko*	*B. boivini*
Ankarafansika NP	1a	Ambonihazo Madagascar Velvet Gecko*	*B. ambonihazo*
Kirindy Forest	1b	Sakalava Madagascar Velvet Gecko	*B. sakalava*
Marojejy NP		Antongil Madagascar Velvet Gecko	*B. antongilensis*
Nosy Mangabe		Antongil Madagascar Velvet Gecko	*B. antongilensis*
Tsingy de Bemaraha NP	1b	Sakalava Madagascar Velvet Gecko	*B. sakalava*
Toliara / Ifaty	1b	Sakalava Madagascar Velvet Gecko	*B. sakalava*
Zombitse-Vohibasia NP	1b	Sakalava Madagascar Velvet Gecko	*B. sakalava*

1c

Northern Madagascar Velvet Gecko is the largest species

1a Ambonihazo Madagascar Velvet Gecko was formally described in 2011

1b Sakalava Madagascar Velvet Geckos, like other velvet geckos, usually hide in crevices during the day.

Leaf-tailed geckos are found in trees, and active at night. Local guides often know the locations of sleeping individuals. Otherwise, you will have to find one at night when they are moving around. Some species give loud, hissing distress calls when disturbed. There are at least 14 species, of which the seven most commonly seen are covered here. Some of the current species may be split into multiple species in the future.

E ① Satanic Leaf-tailed Gecko *Uroplatus phantasticus* M Taharaikitra Madinika

DISTRIBUTION: Eastern rainforest in the southern two thirds of Madagascar.

ID: Colour variable, but always remarkably like a dead leaf. Spikes above the eyes makes it look rather sinister. Distinguished from the very similar Spearpoint Leaf-tailed Geckos by its relatively smaller head and much longer tail.

Length: TL 9 cm | 3·5"

WHERE TO SEE: With luck, can be found at night around Ranomafana, sometimes along the main road through the national park. Also around Andasibe, though less frequently seen there.

E ② Spearpoint leaf-tailed geckos M Taharaikitra Kely
Uroplatus ebenaui / finiavana complex

DISTRIBUTION: This complex of leaf-tailed geckos is found mainly in the understorey of rainforest in the north. It seems to contain several undescribed species. *Uroplatus finiavana* ②ⓐ, which is endemic to Amber Mountain, was described in 2011.

ID: Similar to Satanic Leaf-tailed Gecko, but with a smaller tail and larger head.

VULNERABLE / NEAR-THREATENED

Length: TL 6–8 cm | 2·5–3"

WHERE TO SEE: With some searching, *U. finiavana* ②ⓐ can usually be seen at night around Amber Mountain, while *U. ebenaui* ②ⓑ is occasionally found on Nosy Be.

E ③ Günther's Leaf-tailed Gecko *Uroplatus guentheri* M Tahafisaka Mitsipika

DISTRIBUTION: Patchy distribution in dry forest of the west.

ID: Variable coloration, but usually shows lines along the back, and resembles dry bark. In some places, occurs alongside Henkel's Leaf-tailed Gecko (*page 236*), but is much smaller, lacks 'mossy' fringes, and has spikes around the eye.

ENDANGERED

Length: TL 10–13 cm | 4–5"

WHERE TO SEE: Possible, although rare, in Ankarafantsika and Tsingy de Bemaraha NPs and Kirindy Forest. Most likely during the wet season.

E ④ Lined Leaf–tailed Gecko *Uroplatus lineatus* M Tahafisaka Mavomavo

DISTRIBUTION: Northern part of the eastern rainforest. Often in stands of bamboo.

ID: A distinctive pale yellow colour with faint dark stripes.

Length: TL 16–21 cm | 6–8"

WHERE TO SEE: A very lucky find on night walks around Marojejy and Masoala NPs.

The French name for leaf-tailed geckos is 'uroplates'.

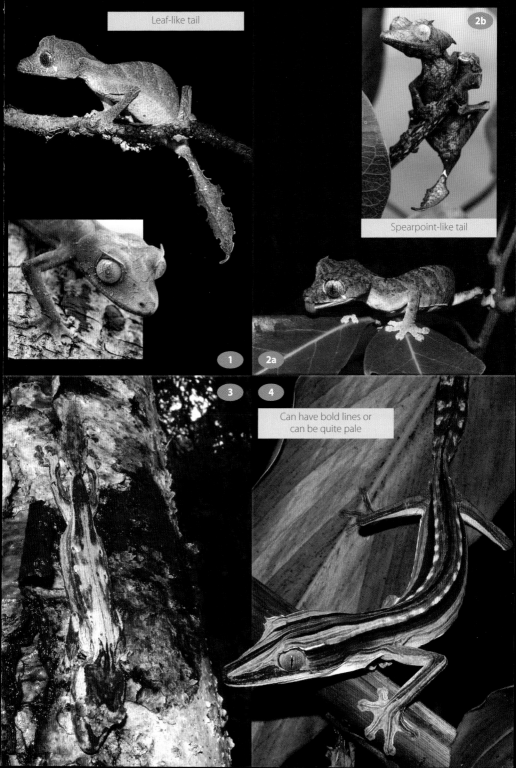

Leaf-like tail

Spearpoint-like tail

Can have bold lines or
can be quite pale

On an island of marvels, leaf-tailed geckos rank among Madagascar's most amazing creatures. They are some of the best-camouflaged creatures on Earth. Not only does their anatomy resemble their environment, but they also have the capacity to change their colour to perfect their disguise. When the mossy-looking species flatten themselves onto a tree trunk and change their colour to match the background, they become almost invisible (see *page 8*).

E **1** **Mossy Leaf-tailed Gecko** *Uroplatus sikorae*   **M** Tandrekitra Maro Loko

DISTRIBUTION: Mid-elevation rainforest in eastern and northern Madagascar.

ID: Mid-sized gecko with fringes that make it look like mossy bark (see *page 8*). Colour highly variable. Can be similar to Common/Giant Leaf-tailed Geckos, but always smaller, and without those species' distinctive eye pattern. The very similar *Uroplatus sameiti* (not illustrated) is found in low-elevation rainforest. Henkel's Leaf-tailed Gecko can be very similar, although it is usually larger, and the two species overlap only in the north.

BEHAVIOUR: Nocturnal; sleeps on tree trunks during the day.

Length: TL < 19 cm | 7·5"

WHERE TO SEE: Quite common in Amber Mountain NP, often on trees around the ticket office. Also possible in the most eastern rainforest sites including Marojejy, Andasibe and Ranomafana.

E **2** **Henkel's Leaf-tailed Gecko** *Uroplatus henkeli*   **M** Tahafisaka Razam-Boay

DISTRIBUTION: Patchy distribution in Sambirano forest of the north and dry forest of the west.

ID: Larger than Mossy Leaf-tailed Gecko. Similar to Giant Leaf-tailed Gecko, but smaller, with a different eye pattern: pale yellow with irregular red zigzags instead of curved red lines.

BEHAVIOUR: Similar to Mossy Leaf-tailed Gecko.

VULNERABLE

Length: TL < 26 cm | 10"

WHERE TO SEE: Nosy Be, especially Lokobe community forest (distinct from the national park). Less frequently sighted in Ankarafantsika and Tsingy de Bemaraha NPs.

E **3** **Common / Giant Leaf-tailed Gecko**   **M** Tahafisaka
Uroplatus fimbriatus / giganteus

DISTRIBUTION: Rainforest in eastern and northern Madagascar.

ID: Huge geckos – the second largest on Earth – with a distinctive eye pattern: pale base colour with dark curved lines on either side of the pupil.

BEHAVIOUR: Sleeps on a tree trunk during the day, usually with its head pointing down. If threatened, it can make a surprising display in which it opens its mouth and shows its bright red tongue. At night, moves around on smaller branches.

Length: TL 24–32 cm | 9–13"

WHERE TO SEE: Common Leaf-tailed Gecko *U. fimbriatus* **3a** is easy to see on Nosy Mangabe. Also possible at many other eastern rainforest sites, including Ranomafana NP. **Giant Leaf-tailed Gecko** *U. giganteus* **3b** is uncommon in Amber Mountain NP. It also seems to be the large leaf-tailed gecko that occurs in Marojejy NP, but the taxonomy and separation of these species is unclear.

Eye details are useful for separating leaf-tailed geckos

1 brown or yellow

3b whitish with dark brown lines

2 ale with wavy red lines

3a beige with reddish-brown lines

1 Mid-sized 'mossy' species

2 Intermediate between Mossy and Giant Leaf-tailed Geckos in many respects

3b

3a

These large snakes are one of Madagascar's biogeographical mysteries. Their exact affinities have long been debated, but recent studies suggest that their closest relative is the very different Calabar Boa *Calabaria reinhardtii* (formerly called 'python') of Africa. They form a family that is endemic to Madagascar (Sanziniidae), although this is often still considered a subfamily of Boiidae.

E **1** Madagascar tree boas
Sanzinia madagascariensis / volontany

M Manditra
F Boa des Forêts de Madagascar

DISTRIBUTION: Throughout most of the island, though scarce in the central highlands. Found in forest, secondary habitat, and plantations. Western populations belong to *S. volontany* **1a**, while eastern populations belong to *S. madagascariensis* **1b**. These species are both often treated as subspecies of *S. madagascariensis*.

ID: Large snake with a distinctive structure. The triangular head features deep grooves on the upper lip, which probably contain thermal receptors used in nocturnal hunting. Young boas are small, but are still identifiable by their structure. *S. volontany* is brownish, while *S. madagascariensis* is greenish.

Length:	TL <2m|6'

WHERE TO SEE: One of the most widespread Malagasy snakes. Possible in almost any protected area, and in many heavily human-modified areas as well.

BEHAVIOUR: Generally found in trees during the day and on the ground at night. Hunt mainly mammals (rats, tenrecs and small lemurs), but also birds and amphibians. Give birth to 1–19 live young.

E **2** Madagascar Ground Boa
Acrantophis madagascariensis

M Do
F Boa de Madagascar

DISTRIBUTION: Inhabits various types of forest, mainly in the northern third of Madagascar, although also in the central-west.

ID: A large snake with intricate dark patterning on a pale brown base. Lacks the upper lip grooves of Madagascar Tree Boas. Larger than Duméril's Ground Boa, and very little overlap in range.

Length:	TL <3·2m	10.5'

WHERE TO SEE: With luck, can be found in Ankarafantsika, Ankarana, Masoala and Tsingy de Bemaraha NPs.

BEHAVIOUR: Nocturnal and ground-dwelling. Usually hides during the day. Hunts for mammals, from tenrecs up to the largest lemurs and birds. Gives birth to 2–6 large live young.

E **3** Duméril's Ground Boa
Acrantophis dumerili

M Fagnano
F Boa de Duméril

DISTRIBUTION: Found in various kinds of habitat, from spiny forest to open savannah, mainly in the southern half of Madagascar. Absent from the eastern rainforest.

ID: Very similar in colour to Madagascar Ground Boa, but its range barely overlaps that species, its average size is smaller, and the dark markings on its flanks are more distinctly 'vertebra'-shaped. Lacks the distinctive upper lip grooves of Madagascar tree boas.

Length:	TL <3m	10'

WHERE TO SEE: With luck or persistence, can be found in and around Toliara and Ifaty, Zombitse-Vohibasia NP, Parc Anja, and Berenty.

BEHAVIOUR: Nocturnal and ground-dwelling. Gives birth to 6–13 live young, much smaller than those of Madagascar Ground Boa.

Diamond-shaped marks with white centres along sides

Tree boas are told from ground boas by grooves on upper lip

1b

2

1a Brownish base colour

1b Greenish base colour

Ground boa lacks grooves on upper lip

3

Pattern like Madagascar Ground Boa, but smaller; little overlap in range

Madagascar's snakes, other than the boas, are in the widespread Lamprophiidae family. All but one species (*Mimophis mahfalensis*) belong to a regionally endemic subfamily (Pseudoxyrhophiinae).

Madagascar has no dangerously venomous snakes, but the hognose, leaf-nosed and cat-eyed snakes, and members of the genus *Ithycyphus* (not illustrated), do seem to possess mild venom, albeit with fangs that are at the back of the mouth, making it very difficult to inject venom into humans.

E **1** Giant Hognose Snake *Leioheterodon madagascariensis*   **M** Menarana

DISTRIBUTION: Common throughout in many different habitats, including those heavily modified by humans. Introduced on Grande Comore.

ID: Colour and structure are distinctive: bold black-and-yellow pattern, and an up-turned 'hog nose' which is used for digging.

BEHAVIOUR: Diurnal and ground-dwelling. Often basks in the sun, for example along roads and paths. Diet includes a range of vertebrates and the eggs of Madagascar swift lizards (*pages 208–211*).

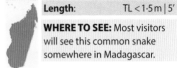

| Length: | TL < 1·5 m | 5′ |

WHERE TO SEE: Most visitors will see this common snake somewhere in Madagascar.

E **2** Blonde Hognose Snake *Leioheterodon modestus*   **M** Mandipotsy

DISTRIBUTION: Patchy distribution throughout much of the island, although absent from the far north and the eastern rainforest. Found mainly in dry habitats, both forest and human-modified ones.

ID: Shares the 'hog nose' of Giant Hognose Snake, but is much more uniform beige in colour.

BEHAVIOUR: Similar to Giant Hognose Snake.

| Length: | TL < 1·2 m | 4′ |

WHERE TO SEE: Best sought in western dry forest, especially Ankarafantsika NP.

E **3** Leaf-nosed snakes *Langaha* spp. [3 species]   **M** Filoala

DISTRIBUTION: Generally rare, but found in forest throughout most of Madagascar.

ID: Another bizarre and unmistakable Malagasy animal: the males have a spear-like projection on their nose, while the females have a club-like projection. *L. madagascariensis* is the only leaf-nosed snake that is encountered frequently.

BEHAVIOUR: Mainly diurnal and arboreal.

| Length: | TL < 1·3 m | 4′ |

WHERE TO SEE: Rarely seen, though present in almost any forest. Perhaps easiest to see in western dry forest as found at Ankarafantsika and Tsingy de Bemaraha NPs.

E **4** Madagascar tree snakes   **M** Fandrefiala
Parastenophis / Phisalixella / Lycodryas spp. [12 species]

DISTRIBUTION: Throughout Madagascar. Most species are restricted to forest, but some are also found in montane habitat, and in heavily human-modified areas.

ID: Short snouts, and big eyes with vertical pupils. Leaf-nosed snakes also have vertical pupils, but have odd facial projections. Madagascar cat-eyed snakes (*page 242*) also have vertical pupils, but are found mainly on the ground and they have thicker bodies than most Madagascar tree snakes.

BEHAVIOUR: Nocturnal and arboreal.

| Length: | Largest species TL < 1·5 m | 5′ Most species TL < 1 m | 3·3′ |

WHERE TO SEE: Generally uncommon, but night walks in the rainforest or western dry forest during the wet season give some chance.

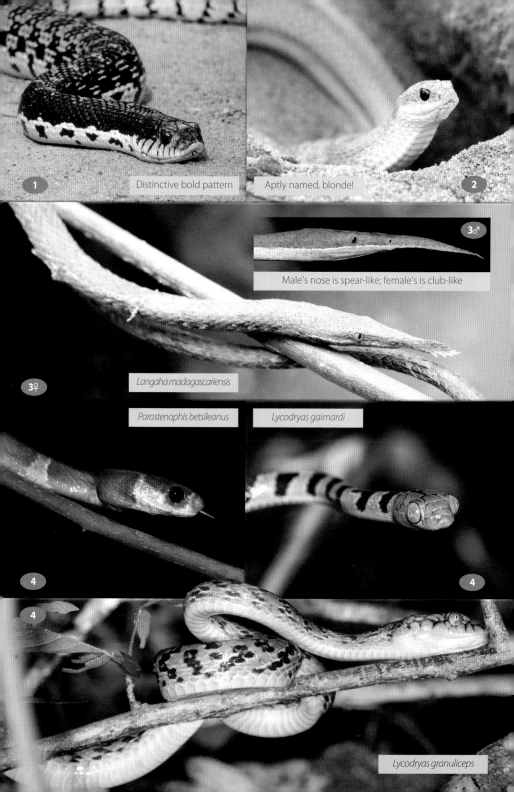

1

Distinctive bold pattern

Aptly named, blonde!

2

3♂

Male's nose is spear-like; female's is club-like

Langaha madagascariensis

3♀

Parastenophis betsileanus

Lycodryas gaimardi

4

4

4

Lycodryas granuliceps

Along with the hognose snakes (*page 240*) and Madagascar tree boas (*page 238*), these are the most common and widespread snakes in Madagascar.

🅴 ① Madagascar cat-eyed snakes *Madagascarophis* spp. [4 species] 🅼 Lapata

DISTRIBUTION: Two species are confined mainly to the arid southwest, and one to the far north, while *M. colubrinus* ①ᵃ occurs throughout the rest of the country in many habitats, and is probably the most common Malagasy snake. Often around water.

Length:	TL < 1 m	3·3′

WHERE TO SEE: Quite common, and seen by most visitors who go on night walks.

ID: Variable, but always show a pale base colour, with fine dashed dark markings superimposed throughout. The eyes have a vertical pupil (hence 'cat-eyed'). Madagascar tree snakes (*page 240*) also have vertical pupils, but are found mainly in trees.

BEHAVIOUR: Active from dusk to dawn. Feed on small reptiles, amphibians and birds. When threatened, they bite readily, so are best treated with caution.

🅴 ② Striped Madagascar Garter Snake* 🅼 Bibindrano
Thamnosophis lateralis

DISTRIBUTION: Found throughout Madagascar in open and often wet habitats. Most common on the High Plateau and in the east.

Length:	TL < 0·8 m	2·5′

WHERE TO SEE: Common in many places; even possible to see it in Tana.

ID: Boldly marked with black and white or yellow. Gold-collared Snake (*page 244*) also has stripes, but shows a red belly, and usually a collar.

BEHAVIOUR: Terrestrial and diurnal. Feeds on frogs.

🅴 ③ Bernier's Striped Snake *Dromicodryas bernieri* 🅼 Maroandavaka

DISTRIBUTION: Found throughout in most habitats, although absent from the interior of eastern rainforest.

Length:	TL < 1·1 m	3·6′

WHERE TO SEE: Easiest to find in the dry west, as around Toliara and Morondava.

ID: One stripe along the back, and two on the sides. Similar pattern to Striped Madagascar Garter Snake, but generally more brown-and-buff, rather than black-and-yellow or black-and-white.

BEHAVIOUR: Terrestrial and diurnal.

🅴 ④ Mahafaly Sand Snake *Mimophis mahfalensis* 🅼 Bibimora

DISTRIBUTION: Absent only from the east. Uses almost all types of habitat except eastern rainforest.

Length:	TL < 1 m	3·3′

WHERE TO SEE: Common in the west and southwest, even in towns and villages.

ID: Most individuals have intricate and distinctive buff and brown markings. Male usually distinctly striped, while female is plainer.

BEHAVIOUR: Mainly terrestrial and diurnal. Prey items include other reptiles and amphibians.

🅴 ⑤ Four-striped Snake *Dromicodryas quadrilineatus* 🅼 Marolongo

DISTRIBUTION: Found in forest and human-modified habitat in the northern half of Madagascar.

Length:	TL < 1·2 m	4′

WHERE TO SEE: One of the most common snakes in the north.

ID: Pattern of four dark stripes is distinctive.

BEHAVIOUR: Terrestrial and diurnal.

1a

1 'Cat eyes' are unique among ground-dwelling Malagasy snakes

2

2 Blackish stripes

3

3 Brownish stripes

4 The **Mahafaly Sand Snake** belongs to a different sub-family and genus from the other snakes of Madagascar; it probably reached Madagascar from Africa much more recently than the other species

Can be quite plain or boldly marked; complex markings on top of head

5 Four dark stripes on back

These are some of the most common snakes that are found exclusively or primarily in rainforest. All are diurnal except the Gluttonous Bighead Snake. Note that Madagascar cat-eyed snakes and Four-striped Snake (*page 242*) also occur inside rainforest.

E 1 Gold-collared Snake* *Liophidium rhodogaster*   M Tompontany Menakibo

DISTRIBUTION: Rainforest in the east and north.
ID: Striped pattern above, with a reddish belly. Usually shows a pale collar.
BEHAVIOUR: Diurnal and terrestrial.

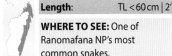

| Length: | TL <60 cm | 2′ |

WHERE TO SEE: One of Ranomafana NP's most common snakes.

E 2 Collared Bright Snake *Liophidium torquatum*   M Tompontany Miovaloko

DISTRIBUTION: Mainly in eastern and northern rainforest, but also locally in dry western forest.
ID: Brown or grey, often with a darker head and a black collar. The upper lip is white, and the pale belly has black speckles.
BEHAVIOUR: Diurnal and terrestrial.

| Length: | TL <70 cm | 2·3′ |

WHERE TO SEE: Shy and inconspicuous, but possible in most forest sites, including Ranomafana, Amber Mountain, Lokobe, and Ankarafantsika NPs.

E 3 Forest Madagascar Garter Snake   M Bibilava Volamena
Thamnosophis infrasignatus

DISTRIBUTION: Eastern rainforest and secondary habitats.
ID: A plain brownish snake with faint yellowish lines down the back and black marks behind the eye. Coloration can be similar to Madagascar cat-eyed snakes (*page 242*) but those species have distinctive 'cat eyes' with vertical pupils.
BEHAVIOUR: Diurnal and terrestrial. Known to eat frogs and small chameleons.

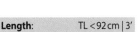

| Length: | TL <1 m | 3′ |

WHERE TO SEE: Andasibe and Ranomafana areas.

E 4 Trail Madagascar Garter Snake*   M Bibilava Mavo
Thamnosophis epistibes

DISTRIBUTION: Eastern rainforest and secondary habitat. Often near streams.
ID: Similar pattern, but paler and not as boldly marked as Striped Madagascar Garter Snake (*page 242*), which has a perference for open areas.
BEHAVIOUR: Diurnal and terrestrial. Hunts frogs.

| Length: | TL <92 cm | 3′ |

WHERE TO SEE: Andasibe and Ranomafana areas.

E 5 Gluttonous Bighead Snake *Compsophis laphystius*   M Bibimaimbo Vangavanga

DISTRIBUTION: Mid-elevation eastern rainforest. One of the species most likely to be seen at night in the rainforest, usually along small streams.
ID: Yellow-brown with faint dark lines.
BEHAVIOUR: Nocturnal, and both arboreal and terrestrial. Feeds on frogs and their eggs.

| Length: | TL <62 cm | 2′ |

WHERE TO SEE: Night walks in Ranomafana, Andasibe, and Marojejy areas.

1 Stripes on back; pale collar; pink belly

2 Dark line through eye and along spine; collar lacking in some; black spots on belly

3 Black line behind eye; yellow stripes on back

4 Yellowish with dark brown stripes

5 Yellow base colour; fine dark stripes

Frogs

- More than 300 species of frog have been described from Madagascar, but DNA barcoding has revealed more than 500 species on the island, so at least 200 remain to be formally described!

- Almost 10% of the world's frogs are endemic to Madagascar, an extraordinary richness of amphibians for an island that makes up only 0·4% of the land area of the globe.

- There are three orders of amphibian in the world: frogs, salamanders and caecilians. Only frogs are found in Madagascar. Six families are represented:

Mantellidae (*pages 254–281*). Endemic to Madagascar and Mayotte. The largest Malagasy frog family. Diverse members include colourful mantellas, terrestrial Madagascar frogs, and arboreal bright-eyed frogs.

Microhylidae (*pages 250–253*). Worldwide tropical family. Madagascar has three endemic subfamilies that include some of its most interesting frogs – beautiful rain frogs, the tiny stump-toed frogs and bizarre Tomato Frog.

Hyperoliidae (*page 248*). A mainly African family represented in Madagascar by the reed frogs.

Starry Night Reed Frog

Ptychadenidae (*page 248*). Mainly African family represented in Madagascar by one species: the Mascarene Ridged Frog, the most common frog on the island.

Golden Mantella

Green Bright-eyed Frog

Madagascar fringed frog

Marbled Rain Frog

Stump-toed frog
Stumffia pygmaea

Tomato Frog

Bufonidae. Madagascar's only toad is the **Asian Toad** *Duttaphrynus melanostictus* (not illustrated), a recently introduced invasive species whose effects on Malagasy wildlife may be disastrous.

Dicroglossidae. The **Indian Bullfrog** *Hoplobatrachus tigerinus* (not illustrated), probably another recent introduction.

- The origins of Malagasy frogs can be traced to seven separate colonization events. The first was some 60 million years ago, while the most recent was within the last couple of years (the Asian Toad).

- Most frogs are vocal, and voice is one of the best ways to find and identify them. But their small size, frequently concealed calling locations, and the ventriloquial quality of their voices can make them bafflingly difficult to see.

- Most frogs are not active during the day and are best searched for at night. However, there are some exceptions, including the mantellas (see *pages 254–265*) and some of the Madagascar frogs (see *pages 274–281*).

- Most frogs call only during the wet season, and many disappear entirely during the dry season, possibly retreating to burrows and becoming torpid. This is especially true in the dry western parts of the island. In the eastern rainforest, some species are active and vocal year-round. But even there, a night walk on a dry night can be quiet, while there can be a cacophony of frog voices on a rainy night. The dry season timing of the main May to October tourist season means that many visitors leave the island without seeing many frogs: the frogs come into their own after the tourists have left.

- Although only adult frogs are covered in this guide, frog reproduction is fascinating. All Malagasy frogs lay eggs, which in most species develop into aquatic tadpoles, then adult frogs. But within these basic parameters, they use an incredible diversity of reproductive strategies: at least 11 of the world's 30 known modes of frog reproduction are used by Malagasy frogs.

- Frog identification can be challenging. There is tremendous colour variation within many species, such that details of colour may be virtually useless for identification. For casual observers, the things to focus on are:
  – Size and shape (although beware of juveniles)
  – The quality of the skin (is it smooth, or bumpy and/or ridged?)
  – The call (if heard)
  – The general colour pattern

- In most Malagasy frogs, females are larger than males. In the following species accounts, male and female dimensions are given separately for species with a large size difference.

- This guide covers less than 20% of Madagascar's described frogs, but the species covered here will account for the majority of sightings in frequently visited sites. Refer to *Amphibians and Reptiles of Madagascar* by Glaw and Vences for thorough coverage (see Further reading on *page 327* for details).

- There is no up-to-date standardization of common names for frogs, but this guide includes common names for the benefit of those who find scientific names off-putting. Where there is a logical existing common name, that one is used. In some cases, it was necessary to invent a new common name, or to replace or modify one that is a misnomer. These new common names are marked with asterisks. Be aware that herpetologists and most local guides use scientific names exclusively.

- Frog diversity is very low in the dry southwest, and fairly low in most of the west. The eastern rainforest is remarkably rich in frogs. Within this biome, the rarely visited Tsaratanana massif of the north supports the highest diversity.

1 Mascarene Ridged Frog *Ptychadena mascareniensis*

M Sahona an-Tanimbary

Length:	<5·5cm | 2·2"

WHERE TO SEE: Day or night, almost anywhere! Often in rice paddies.

DISTRIBUTION: Across Africa, Madagascar, and other Indian Ocean islands. This is the most common and widespread frog in Madagascar. It is found around almost any kind of stagnant water, although it is absent from rainforest interior.

ID: Pointed nose. Raised ridges along the back. Colour extremely variable: the base colour is normally brown, with a paler stripe along the middle of the back. This stripe can be yellow or lime green. Distinguished from the **Indian Bullfrog** *Hoplobatrachus tigerinus* (not illustrated) by its smaller size and straight ridges as opposed to discontinuous bumps along the back.

VOICE: Loud, harsh calls that are often repeated quickly. One of the call types resembles the bleat of an angry goat.

BEHAVIOUR: Lives on the ground, in or near water. Active both day and night.

E **2** Starry-night Reed Frog *Heterixalus alboguttatus*

Length:	♀ 3cm | 1·2"
	♂ smaller

WHERE TO SEE: At night around the village of Ranomafana. Good local guides know places to search for this species.

DISTRIBUTION: Swamps and rice fields in the southern third of eastern Madagascar. Not found inside forest habitats. Often found in bananas trees.

ID: Female sports an amazing 'starry night' pattern. Male is often plainer; some are plain buff. Members of this genus can always be recognized by their nearly triangular pupils.

VOICE: Slow, rattling trill.

BEHAVIOUR: Arboreal and nocturnal. Sleeps next to bodies of water during the day, sometimes in the open.

E **3** Betsileo Reed Frog *Heterixalus betsileo*

Length:	<3cm | 1·2"

WHERE TO SEE: At night in the Andasibe and Anjozorobe areas. Also found in highland towns such as Fianarantsoa.

DISTRIBUTION: Swamps, rice fields, and secondary forest in central Madagascar. Occurs both around forested areas on the east slope and on the High Plateau.

ID: Distinctive triangular pupil shape identifies it as a *Heterixalus* species. Base colour varies from pale green to yellow, often with paler stripes along the sides of the back and fine dark speckles. Can resemble Green Bright-eyed Frog (*page 260*) in colour, but that species has red-and-blue eyes and rounded pupils.

VOICE: Single loud, rasping note, regularly repeated.

BEHAVIOUR: Similar to Starry-night Reed Frog.

2♀

Heterixalus frogs have a distinctive pupil shape

1 Colour highly variable; often a pale stripe down centre of back; ridges on back

2♀ Females are unmistakable

2♂ Male much duller than female

3 Usually speckled, and often has yellow lines on sides of back

❸ ① Tomato Frog *Dyscophus antongilii*   M Sangongogno

DISTRIBUTION: Mainly around the Bay of Antongil, in the northeast. Seems to prefer human-modified habitat.
ID: Large all-red frog. Redder than the closely related and possibly conspecific **Sambava Tomato Frog** *Dyscophus guineti* (not illustrated), which is typically orange.
VOICE: An unusual series of hollow, low-pitched notes.
BEHAVIOUR: Nocturnal and terrestrial.

NEAR THREATENED
Length: ♂ 6–6·5 cm | 2·5"
                ♀ 8·5–10·5 cm | 3·4–4·1"
WHERE TO SEE: Wet habitat around the town of Maroantsetra.

❸ ② Web-foot Frog *Paradoxophyla palmata*

DISTRIBUTION: Eastern rainforest and adjacent disturbed habitat.
ID: Small frog with a bizarre shape: a small triangular head on a fat body.
VOICE: Very cricket-like.
BEHAVIOUR: Both terrestrial and aquatic. Breeds explosively when there is rain, and can suddenly become common, hopping around on roads and other open areas. Rather shy, and capable of long leaps to escape from danger.

Length: 1·9–2·6 cm | 0·7–1"
WHERE TO SEE: In the Andasibe and Ranomafana areas during and just after rain. Mainly at night.

❸ ③ Marbled Rain Frog *Scaphiophryne marmorata*

DISTRIBUTION: Mid-elevation eastern rainforest and adjacent secondary habitat.
ID: Beautiful frog with a fat body, marbled green-and-brown colour pattern, and very bumpy skin. Some other members of this genus are similar, but less frequently encountered.
VOICE: Hollow trill. Not frequently heard.
BEHAVIOUR: Nocturnal and terrestrial. Breeds explosively in the rains.

VULNERABLE
Length: 3·2–4·4 cm | 1·3–1·7"
WHERE TO SEE: At night around Andasibe after recent rain, when it can sometimes be found hopping around everywhere.

❸ ④ Stump-toed frogs *Stumpffia* [16 species]

DISTRIBUTION: Mainly in eastern and northern rainforest, although some species are found in the west and centre, and in human-modified habitats.
ID: Small to tiny in size. Can often be tentatively identified by their size and reduced digits, but beware juveniles of other frog species.
VOICE: Most species have a single high-pitched chirping call that is frequently repeated at short intervals.
BEHAVIOUR: Terrestrial. Active during the day; most vocal at dusk.

Length: 1–2 cm | 0·4–0·8"
WHERE TO SEE: Easily overlooked due to their small size. *S. pygmaea* ④ₐ is common in Lokobe NP. *Stumpffia* of undescribed species are fairly common on Masoala. A couple of species occur in the Andasibe and Ranomafana areas. Can be seen during the day.

All *Stumpffia* frogs are small, and *S. pygmaea* ④ₐ and *S. tridactyla* are tiny. They are among the world's smallest vertebrates, only about one centimetre (less than half an inch) long.

1 ♀

Females red;
males yellowish

2   Pointed head

3   Wide body

4a

4   Undescribed
species from
Andasibe

ⓔ ① Boulenger's Giant Treefrog *Platypelis grandis*

DISTRIBUTION: Eastern and northern rainforest. Usually seen in or adjacent to tree holes.

ID: One of the world's largest arboreal frogs. As with most tree-dwelling frogs, has large tips to the toes. Grainy-looking back, with many large bumps. Adult is brown, with irregular paler markings. Juvenile starts bright green, then darkens to olive, then brown.

VOICE: Atypical for a frog; sounds more like a bird or mammal. A very loud single note that sounds like chopping wood. Sometimes calls during the day.

BEHAVIOUR: Arboreal and nocturnal.

Length:	♂ 5–9 cm | 2–3·5"
	♀ 4–6 cm | 1·6–2·4"

WHERE TO SEE: Possible in most rainforest sites including Ranomafana, Andasibe, Nosy Mangabe and Amber Mountain. Can be seen asleep in tree holes during the day, or active nearby at night.

In 90% of frog species, females are larger than males. This enables the 'amplexus' mating embrace in which the male sits on the female's back. Boulenger's Giant Treefrog is one of the exceptions: males are larger, which seems to give them advantage in territorial battles.

ⓔ ② Mahanoro Tree-hole Frog* *Plethodontohyla notosticta*

DISTRIBUTION: Eastern rainforest. Found in tree holes and the axils of tree ferns and Pandanus (*page 316*).

ID: A rather wide, squat frog that is likely to be seen in holes in trees. Brownish colour, with a fine white line running along the junction of the side and the back. Around Andasibe, some individuals have a green back. **Climbing Tree-hole Frog** *Plethodontohyla mihanika* (not illustrated) has longer hindlimbs.

VOICE: A simple hoot that is repeated over and over.

BEHAVIOUR: Arboreal. Calls mainly at night.

Length:	3·5–4·2 cm | 1·4–1·7"

WHERE TO SEE: Possible in most eastern forest sites including Ranomafana, Andasibe and Masoala. During the day often found sitting in tree holes; at night found by call.

ⓔ ③ Ambatoharanana Climbing Frog* *Platypelis tuberifera*

DISTRIBUTION: Found in Pandanus (*page 316*) in the eastern rainforest.

ID: Orange or buff, often with a thin pale line down the spine and a dark line behind the eye. The skin is smooth. Other *Platypelis* and *Cophyla* frogs can be similar, but are smaller and not usually found in Pandanus.

VOICE: Plaintive, rising whistle. Repeated every several seconds.

BEHAVIOUR: Nocturnal and arboreal.

Length:	3–4 cm | 1·2–1·6"

WHERE TO SEE: Can be found during the day in Andasibe-Mantadia and Ranomafana NPs.

ⓔ ④ Barbour's Climbing Frog* *Platypelis barbouri*

DISTRIBUTION: Eastern rainforest between Marojejy and Andasibe.

ID: A small frog covered in big bumps. Variable but generally pale brown colour, often with darker markings interspersed.

VOICE: Single high-pitched *"peet"* repeated about every three seconds.

BEHAVIOUR: Nocturnal and arboreal.

Length:	♂ 1·9–2·3 cm | 0·8–0·9"

WHERE TO SEE: At night around Andasibe.

1 Adults are brown

1ju Juveniles start bright green, then transition to brown

2 White lines along edges of back

3 Buffy Pandanus-dwelling frog

4 Small frog with big bumps

All the frogs covered on this and subsequent pages are in the Mantellidae family, endemic to Madagascar and Mayotte. The most famous of these are the mantellas: colourful, toxic frogs that resemble the unrelated poison dart frogs of the Neotropics, a striking example of convergent evolution. Even local guides who know little about frogs will seek out mantellas, so most visitors will see at least one species. All mantellas are active during the day, and most live on the ground.

E **1** Baron's Mantella *Mantella baroni*   M Anakova

DISTRIBUTION: In rainforest and adjacent secondary habitat in the central and southern portions of eastern Madagascar. Prefers stream banks and other wet areas.
ID: A Beautiful multi-coloured species. **Madagascar Mantella** *Mantella madagascariensis* (not illustrated) is similar, but much less common. They occur together in the Vohiparara region of Ranomafana NP, but Baron's Mantella is more abundant even there. The two species are best identified by the pattern on the underside of their hindlegs: Madagascar Mantella shows red all the way up the legs, with orange patches interspersed, while Baron's Mantella has red only up to the thighs, and usually shows no orange. Madagascar Mantella also shows a horseshoe-shaped blue mark on the throat whereas Baron's Mantella shows either no mark or a blue spot.
VOICE: Metallic single click. Often repeated.
BEHAVIOUR: Active and vocal during the day; sometimes calls at night.

Length:	2·2–3 cm | 0·8–1·2"

WHERE TO SEE: In the Mantadia sector of Andasibe-Mantadia NP, and Ranomafana NP, mainly from November to March.

E **2** Orange-backed Mantella *Mantella ebenaui*

DISTRIBUTION: Various types of forest and secondary habitat in the northern third of Madagascar.
ID: Orange and black, with blue highlights.
VOICE: High-pitched double click. Frequently repeated.
BEHAVIOUR: Active and vocal day and night.

Length:	1·8–2·6 cm | 0·7–1"

WHERE TO SEE: Abundant on Nosy Be and Nosy Komba. Also possible on St. Marie Island, around Maroantsetra, and in Ankarafantsika NP.

E **3** Betsileo Mantella *Mantella betsileo*

DISTRIBUTION: In wet areas within western dry forest and secondary habitat.
ID: Virtually identical to Orange-backed Mantella, but they do not overlap in range.
VOICE: Double click, like Orange-backed Mantella.
BEHAVIOUR: Active and vocal day and night.

Length:	1·8–2·6 cm | 0·7–1"

WHERE TO SEE: Tsingy de Bemaraha NP and Kirindy Forest.

E **4** Golden Mantella *Mantella aurantiaca*   M Sahona Mena

DISTRIBUTION: Tiny range in central-eastern Madagascar. Prefers marsh edges and wet forest.
ID: Unmistakable orange frog: one of Madagascar's 'flagship' conservation species.
VOICE: High-pitched clicks. Sometimes doubled.
BEHAVIOUR: Active and vocal during the day, especially in the morning.

CRITICALLY ENDANGERED	
Length:	1·9–2·4 cm | 0·8–0·9"

WHERE TO SEE: Torotorofotsy Marsh, northwest of Andasibe village, from November to January.

1 Red thighs without orange markings interspersed separate this frog from the similar but much less common Madagascar Mantella

2 Electric blue markings below

Orange back

3 Virtually identical to Orange-backed Mantella

4 The site for Golden Mantella at Torotorofotsy Marsh is managed by the NGO Mitsinjo. Entrance permits and a local guide can be arranged at their office just south of Andasibe.

❸ ① Climbing Mantella *Mantella laevigata*

DISTRIBUTION: Eastern rainforest in the north of Madagascar. Unlike most mantellas, it climbs trees, and can be found anywhere from the forest floor up into the mid-storey.
ID: Shares black-and-green coloration with Guibé's Mantella, but has a much more clearly defined pattern: mostly black, with a broad band of green or yellow-green on the back.
VOICE: Double clicks. Frequently repeated.
BEHAVIOUR: Active during the day. Breeds in water-filled tree holes.

NEAR THREATENED	
Length:	2·2–2·9 cm | 0·9–1·1"

WHERE TO SEE: Nosy Mangabe is the classic site. Can also be found in Marojejy NP.

❸ ② Blue-legged Mantella *Mantella expectata*

DISTRIBUTION: Found along streams and other wet areas within the Isalo sandstone massif of the southwest.
ID: Yellow back, black sides and blue or blue-grey legs: unmistakable within its tiny range.
VOICE: Rattling double click.

ENDANGERED	
Length:	2–2·6 cm | 0·8–1"

WHERE TO SEE: Can be found in Isalo NP during the wet season, from November to early January. Best sought in the flooded, grassy areas at the entrance and outlet of canyons.

❸ ③ Guibé's Mantella *Mantella nigricans*

DISTRIBUTION: Eastern rainforest in the north of Madagascar. Found along streams.
ID: Limbs mostly fluorescent green, and the back colour varies between mostly black and mostly green.
VOICE: Metallic single *"tick"* like a tiny hammer striking metal.
BEHAVIOUR: Active during the day.

Length:	2·7–2·8 cm | 1·1"

WHERE TO SEE: Marojejy NP, especially around Camp Marojejia, the middle of the park's three camps.

❸ ④ Green Mantella *Mantella viridis*

DISTRIBUTION: Tiny distribution in both dry and humid forest at the northern tip of Madagascar. Found in wet areas, for example along streams.
ID: Pale green, with black along the sides.
VOICE: Metallic double clicks.
BEHAVIOUR: Active day and night.

ENDANGERED	
Length:	2·2–3 cm | 0·9–1·2"

WHERE TO SEE: Near Diego-Suarez at Montagne des Français, which can be accessed via the Jungle Park lodge. Common along the little stream that runs through that camp. Also possible in Amber Mountain NP.

Streams running through eastern rainforest are Madagascar's richest habitat for frogs

One of the largest genera within the Mantellidae family is *Boophis*, the 'bright-eyed frogs': classic tree frogs with enlarged tips to their toes, large eyes, and nocturnal habits.

E 1 Central Bright-eyed Frog *Boophis rappiodes*

DISTRIBUTION: Eastern rainforest and forest edge.
ID: Small and colourful. Green base colour; yellow stripes that start on the nose, then fade along the sides of the body; and reddish dots and blotches. Lacks dark brown markings of similar Bott's Bright-eyed Frog.
VOICE: Quiet double click.
BEHAVIOUR: Nocturnal. Calling males usually sit in the forest understorey along rivers and streams.

Length: ♂ 2–2.5 cm | 0.8–1"
♀ 3–3.4 cm | 1.2–1.3"

WHERE TO SEE: One of the more common frogs on rainy nights around Andasibe and Ranomafana.

E 2 Bott's Bright-eyed Frog* *Boophis bottae*

DISTRIBUTION: Eastern rainforest and forest edge.
ID: Very similar to Central Bright-eyed Frog, but usually has some dark brown coloration on the back.
VOICE: A short trill followed by a series of clicks that are similar to those given by Central Bright-eyed Frog.
BEHAVIOUR: Similar to Central Bright-eyed Frog. Male calls from fairly low down within forest.

Length: ♂ 2.1–2.4 cm | 0.8–0.9"
♀ 3.5 cm | 1.4"

WHERE TO SEE: Like Central Bright-eyed Frog, one of the more common frogs on rainy nights around Andasibe and Ranomafana.

1 Little or no dark brown coloration

2 Very similar to Central Bright-eyed Frog, but shows some brown: often a dark bar between the eyes

E **1** Fiery Bright-eyed Frog* *Boophis pyrrhus*

DISTRIBUTION: Around slow-moving water in eastern rainforest and forest edge.

ID: Unique coloration: red or orange base colour with red dots and a darker 'hourglass' pattern on the back.

VOICE: Series of more than ten harsh, metallic notes that become more intense towards the end.

BEHAVIOUR: Nocturnal. Male calls from fairly low down within forest.

Length: ♂ 2·6–3·2 cm | 1–1·3"
♀ 3·7 cm | 1·5"

WHERE TO SEE: One of the most common frogs at night around Andasibe.

E **2** Green Bright-eyed Frog *Boophis viridis*

DISTRIBUTION: Around slow-moving water in eastern rainforest and along forest edge.

ID: Pale green, often with tiny red spots.

VOICE: Harsh, high-pitched croaking notes repeated in either long or short series.

BEHAVIOUR: Nocturnal. Male calls from fairly low down within forest.

Length: 3–3·5 cm | 1·2–1·4"

WHERE TO SEE: One of the more common frogs on rainy nights around Andasibe.

E **3** Red-eyed Bright-eyed Frog *Boophis luteus*

DISTRIBUTION: Forest canopy in eastern rainforest and adjacent degraded habitats. Isolated populations also exist in riparian forest in the centre and south.

ID: Bright green, with the outer part of the iris red.

VOICE: A conspicuous part of the nocturnal soundscape. Loud and fast series of notes that has been likened to an American police car siren, or to a quick repetition of the French numbers *"vingt-sept, vingt-huit"*.

BEHAVIOUR: Nocturnal. Males call from high perches along streams, making it difficult to find.

Length: ♂ 3·5–4 cm | 1·4–1·6"
♀ 5·1 cm | 2"

WHERE TO SEE: Night walks around Andasibe and Ranomafana. Easy to hear, but difficult to see. Most often seen when it is washed out of the canopy on nights of heavy rain.

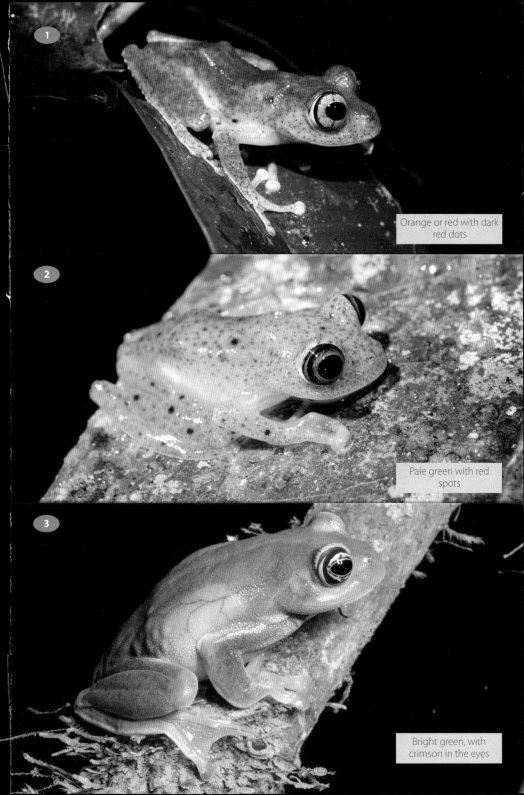

Orange or red with dark red dots

Pale green with red spots

Bright green, with crimson in the eyes

E **1** **Western Bright-eyed Frog*** *Boophis doulioti*

DISTRIBUTION: Found around almost any non-flowing water in the west and southwest. Often on banana plants and inside man-made structures.

ID: The only widespread western species of bright-eyed frog. The base colour is brown; some individuals have two yellow bands along the sides of the back. Almost identical to Duméril's Bright-eyed Frog, but they do not overlap in range.

VOICE: Often-repeated yelps, and occasional trills.

BEHAVIOUR: Nocturnal.

Length: ♂ 3·5–4·2 cm | 1·4–1·7"
♀ 4·1–5 cm | 1·6–2"

WHERE TO SEE: Ankarafantsika NP, often in the camp bathrooms. Also possible in most western towns.

E **2** **Duméril's Bright-eyed Frog** *Boophis tephraeomystax*

DISTRIBUTION: Uses the same habitats as Western Bright-eyed Frog, but in the east and north. Frequently found in rice paddies, villages, and other human-modified habitats.

ID: Almost identical to Western Bright-eyed Frog, but with a different range.

VOICE: Yelps and trills, similar to those of Western Bright-eyed Frog, but simpler.

BEHAVIOUR: Nocturnal.

Length: ♂ 3·5–4·2 cm | 1·4–1·7"
♀ 4·1–5 cm | 1·6–2"

WHERE TO SEE: Found in and around all the major eastern and northern rainforest sites.

E **3** **Madagascar Bright-eyed Frog** *Boophis madagascariensis*

DISTRIBUTION: Found along slow-flowing streams through forest and secondary habitat in eastern and central Madagascar.

ID: Fairly large, plain frog with spikes on the elbows and heels. Colour varies between pale brown and rich reddish-brown. Some similar species occur in the north, and *Boophis roseipalmatus* (not illustrated) is often seen on Amber Mountain.

VOICE: Odd, complex combinations of clucks, rattles, and clicks.

BEHAVIOUR: Nocturnal. Male usually calls from eye-level or below along streams.

Length: ♂ 5–6·5 cm | 2–2·6"
♀ 7–8 cm | 2·8–3·2"

WHERE TO SEE: One of the more common frogs on night walks around Andasibe and Ranomafana.

3

1

2

3

Can be reddish-brown, dull brown or pale brown and shades in between

3

Large spikes on heels

3

Ⓔ ① Goudot's Bright-eyed Frog *Boophis goudoti*

DISTRIBUTION: Found along streams both on the High Plateau and in the central part of the eastern rainforest belt. Uses both forested and heavily degraded habitats.

ID: Large. Brownish base coloration, with variable darker markings. Lacks the white lip of White-lipped Bright-eyed Frog, and the elbow spike of Madagascar Bright-eyed Frog (*page 262*).

VOICE: Loud, harsh rattles and grunts. Similar to White-lipped Bright-eyed Frog, but slightly lower-pitched and harsher.

BEHAVIOUR: Nocturnal. Male calls from or close to water.

| Length: | ♂ 5–7 cm \| 2–2·8" |
| | ♀ 7·5–10 cm \| 3–3·9" |

WHERE TO SEE: Most likely away from protected areas, at night around towns like Moramanga and Ambositra. Might show up on your plate if you order 'cuisse de nymph' in a restaurant!

Ⓔ ② White-lipped Bright-eyed Frog *Boophis albilabris*

DISTRIBUTION: Along streams in eastern and northern rainforest and gallery forest. Generally found in the forest mid-storey.

ID: Large. Usually green, although some individuals are brown, but always has a white upper lip. Green individuals are much larger than other green species of bright-eyed frog. Brown individuals can resemble Madagascar Bright-eyed Frog (*page 262*) but do not have elbow or heel spikes.

VOICE: Loud, harsh rattles and grunts.

BEHAVIOUR: Nocturnal.

| Length: | ♂ <7·3 cm \| 2·9" |
| | ♀ <8·1 cm \| 3·2" |

WHERE TO SEE: At night around Ranomafana and Masoala.

Larger *Boophis* species inflate themselves when threatened, perhaps to make it more difficult for a snake to swallow them!

Generally large and brownish
but colour variable

Usually green (see *opposite*)
but can be brownish

Lacks spikes on heels

🄔 ① Pandanus frogs *Guibemantis* subgenus *Pandanusicola* spp. [9+ species]

M Sahonavakoana

DISTRIBUTION: Found in Pandanus (*page 316*) plants within the rainforest. Most species are restricted to the east, although some also occur in the northern and central parts of Madagascar. This complex is still poorly understood, and many species remain to be described or split.

ID: Usually found in Pandanus. Ambatoharanana Climbing Frog (*page 252*) and other *Platypelis* species also live in Pandanus, but have flatter bodies and different coloration. Pandanus frogs are extremely variable: the most common colours are green or pale yellow, with darker brown markings. The skin is smooth, and looks almost gelatinous.

VOICE: Series of notes with the quality of pebbles being clicked together. Some species give these notes in quick series, while others deliver them more slowly.

BEHAVIOUR: Sometimes calls during the day, but most active and vocal at night.

Length: 2·3–3·3 cm | 0·9–1·3"

WHERE TO SEE: Almost any rainforest site, including Amber Mountain, Marojejy, Masoala, Andasibe-Mantadia, and Ranomafana NPs.

Probable *Guibemantis variabilis* from Mantadia

🄔 ② Madagascar fringed frogs* *Spinomantis* [4 fringed species]

DISTRIBUTION: Along streams in eastern rainforest. Usually in the mid-storey, often quite high.

ID: Masters of disguise, clad in spines, fringes, and cryptic coloration that resembles moss; similar to the camouflage of leaf-tailed geckos (*pages 234–237*).

VOICE: Loud, metallic calls given in series, almost like a small hammer beating on metal.

BEHAVIOUR: Nocturnal and arboreal.

Length: 3·1–5·1 cm | 1·2–2"

WHERE TO SEE: Night walks around Andasibe, Ranomafana, and Masoala. Sometimes local guides will point out well-camouflaged individuals sleeping on tree trunks during the day.

🄔 ③ Pointy frogs* *Blommersia* spp. [10 species]

DISTRIBUTION: Most species are eastern, but a few are found in the north, west, and centre. Habitats range from open wetlands to forest edge.

ID: Small frogs with a rather long, pointed nose. Most species are brownish and/or greyish, but extremely variable. Often a dark 'mask' behind the eye.

VOICE: Sharp, raspy clicks. Given in series by most species.

BEHAVIOUR: Call mainly at night, but sometimes also during the day. Often on vegetation in the lower part of the forest, but can also be found hopping on the ground.

Length: 1·4–2·6 cm | 0·6–1"

Blommersia domerguei

WHERE TO SEE: *Blommersia blommersae* ③a is the species that is most frequently seen, especially at night around Andsibe and Ranomafana. *B. wittei* (not illustrated) is fairly common in much of the north and west, usually in human-modified habitat, including villages. *B. domerguei* ③b is fairly common on the High Plateau and in higher parts of the eastern zone.

1 *Guibemantis liber* from Amber Mountain NP

1 *Guibemantis pulcher* from near Ranomafana

2

2 *Spinomantis aglavei* is one of the most frequently seen Madagascar fringed frogs

3a *Blommersia blommersae*

3a

Finding frogs In Madagascar, you 'bump into' frogs much less often than mammals, birds, and reptiles. Although some species are active during the day, most are nocturnal. Even the species that are day-active may be missed by observers who are more attuned to the movement of birds or mammals in the canopy than to jumping frogs at their feet. Frog sightings are also highly rain-dependent, especially in dry habitats, but even in the eastern rainforest. The peak season for frogs is the November to March wet season, after most visitors have left. Doing night walks with skilled local guides who know frog calls and microhabitats will greatly increase the number of species that you see. Night walks are currently not allowed within national parks but can be taken in areas close by (for example along the main road at Ranomafana NP) or in adjacent non-MNP reserves (such as the ones near Andasibe that are run by Mitsinjo and the local community association).

E **1** Madagascar Bullfrog *Laliostoma labrosum*

DISTRIBUTION: Most of Madagascar, apart from the eastern rainforest and most of the High Plateau.
ID: A medium-sized and very broad frog. Variable in colour, grey or brown, with some darker markings.
VOICE: Fast trill of rough notes that lasts about two seconds.
BEHAVIOUR: Terrestrial. Calls at night around water. Breeds explosively in temporary ponds after heavy rains.

Length: ♂ 4·2–4·8 cm | 1·7–1·9" ♀ 6–8 cm | 2·4–3·2"

WHERE TO SEE: Can be common in the north, west and southwest after heavy rain. Look for it around Ankarana, Ankarafantsika and Zombitse-Vohibasia NPs, Kirindy Forest, Toliara and Berenty.

E **2** Madagascar jumping frogs *Aglyptodactylus* spp. [3+ species]

DISTRIBUTION: Found on the floor of eastern, northern, and western forest.
ID: Brown to buff base colour, some with darker markings interspersed. The distinctive black markings in front of and behind the eyes, and adjacent to the hindlimbs, are often enough to identify them as Madagascar jumping frogs. Males turn yellow during breeding season.
VOICE: Croaked notes given in series.
BEHAVIOUR: Terrestrial and largely diurnal. Often seen as they make impressive leaps across the forest floor. Explosive breeders.

Length: 3·5–6 cm | 1·4–2·4"

WHERE TO SEE: At least one species occurs in most protected areas. *Aglyptodactylus madagascariensis* **2a** is the common species in the east and north, while *A. securifer* **2b** is common in the north and west. The large, rare, *A. laticeps* (not illustrated) can be found in Kirindy Forest.

2b

Black marks on both sides of the eyes and adjacent to the hindlimbs

268

1

Can be plain or boldly marked

2a

For a long time, there was thought to be only one species of Madagascar jumping frog. However, recent investigations have shown that this genus actually contains multiple species. In particular, *Aglyptodactylus madagascariensis* seems to represent a complex of several species.

Breeding male yellow below

In general, bridge frogs are earth-coloured, with bumps and/or ridges on their backs. They are mainly terrestrial, although some species call at night from low perches above the ground. Most species are active and vocal during the day, so these frogs are frequently encountered during daytime forest walks.

Identifying bridge frogs can be difficult. Call is one of the most important ID clues. This section can only touch on this diverse and complicated group, which often confuses even amphibian experts. The new name 'bridge frogs' is used here, as the former name 'Madagascar frogs' refers now only to members of the genus *Mantidactylus*.

E **1** Boulenger's Bridge Frog *Gephyromantis boulengeri*

DISTRIBUTION: Eastern rainforest and secondary habitats.

ID: A small, plain, brown frog, with bumps, but no ridges, on the back. Variable in colour; can have a pale stripe on the back.

VOICE: A characteristic voice of eastern rainforest: a quick series of several "*tsek*" notes.

Length:	2·5–3 cm	1–1·2"

WHERE TO SEE: Common during the day on Nosy Mangabe and St. Marie Island, and around Andasibe and Masoala.

E **2** Webb's Bridge Frog *Gephyromantis webbi*

DISTRIBUTION: Small area of eastern rainforest around the Bay of Antongil.

ID: A beautiful but cryptic species with colours matching those of its mossy rock habitat.

VOICE: Series of several harsh "*tcheck*" notes.

ENDANGERED	
Length:	♂ 2·5 cm	1" ♀ 3·1 cm	1·2"

WHERE TO SEE: Common during the day on rocks along small streams on Nosy Mangabe and Masoala.

E **3** Massif Bridge Frog *Gephyromantis pseudoasper*

DISTRIBUTION: Both Sambirano and eastern rainforest in the far north.

ID: A small brownish frog with bumpy skin. Can be superficially similar to Boulenger's Bridge Frog, but their ranges are largely discrete, and Massif Bridge Frog is paler below, often with some yellow.

VOICE: Typical call is three quick series of three notes (nine notes in total).

Length:	3·3 cm	1·3"

WHERE TO SEE: Lokobe, Ankarana, Amber Mountain, and Marojejy NPs.

Boulenger's and Webb's Bridge Frogs can be found on the island of Nosy Mangabe, adjacent to Masoala.

Brownish and bumpy; can be plain or boldly marked

Mossy-looking coloration

Pale underneath, often with yellowish coloration, unlike Boulenger's Madagascar Frog which is darker below

🇪 ① **Rough Bridge Frog*** *Gephyromantis asper*

DISTRIBUTION: Around streams in eastern rainforest.
ID: Very rough skin: bumps throughout, ridges on the back, and spikes above the eyes and on the heels. Highly variable in colour, from buff to dark brown.
VOICE: Very quick series of 2–4 "*tik*" notes, often repeated several times.

Length:	2·7–3·1 cm | 1–1·2"

WHERE TO SEE: During the day in Ranomafana and Andasibe-Mantadia NPs.

🇪 ② **Engraved Bridge Frog*** *Gephyromantis sculpturatus*

DISTRIBUTION: Mid-elevation eastern rainforest.
ID: Very similar to Beige Bridge Frog, which this species replaces at middle elevations.
VOICE: Similar to Beige Bridge Frog, but notes are harsher.

Length:	♂ 3·8–4·3 cm | 1·5–1·7"

WHERE TO SEE: Ranomafana NP. Also present around Andasibe, although less common.

🇪 ③ **Beige Bridge Frog*** *Gephyromantis luteus*

DISTRIBUTION: Low-elevation eastern rainforest and secondary habitat.
ID: Usually pale brown, with some darker markings. The skin is fairly smooth, but there are ridges on the back. A pair of black-edged ridges runs from behind the eyes, nearly converging on the back.
VOICE: Long series of up to 21 fairly musical notes.

Length:	♂ 3·6–4·3 cm | 1·4–1·7"
	♀ 4·1–4·7 cm | 1·6–1·9"

WHERE TO SEE: One of the most common frogs on Nosy Mangabe and Masoala.

The bridge frogs and Madagascar frogs are the 'LBJs' ('little brown jobs', a colloquial term for confusingly cryptic brownish birds) of the frog world!

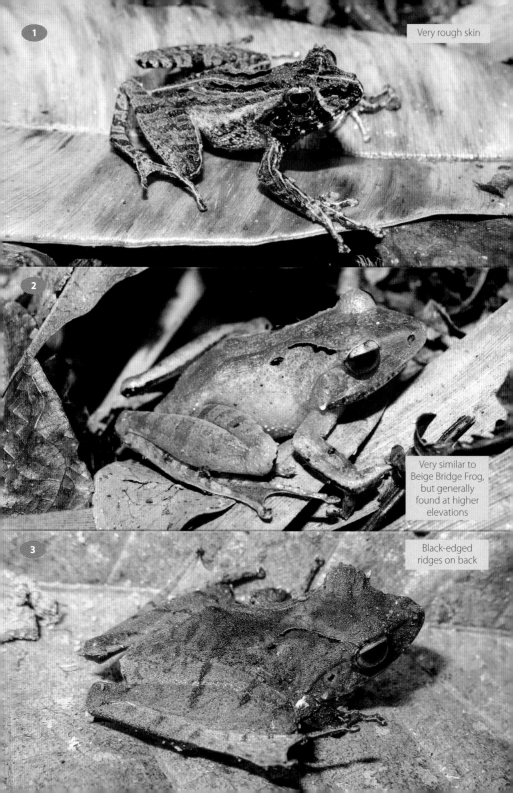

1 Very rough skin

2 Very similar to Beige Bridge Frog, but generally found at higher elevations

3 Black-edged ridges on back

Mantidactylus is another of Madagascar's largest frog genera. Like *Gephyromantis*, they are mainly ground-dwelling, and many species are vocal during the day. To a casual observer the two genera look very similar, although *Mantidactylus* tend to breed in streams and are usually more closely associated with water. They are 'classic' aquatic frogs, whereas *Gephyromantis* are more delicate and terrestrial.

Many *Mantidactylus* are plain and earth-coloured, while others are slightly more colourful and distinctive. Some plainer species are covered here and on *pages 276–277*, while more distinctive ones follow.

E **1** Ivohimanitra Madagascar Frog *Mantidactylus majori*

DISTRIBUTION: Along streams in rainforest in southeastern Madagascar.

ID: A medium-sized frog, with fairly smooth skin. Sharply bicoloured: dark above and pale below.

VOICE: Quick series of about ten creaky notes.

Length:	4·1–4·7 cm | 1·6–1·9"

WHERE TO SEE: Commonly encountered in Ranomafana NP, even during the day.

E **2** Grandidier's Madagascar Frog *Mantidactylus grandidieri*   **M** Radaka

DISTRIBUTION: Deep and slow-flowing portions of eastern rainforest streams, north to the Masoala area.

ID: A large brown frog, usually with pale spotting, identifiable by its size and habitat. Probably a complex that contains multiple species. *Mantidactylus guttulatus* (not illustrated) is very similar, but has a more northern distribution, from the Marojejy area north. Goudot's Bright-eyed Frog (*page 264*) also lives along streams, and can be superficially similar, but is smaller and slimmer, and has the enlarged tips to the toes that are typical of bright-eyed frogs.

Length:	7·5–10·8 cm | 3–4·3"

WHERE TO SEE: At night in eastern rainforest, including Ranomafana, Andasibe, and Masoala areas.

2

A large, stream-dwelling frog

1 Pointed nose; often sits on snags along stream edges

1

2

2ju Identifying juvenile frogs can be very confusing, as they are smaller and often a different colour and pattern from the adults.

🇪 ① Fort / Mocquard's Madagascar Frog
Mantidactylus femoralis / mocquardi

DISTRIBUTION: These two 'species' seem actually to form a poorly understood complex of species. Members of this group are common along rainforest streams in eastern and northern Madagascar, and locally in wet refuges in the west.
ID: Highly variable, but generally mid-sized, brown frogs, ranging from buff to very dark brown, usually with darker markings interspersed; some individuals have a pale stripe along the spine.
VOICE: Varies across the complex, but in general, give grumpy, unmusical notes in a series of variable length.

Length: ♂ 3·1–3·7 cm | 1·2–1·5"
♀ 4·5–5·5 cm | 1·8–2·2"

WHERE TO SEE: Possible along almost any rainforest stream, even during the day.

🇪 ② Warty Madagascar Frog *Mantidactylus ulcerosus*

DISTRIBUTION: Found in the northwest in a variety of wet habitats, including highly human-modified ones.
ID: Covered in large 'warts', which form ridges on the back. Plain brown in colour. Can be very similar to Betsileo Madagascar Frog, but seemingly little overlap in range.
VOICE: A quick series of several creaky, trilled notes.

Length: 3·2–4·1 cm | 1·2–1·6"

WHERE TO SEE: Ankarafantsika NP and the Nosy Be area. Can be seen during the day.

🇪 ③ Betsileo Madagascar Frog *Mantidactylus betsileanus*

DISTRIBUTION: Along streams and swampy areas in and adjacent to eastern rainforest. Seemingly restricted to the central and southern part of the rainforest belt, but very similar undescribed species occur farther north.
ID: Actually a complex of species whose definitive identification is difficult. Small, with bumps and ridges on the back. Generally pale brown with darker markings, with some having a paler stripe along the spine. Usually has a white spot on the tip of the nose.
VOICE: Very fast, hollow trill that lasts about three seconds.

Length: ♂ 2·3–2·8 cm | 0·9–1·1"
♀ 2·8–3·5 cm | 1·1–1·4"

WHERE TO SEE: Andasibe and Ranomafana areas, even during the day, although more vocal at night.

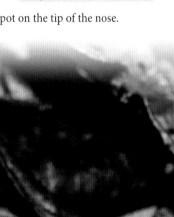

1. Variable; often but not always has a pale stripe on the back

2. Warty ridges on back

3. Highly variable; usually has a white tip to the nose, with some having a pale stripe all along the spine

ⓔ ① Charlotte's Madagascar Frog* *Mantidactylus charlotteae*

DISTRIBUTION: Near streams in low-elevation rainforest in the northeast.

| Length: | 2·2–3·2 cm | 0·9–1·3" |

WHERE TO SEE: Common in the northeast, on the islands of St. Marie and Nosy Mangabe, and in Marojejy and Masoala NPs.

ID: This species and the other two shown here share the same basic colour pattern: dark brown (almost black) on the sides, pale brown on the back, and a white stripe under the eye. Compared with White-whiskered Madagascar Frog, Charlotte's Madagascar Frog is usually smaller, and the white stripe below the eye fades before reaching the nostril.

VOICE: Quick series of creaky notes, more complex than those of White-whiskered Madagascar Frog, and delivered more slowly.

BEHAVIOUR: Active and vocal during the day.

ⓔ ② White-whiskered Madagascar Frog* *Mantidactylus melanopleura*

DISTRIBUTION: In the vicinity of streams within eastern rainforest.

| Length: | 3–4·1 cm | 1·2–1·6" |

WHERE TO SEE: During the day at most eastern rainforest sites including Ranomafana, Andasibe, Masoala and Marojejy.

ID: This is the largest and most boldly marked of the three species shown here, and the only one with a white stripe that reaches its nostril.

VOICE: Long series of "*tak*" notes, delivered quickly.

BEHAVIOUR: Active and vocal during the day.

ⓔ ③ Central Madagascar Frog *Mantidactylus opiparis*

DISTRIBUTION: In the vicinity of streams within eastern rainforest.

| Length: | 2·4–3·3 cm | 0·9–1·3" |

WHERE TO SEE: During the day at most eastern rainforest sites including Ranomafana, Andasibe, and Marojejy. Usually less common than White-whiskered Madagascar Frog.

ID: Similar to Charlotte's and White-whiskered Madagascar Frogs, but less boldly patterned; in particular the white stripe below the eye is usually blurred. Often shows a diamond-shaped marking within the pale brown patch on the back (like White-whiskered Madagascar Frog, but unlike Charlotte's Madagascar Frog).

VOICE: Very similar to White-whiskered Madagascar Frog, but the series is delivered much more slowly.

BEHAVIOUR: Active and vocal during the day.

2

1 White stripe fades before nostril

1ju Juvenile, probably Charlotte's Madagascar Frog

2 White stripe reaches nostril

3 Indistinct white line below eye

E 1 Folohy Madagascar Frog *Mantidactylus argenteus*

DISTRIBUTION: Along streams in eastern rainforest.
ID: Smooth skin is green with brown markings. Silvery below. Looks more like a pandanus frog (*page 266*) than the other Madagascar frogs.
VOICE: Series of 6–15 quiet "*tick*" notes, slightly fading at the end.
BEHAVIOUR: The only Madagascar frog that is largely arboreal. Calls from trees along rainforest streams during the day.

Length: ♂ 2·7 cm | 1·1"
♀ 3·1 cm | 1·2"

WHERE TO SEE: During the day in the Mantadia sector of Andasibe-Mantadia NP.

E 2 Duméril's Madagascar Frog *Mantidactylus lugubris* complex

DISTRIBUTION: A complex of species that occurs across the eastern rainforest and locally elsewhere. Found along streams, usually sitting on rocks very close to the water.
ID: Skin smoother than most Madagascar frogs, although there are some bumps. Colour highly variable, but beautiful, and matches their rocky streamside habitat. Typically shows black, brown and olive bands across the back.
VOICE: A single short, rasping trill.
BEHAVIOUR: Vocal at night.

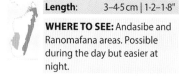

Length: 3–4·5 cm | 1·2–1·8"

WHERE TO SEE: Andasibe and Ranomafana areas. Possible during the day but easier at night.

2

Mostly arboreal

Smooth skin, bands across back

The vast majority of living things are invertebrates, with arthropods alone representing over 75% of Earth's biodiversity. Madagascar supports well over 100,000 species of invertebrate, most of which are endemic. This represents an extraordinarily high proportion of the world's 1·3 million or so described animal species, and serves to demonstrate again the importance of Madagascar as a repository of biodiversity. A handful of the more conspicuous and exceptional invertebrates is covered below.

❶ ① Giant African Land Snail *Achatina fulica*

M Sifotra
F Escargot Géant Africain

DISTRIBUTION: Found throughout the island except in very dry environments. Occurs in most habitats, from gardens to primary forest. Unfortunately, this introduced species is the most common and conspicuous of the island's almost 700 terrestrial snails, most of which are endemic.

ID: A large snail that is usually brown, although highly variable in colour.

Length:	<20 cm | 8"
Weight:	<1·5 kg | 3·3 lb
	(Average size much smaller)

WHERE TO SEE: Almost anywhere.

❸ ② Giant pill millipedes

Zoosphaerium / Sphaeromimus / Microsphaerotherium spp.

M Tainkintana

DISTRIBUTION: There are about 40 species of giant pill millipede found all around Madagascar, mainly in forest. They belong to an ancient family that is also found in southern India and Sri Lanka, and which was split apart by the breakup of Gondwanaland.

ID: They look like giant pillbugs or woodlice, but are in a completely different subphylum of organisms. Variable in colour; most commonly dark brown, buff or dark green.

| Length: | <10 cm \| 4" |

WHERE TO SEE: Possible in most forest sites, but most often seen in eastern and northern rainforest.

②

'Normal' millipedes are also abundant and conspicuous in Malagasy forests. Some are quite beautiful, sporting yellow bands or bright red colours

Rolls up in defence, like a pillbug or woodlouse

Often shows brown coloration
and banding

1 Golden orb-web spiders *Nephila* spp.

M Hala

DISTRIBUTION: Spiders of this genus are found throughout the world in warm climates. Occur across Madagascar, although most common in the east. Often in close association with humans, sometimes building webs on electric lines and poles.

ID: Black body with yellow markings and red-and-black-striped legs. Females dwarf males.

BEHAVIOUR: Constructs huge webs with golden strands.

| Length (legspan): | ♂ 1–2 cm \| 0·4–0·8" |
| | ♀ < 20 cm \| 8" |

WHERE TO SEE: Very common and widespread, often in towns.

E 2 Giraffe-necked Weevil *Trachelophorus giraffa*

M Gisagisa
F Scarabée Girafe

DISTRIBUTION: Found mainly along forest edge and in secondary habitat. The Malagasy species is the most famous, but other very long-necked weevils occur elsewhere in the world.

ID: Incredible and unmistakable long-necked weevil with a red back. Males have much longer necks than females.

BEHAVIOUR: Males fight with their extremely long necks, while females' more modest necks assist in making their favoured food plants into leaf rolls, in which they lay eggs.

| Length: | ♂ ~2·5 cm \| 1" |

WHERE TO SEE: Fairly common in the Andasibe and Ranomafana areas. Often pointed out by local guides.

E 3 Flatid Leaf Insect *Phromnia rosea*

DISTRIBUTION: Found in forest throughout Madagascar.

ID: Usually found in large aggregations. Adults are red and flat, while the nymphs look like white flowers due to a waxy substance that they extrude to deter predators.

| Length: | ~2 cm \| 0·8" |

WHERE TO SEE: Common in most protected areas.

3ju

Both adults (*opposite*) and nymphs form groups and look almost like flowers at a distance!

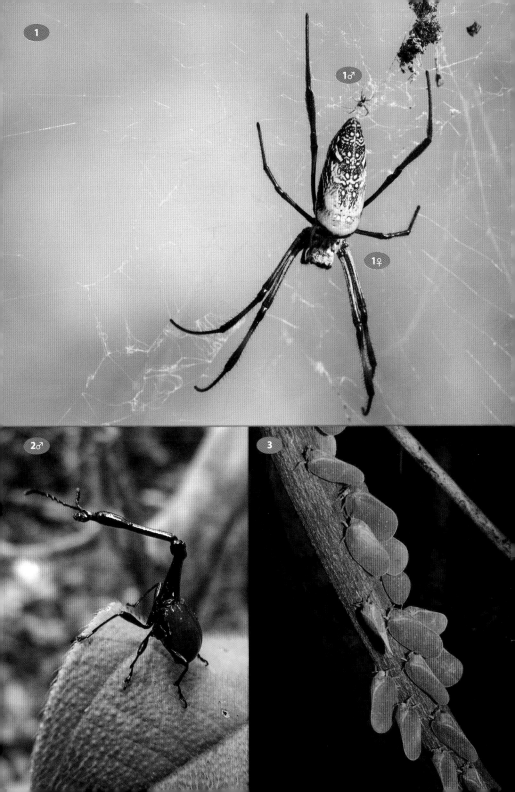

There are about 300 butterflies described from Madagascar, about three quarters of which are endemic. This section includes the most widespread and obvious species and groups. It will allow you to identify most of the butterflies that you see on a typical nature tour, at least to genus.

There is no standardization of common names for butterflies; common names novel to this guide are marked with an asterisk. Wingspan (WS) is the measurement given for butterflies.

1 Citrus Swallowtail *Papilio demodocus*

M Lolomboasary
F Papillon de Vinson

DISTRIBUTION: Sub-Saharan Africa. One of Madagascar's most common butterflies. Found in all open habitats except high mountains.

ID: Large and distinctive black-and-cream butterfly with elaborate markings. Lacks 'swallow tails'.

BEHAVIOUR: Some of its food plants are cultivated citrus trees.

Length:	WS 10–13 cm | 4–5"

WHERE TO SEE: Can be found in almost any garden or village. Common even in Tana.

e 2 Mocker Swallowtail *Papilio dardanus meriones*

DISTRIBUTION: Sub-Saharan Africa. Found in forest and edge habitat throughout Madagascar.

ID: Black-and-cream buterfly with less complex pattern than Citrus Swallowtail, and pale-tipped 'swallow tails'. In mainland Africa, the female mimics unpalatable species such as African Monarch (*page 298*), but on Madagascar, there is no mimicry and both sexes are similar.

BEHAVIOUR: Typical swallowtail: flighty and rarely lands for long.

Length:	WS 8–11 cm | 3–4.5"

WHERE TO SEE: Generally uncommon. Masoala is a good site.

E 3 Cream-lined Swallowtail *Papilio delalandei*

DISTRIBUTION: Found in rainforest and dry forest.

ID: Distinctive swallowtail with dark base coloration and cream bands through the wings, which are visible both above and below.

Length:	WS ~8–11 cm | 3–4.5"

WHERE TO SEE: Most common in eastern rainforest, such as around Ranomafana and Andasibe.

The largely deforested High Plateau does not hold many butterflies, but does play host to the common and familiar Citrus Swallowtail.

Lacks tails

Cream base colour

® ① Spotted Blue Swallowtail* *Papilio epiphorbas*

DISTRIBUTION: Madagascar and the Comoros. Widespread and common, both in forest and human-modified habitat, although absent from the dry southwest.
ID: A dark swallowtail with blue markings on the top of the wings. Similar to Banded Blue Swallowtail, but has discrete blue spots on each wing instead of blue lines. through both wings.

| Length: | WS ~8–11 cm \| 3–4.5" |

WHERE TO SEE: Especially common in the west and on the High Plateau. Can be seen in gardens in Tana.

❸ ② Banded Blue Swallowtail *Papilio oribazus*

DISTRIBUTION: Found in and around rainforest.
ID: See Spotted Blue Swallowtail. Most common in rainforest, whereas Spotted Blue Swallowtail prefers drier and more open habitats.

| Length: | WS ~8–11 cm \| 3–4.5" |

WHERE TO SEE: Common in most rainforest sites, including Andasibe.

® ③ Madagascar Swordtail* *Graphium evombar*

DISTRIBUTION: Comoros and Madagascar, in rainforest and western dry forest.
ID: Intricate patterning and very long tails. The pale parts of the wings range from pale yellow to pale blue.
BEHAVIOUR: Very fast flier. Sometimes lands on mud.

| Length: | WS ~7–8 cm \| 3" |

WHERE TO SEE: Perhaps easiest to see in western forest, as in Ankarafantsika NP and Kirindy Forest.

Plain below

Occasionally lacks tails

Very long tails

ⓔ ① Green Lady* *Graphium cyrnus*

DISTRIBUTION: Found throughout Madagascar in all types of forest.
ID: Handsome tailless swallowtail. Black and pale green above; dark brown and pale green below, with variable red highlights.

Length:	WS ~6–7 cm | 2·5–3"

WHERE TO SEE: Possible in most forest sites. Frequent in Andasibe-Mantadia NP.

ⓔ ② Madagascar Giant Swallowtail *Pharmacophagus antenor*

DISTRIBUTION: Found in open habitats, including towns and gardens. Absent from the east, and most common in the west and southwest.
ID: This huge swallowtail can be identified simply by its size. The base colour is black, with pale yellow spots, and some red highlights. The forewings are extremely long.
BEHAVIOUR: Wanders widely, and often flies high.

Length:	WS 12–14 cm | 4·5–5·5"

WHERE TO SEE: Fairly common around Toliara, Ifaty, and Morondava.

Most often seen in flight

1

2

Lacks tails

Huge, dark
swallowtail

Ⓡ ① Madagascar Orange Tip* *Colotis evanthe*

DISTRIBUTION: Madagascar and the Comoros. Found both in forest and open, human-modified areas.
ID: Mostly white. Male has bright orange markings on the tip of the upperside of the forewing; the forewing tips of the female are duller. After landing, closes wings, when only a speckled white pattern is visible below.
BEHAVIOUR: Flies weakly and usually stays close to the ground.

Length:	WS ~3–4 cm | 1–1·5"
WHERE TO SEE: Especially common in the west and north.	

② Grass yellows *Eurema* spp. [4 species]

DISTRIBUTION: Members of this genus are found throughout much of the world in open habitats, including those that are human-modified.
ID: Small, yellow butterflies, with black edges to the upperside of the wings. Separation of the four Malagasy species can be tricky. **Broad-bordered Grass Yellow** *Eurema brigitta* ② is the most common and widespread species. It has broad dark borders to the forewing (and often the hindwing) above, and is dull yellow with broad greyish or pinkish borders and simple speckling below. **Malagasy Grass Yellow** *E. floricola* ②ₐ has complex spots below, including a roughly 'T'-shaped mark near the centre of the hindwing. **Angled Grass Yellow** *E. desjardinsii* ②c can be very similar to Malagasy Grass Yellow, but shows an angled rather than evenly rounded hindwing. **Marsh Grass Yellow** *E. hapale* (not illustrated) can also be very similar to the preceding two species, but is generally paler, and shows linear (not 'T'-shaped) outlined marks near the centre of the hindwing and the front of the forewing below.
BEHAVIOUR: Fairly weak flight, usually close to the ground.

Length:	WS 3–4 cm | 1–1·5"
WHERE TO SEE: Almost anywhere.	

③ Migrants *Catopsilia* spp. [2 species]

DISTRIBUTION: *C. thauruma* ③ₐ is a regional endemic, while *C. florella* ③b has a wide Old World distribution. Found in all open habitats.
ID: Male is greenish-white, while the female is yellowish. Whiter individuals can be mistaken for whites (*page 294*), but black markings not obvious. The two Malagasy species are hard to distinguish. *C. florella* is slightly smaller than *C. thauruma* and has more pointed forewings. *C. thauruma* is more common; often observed around villages.
BEHAVIOUR: Strong fliers.

Length:	WS 5–7 cm | 2–2·5"
WHERE TO SEE: Most towns and gardens.	

③ₐ♀   Probable *Catopsilia florella*

1♂

1♀

2a

2b

Grass yellows are yellow with
black wing edges above

2c

3a♂   Males greenish-white

3b♀   Females yellow

(e) (1) **African Wood White** *Leptosia alcesta sylvicola*

DISTRIBUTION: Afrotropical forest.
ID: Mostly plain white, with faint speckles below, and one black spot on the forewing.
BEHAVIOUR: Very weak flight gives rise to its colloquial name 'Flip-flop'.

Length:	WS 3–4 cm | 1–1·5"

WHERE TO SEE: Present in most forest sites, but inconspicuous.

(E) (2) **Grandidier's Caper White*** *Belenois grandidieri*

DISTRIBUTION: Dry forest and adjacent secondary habitat. Absent from the east.
ID: Delicate black tracery and scattered hints of yellow below.

Length:	WS ~4 cm | 1·5"

WHERE TO SEE: Fairly common in western forest, as in Kirindy Forest and around Toliara.

(E) (3) **Madagascar Dotted Border*** *Mylothris phileris*

DISTRIBUTION: Forest throughout Madagascar.
ID: White, with black spots along the edges of the wings, and a variable orange blaze at the base of the hindwing In rainforest, occurs alongside **Albatross White** *Appias sabina* (not illustrated). That species shows smaller spots along the hindwing, and more wedge-shaped marks along the edge of the forewing.
BEHAVIOUR: More languid flight, and more often in the forest canopy than other pierids.

Length:	WS ~5 cm | 2"

WHERE TO SEE: Fairly common in most forest sites.

(E) (4) **Yellow-painted Caper White*** *Belenois helcida*

DISTRIBUTION: Rainforest, mainly in the east and north.
ID: Broad black edges to both wings. Orange blaze at the base of the forewing below.

Length:	WS ~4–5 cm | 1·5–2"

WHERE TO SEE: Rainforest sites such as Andasibe.

1 Black spot and black edge on forewing above

1 White with speckles below

2 Lacy pattern below

3 Dots along wing edges

4 Pattern similar on top and bottom of wings

E **1** Madagascar metalmarks *Saribia* spp. [4 species]

DISTRIBUTION: Rainforest, mainly in the east and north.
ID: Intricate, distinctive pattern of zig-zags, bars and
eye spots below. The plainer topside is rarely seen, as
the wings are usually held closed when perched.
There are multiple tails at the back of the hindwing.
BEHAVIOUR: Flies low, inside of the forest.

Length: WS ~4 cm | 1·5"

WHERE TO SEE: Amber
Mountain, Andasibe-Mantadia,
and Ranomafana NPs.

2 Blues / hairstreaks 16 genera [~ 46 species]

DISTRIBUTION: Various species found throughout
Madagascar in most habitats.
ID: Large group of small butterflies. Most are blue or
purple above, and pale grey below. Many have 'false eye'
spots on their hindwing, while some have thin tails, or
'false antennae'. After landing, the hindwings are waved in
circles, enhancing the impression of a false head to misdirect the attacks of predators.
BEHAVIOUR: Most species have low, weak, fluttery flight.

Length: WS mostly 2–3 cm | 1"

WHERE TO SEE: Blues are
very common, even in Tana;
hairstreaks are harder to find.

Common Smoky Blue *Euchrysops malathana*

Cloudy Blue *Zizina antanossa*

Hairstreak *Hemiolaus cobaltina*

Brown Playboy *Deudorix antalus*

Definitively identifying Madagascar metalmarks usually requires dissection and/or DNA sequencing!

1 Probable *Saribia perroti* from Ranomafana NP

1 Possible *Saribia tepahi* from Amber Mountain NP

2 Hairstreak, probably *Deudorix batikeli* (female)

2 **Common Zebra Blue** *Leptotes pirithous*

2 **Sooty Blue** *Zizeeria knysna*

2 **Gaika Blue** *Zizula hylax*

The Nymphalidae or 'brush-footed butterfly' family contains some of the most colourful and conspicuous Malagasy butterflies.

1 African Monarch *Danaus chrysippus*

DISTRIBUTION: Widespread Old World species. Found throughout Madagascar except in the high mountains.
ID: Large and distinctive orange, black-and-white butterfly. Mimicked by female Common Diadem (*page 310*); see that species for separation.
BEHAVIOUR: Flies strongly, but with frequent glides.

Length:	WS 5–7·5 cm | 2–3"

WHERE TO SEE: Almost anywhere.

E 2 Madagascar Forest Nymph* *Aterica rabena*

DISTRIBUTION: Forest throughout.
ID: Distinctive pattern: largely dark brown forewing with white markings, and largely orange hindwing.
BEHAVIOUR: Flies low within forest, and frequently perches on the ground with wings open.

Length:	WS ~6–7 cm | 2·5"

WHERE TO SEE: Fairly common in small numbers in most forest sites.

E 3 Madagascar Beauty* *Salamis anteva*

DISTRIBUTION: Forest throughout.
ID: Beautiful orange, black, and white pattern above, but usually lands with wings closed, when only the cryptic leaf-like underside of the wings is visible.
BEHAVIOUR: Floppy flight.

Length:	WS ~6 cm | 2·5"

WHERE TO SEE: Most conspicuous in western forest, as in Ankarafantsika and Tsingy de Bemaraha NPs.

① **Common Leopard** *Phalanta phalantha*

DISTRIBUTION: Open areas throughout much of the Old World, including Madagascar.
ID: Mid-sized orange butterfly with copious black markings. Very similar to Madagascar Leopard, but prefers open areas (Madagascar Leopard is always in forest). The lines along the edges of the wings are thin and wavy in Common Leopard, and thicker and straighter in Madagascar Leopard.
BEHAVIOUR: Strong, fast flier.

| Length: | WS 4–5 cm | 1·5–2" |

WHERE TO SEE: Almost anywhere.

E ② **Madagascar Leopard*** *Phalanta madagascariensis*

DISTRIBUTION: Forest throughout.
ID: Mid-sized orange butterfly with black markings. Very similar to Common Leopard, but has thicker and straighter black lines at the edges of its wings, and is found in forest, whereas Common Leopard prefers open areas.

| Length: | WS ~4–5 cm | 1·5–2" |

WHERE TO SEE: Less common than Common Leopard, although possible in most forest sites.

③ **Common Joker** *Byblia anvatara*

DISTRIBUTION: Throughout most of Afrotropics. Found in almost any open habitat, especially human-created ones. Absent only from high mountains and rainforest interior.
ID: Distinctive and beautiful pattern of orange, buff, and brown.
BEHAVIOUR: The erratic flight is rather moth-like.

| Length: | WS 4–5 cm | 1·5–2" |

WHERE TO SEE: Almost anywhere, including Tana.

1 — Lines along edges of wings are thin and wavy

2 — Lines along edges of wings are thick and fairly straight

Complex patterning above and below

3

1 Polka Dot *Pardopsis punctatissima*

DISTRIBUTION: From South Africa to Ethiopia, and throughout Madagascar. Prefers open habitats created by humans, such as pastures.
ID: Similar in shape to acraeas, but small, widely spaced, black 'polka dots' are unmistakable.
BEHAVIOUR: Flight is weak and low to ground.

Length: WS 3–4 cm | 1–1·5"
WHERE TO SEE: Possible almost anywhere, although inconspicuous.

2 Tree nymphs *Sevenia* spp. [3 species]

DISTRIBUTION: An Afrotropical genus. All three Malagasy species are endemic, found in forests.
ID: Dull orange above. Underside of hindwing is fuzzy grey with darker spots and bars. *Sevenia howensis* (not illustrated) is dark and heavily marked on the underside of the hindwing; *S. madagascariensis* (not illustrated) is pale and faintly marked; *S. amazoula* **2a** is intermediate, with a pale base colour but fairly bold markings.
BEHAVIOUR: Slow, gliding flight. Often land in trees and hang upside down.

Length: WS ~6 cm | 2·5"
WHERE TO SEE: Present, although inconspicuous, in most forest sites.

3 Acraeas *Acraea* spp. [18 species]

DISTRIBUTION: Large Old World tropical genus. Ten species are endemic to Madagascar. Most species are restricted to forest, but some inhabit open areas.
ID: A diverse group of long-winged butterflies. All show red or orange, with black markings. Many have partially transparent wings.
BEHAVIOUR: Distinctive slow flight with frequent glides. Often in the mid-storey and canopy of forest.

Length: WS 4–7 cm | 1·5–3"
WHERE TO SEE: Multiple species occur in all forest sites, and a few are usually common.

Acraea turna
Ifaty

Sevenia amazoula

Acraea dammii
Lokobe NP

Acraea ranavalona
Lokobe NP

1 Emperors *Charaxes* spp. [9 species]

DISTRIBUTION: A large Old World genus. All of the nine Malagasy species are found exclusively in forest, and eight of them are endemic.

ID: Pointed forewing, and one or two tails on the hindwing. A variable group, but all species show a jagged, complex pattern below, visible when the wings are closed after landing. The upperwing has a black pattern on a base colour of white, beige, or orange.

Length: WS 5–10 cm | 2–4"

WHERE TO SEE: Not often observed, but at least one species is found in most forest sites.

BEHAVIOUR: Distinctive flight alternates powerful wingbeats and quick glides on flat wings. Found mainly in forest canopy. Territorial; will defend food sources.

R 2 Madagascar Brown Pansy* *Junonia goudotii*

DISTRIBUTION: Found in Madagascar, the Comoros, and Mauritius. Present in many habitats, from human-created savannah to forest edge.

ID: Distinctive brown and orange pattern above.

BEHAVIOUR: All pansies slowly open and close their wings when perched.

Length: WS 5 cm | 2"

WHERE TO SEE: Possible almost anywhere, though in small numbers.

E 3 Madagascar Commodore* *Precis andremiaja*

DISTRIBUTION: Rainforest edges and adjacent scrub.

ID: Above, male has a white stripe, and female a broader orange one. Below, both sexes are cryptic and leaf-like.

BEHAVIOUR: Slowly opens and closes wings after landing.

Length: WS ~6 cm | 2.5"

WHERE TO SEE: Common in many places such as around Andasibe and Masoala.

Club-tailed Charaxes
Charaxes zoolina
Zombitse-Vohibasia NP

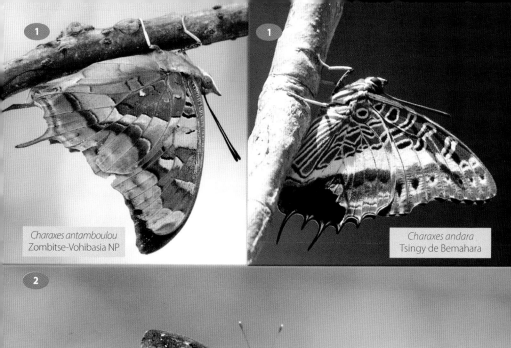

Charaxes antamboulou
Zombitse-Vohibasia NP

Charaxes andara
Tsingy de Bemahara

Female (below); male has
narrower white bands
through both wings

3♀

3♀

Ⓡ ① **Brilliant Blue** *Junonia rhadama*

DISTRIBUTION: Mascarenes, Comoros, Seychelles, and Madagascar. Found at forest edge, and in a variety of open and human–modified habitats.
ID: Shows more blue than other blue pansies, especially in the forewing. Male brighter than female.

Length:	WS ~4–5 cm | 1.5–2"

WHERE TO SEE: Widespread and common, even in the gardens of Tana.

ⓔ ② **Yellow Pansy** *Junonia hierta paris*

DISTRIBUTION: Old World tropics. Found throughout Madagascar in open and human-modified habitats, and forest edge. Absent from rainforest and the High Plateau.
ID: Distinctive pattern of rich buff and dark brown with dark blue or purple spots above. Male has brighter colours than the more subdued female.

Length:	WS 4–5 cm | 1.5–2"

WHERE TO SEE: Almost anywhere in drier habitat.

③ **Blue Pansy** *Junonia oenone*

DISTRIBUTION: Afrotropics. Throughout Madagascar in most open habitats except high mountains and the arid southwest.
ID: Large blue patch on the hindwing above, bigger and brighter on male. Female has several 'eye spots', and can resemble the much less common **Eyed Pansy** *Junonia orithya* (not illustrated), but always shows blue at the wing centre, rather than towards the edges of the wings.
BEHAVIOUR: The male is aggressively territorial.

Length:	WS 4–5 cm | 1.5–2"

WHERE TO SEE: Almost anywhere.

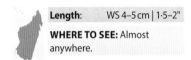

Underwing pattern subdued, but mirrors pattern above

1♂

1♀

Bolder pattern below than other pansies

2♂

2♀

Large buff patches above

3♂

3♀

(e) (1) Clouded Mother-of-Pearl *Protogoniomorpha anacardii duprei*

DISTRIBUTION: Much of Afrotropics. Widespread in forest and secondary habitat in Madagascar.

ID: Pattern above distinctive, even in flight: white with black borders. Female has broader dark edges than male. Below, cryptic and leaf-like.

BEHAVIOUR: Bounding, floppy flight. Generally holds wings closed when perched, but sometimes opens and closes them slowly.

Length: WS 6–7·5 cm | 2–3"

WHERE TO SEE: Most common in rainforest, for example around Amber Mountain and Andasibe.

(E) (2) Madagascar Diadem *Hypolimnas dexithea*

DISTRIBUTION: Eastern and northern rainforest, and locally in western dry forest.

ID: Unmistakable; one of Madagascar's most spectacular butterflies. A complex pattern of white, rufous-brown and black.

BEHAVIOUR: Usually stays high in forest canopy. A strong and high flier.

Length: WS ~7–9 cm | 3–3·5"

WHERE TO SEE: Small numbers in rainforest sites such as Andasibe, Ranomafana, and Amber Mountain NPs.

(e) (3) African Map Butterfly *Cyrestis camillus elegans*

DISTRIBUTION: Afrotropics. In Madagascar, found in rainforest and adjacent secondary habitat.

ID: Beautiful, unmistakable species with a white base colour and vaguely cartographic black and yellowish markings.

BEHAVIOUR: Visits muddy spots, as along roads.

Length: WS 4–5 cm | 1·5–2"

WHERE TO SEE: Generally uncommon. Lokobe NP is one good site.

e **1** **Spotted Sailer** *Neptis saclava saclava*

DISTRIBUTION: Widespread in Afrotropics. Found in both primary forest and disturbed habitats in Madagascar.
ID: See similar Madagascar Sailer. They can occur together, but Spotted Sailer is more likely in secondary habitat.
BEHAVIOUR: Like Madagascar Sailer.

Length: WS 4–5 cm | 1·5–2"

WHERE TO SEE: Fairly common and widespread.

E **2** **Madagascar Sailer*** *Neptis kikideli*

DISTRIBUTION: Found in forest throughout Madagascar.
ID: Sailers have a dark grey base colour and a broad band of white across both wings. They are smaller than other pied butterflies. Madagascar Sailer is very similar to Spotted Sailer, but has a broader band of white on both wings, and a subtly different pattern of white spots on the forewing.
BEHAVIOUR: Slow flight with frequent glides. Usually lands with wings open.

Length: WS ~4–5 cm | 1·5–2"

WHERE TO SEE: Fairly common in most forest sites.

e **3** **False Chief** *Pseudacraea lucretia apaturoides*

DISTRIBUTION: Afrotropics. Found in rainforest in Madagascar.
ID: Bold black-and-white pattern with veins running through the white patches. **Imerina Chief** *Pseudoacraea imerina* (not illustrated) has similar shape and overall colour, but has bluish spots rather than a pattern of veins.
BEHAVIOUR: Unhurried flight. Often glides with wings open.

Length: WS 6–8 cm | 2·5–3"

WHERE TO SEE: Quite common. Good areas include Andasibe, Ranomafana, and Anjozorobe.

4 **Common Diadem** *Hypolimnas misippus*

DISTRIBUTION: Worldwide tropical distribution. Occurs widely in Madagascar, although absent from the High Plateau and the southwest. Found in human-modified habitats.

Length: WS 6–8 cm | 2·5–3"

WHERE TO SEE: Widespread but generally uncommon. Often near coastal towns.

ID: The male has a distinctive pattern: a black base colour, with large white blotches and purplish highlights. The female mimics the unpalatable African Monarch (*page 298*) with remarkable accuracy, but has a heavier build and subtly different shape: a slightly more wavy trailing edge to the hindwing and a slightly more curvaceous trailing edge to the forewing.

1 Evening Brown *Melanitis leda*

DISTRIBUTION: Old World tropics and Australia. Found throughout Madagascar in open habitats and forest edge but absent from high mountains.
ID: A large brown butterfly, with different dry and wet season forms: conspicuous 'eye-spots' in the wet season, and few or none in the dry season. Larger than Madagascar and Indian Ocean satyrs.
BEHAVIOUR: Active at dusk or on cloudy days. Reluctant to fly, and flies weakly.

Length: WS 6–7 cm | 3"

WHERE TO SEE: Widespread but uncommon and inconspicuous.

E 2 Madagascar satyrs* *Strabena* spp. [37 species]

DISTRIBUTION: A large, endemic genus. Various species can be found all around the island. Most live in forest, but some occur in secondary habitat and grasslands, more so than in the Indian Ocean satyrs.
ID: Generally small and brown. Similar to Indian Ocean satyrs, but separated by the pattern on the forewing. Both groups show an orange eyespot ring with a smaller black iris inside. Madagascar satyrs usually have the main eyespot towards the tip rather than the centre of the forewing, and it contains two bluish pupils. In Indian Ocean satyrs, the main eyespot is closer to the centre of the forewing, and has only one whitish pupil inside the black iris.
BEHAVIOUR: Fairly weak, skipping flight, low to the ground. These are among the few butterflies to be found in the understorey of thick forest. Feed on nectar.

Length: WS ~4–6 cm | 1·5–2·5"

WHERE TO SEE: In general, much less commonly seen than Indian Ocean satyrs.

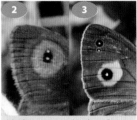

Madagascar and Indian Ocean satyr forewing eyespots

R 3 Indian Ocean satyrs* *Heteropsis* spp. [64 species]

DISTRIBUTION: A large, regionally endemic genus. Various species are found all around the island. Most live in forest, but a few occur in secondary habitat and grasslands.
ID: See Madagascar satyrs.
BEHAVIOUR: Like Madagascar satyrs, but feed mainly on fruit.

Length: WS ~4–6 cm | 1·5–2·5"

WHERE TO SEE: Can be found in most places, although not usually in gardens or towns.

Heteropsis turbans
Ranomafana NP

Heteropsis vola
Andasibe

Wet season form
very plain

1

Dry season form
with eye spots

1

2 *Strabena tamatavae*
High Plateau

2 *Strabena triophthalma*
Anjozorobe-Angavo forest

3

Heteropsis difficilis
Ranomafana NP

Heteropsis subsimilis
Amber Mountain NP

Heteropsis narcissus
Masoala

E **1** Comet Moth *Argema mittrei*

F Papillon Comète de Madagascar

DISTRIBUTION: Endemic to Malagasy rainforest.
ID: Huge spectacular yellow silk moth with large eye-spots and long tails.
BEHAVIOUR: Only lives for a few days.

Length: WS ~ 15–20 cm | 6–8"
WHERE TO SEE: Ranomafana area.

E **2** Madagascar Sunset Moth *Chrysiridia rhipheus*

M Lolo Andriana

DISTRIBUTION: Throughout most of Madagascar in rainforest, western dry forest, and secondary habitats.
ID: A large and beautiful multi-coloured and multi-tailed moth that is often mistaken for a butterfly.
BEHAVIOUR: Flies during the day, unlike most moths.

Length: WS 7–9 cm | 3–3.5"
WHERE TO SEE: Most likely in eastern rainforest sites such as Andasibe and Masoala.

3 Skippers Hesperiidae [56 species]

DISTRIBUTION: Large, worldwide family that is well represented in Madagascar. Most species are found in forest, but some use secondary habitats and grassland.
ID: Moth-like butterflies, with thick bodies and large eyes. Some are fairly colourful, but most are brown, grey, or dull orange.
BEHAVIOUR: Fast, bounding flight gives the family its common name.

Length: WS 2–7 cm | 1–3"
WHERE TO SEE: Widespread, but generally inconspicuous.

Skippers show a variety of postures when at rest: some species hold their wings closed, others open, and some partially spread.

3♂

Some skippers flat-winged: *Eagris sabadius* Amber Mountain NP

Offset wing posture unique to skippers: probable *Fulda coroller* Diego-Suarez

Some skippers quite colourful
Coeliades rama Kirindy Forest

Most skippers plain: *Parnara naso* Diego-Suarez

Madagascar supports over 11,000 species of plant, most of which are endemic. It boasts eight endemic and near-endemic families and over 300 endemic genera. Six of the world's nine species of baobab are found only on the island. It supports about 850 species of orchid, and more than twice the diversity of palms than the continent of Africa. Although this guide is primarily focused on animals, a few of the most conspicuous and distinctive plants are highlighted here.

E **1** Traveller's Palm *Ravenala madagascariensis*

M Ravinala
F Arbre du Voyageur

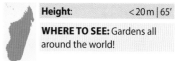

DISTRIBUTION: Originally endemic to Madagascar, but introduced around the warmer parts of the world as an ornamental species. Thrives in human-modified areas and forest edges. There are whole 'forests' of Traveller's Palm in some disturbed areas.

Height:	<20m	65'

WHERE TO SEE: Gardens all around the world!

ID: The mature trees are crowned by a broad fan of palm-like fronds. Its iconic shape is featured on the Air Madagascar logo and in many other places.

The Traveller's Palm was so named because of the water that accumulates at the base of its huge leaves, a godsend for travellers who found themselves without water. It is not actually a palm, but a member of the bird-of-paradise (Strelitziaceae) family. Ruffed lemurs (*page 52*) seem to be this tree's main natural pollinator.

2 Pandanus *Pandanus* spp.

M Vakoana
F Baquois

DISTRIBUTION: Almost 100 of the world's 700 *Pandanus* species are endemic to Madagascar. On the island, they are found in all types of forest, from spiny forest to rainforest. Many species thrive in swamps.

Height:	<20m	65'

WHERE TO SEE: Any Malagasy forest, from spiny forest to rainforest.

ID: Some species are shrubs, while other can be tall trees. Most have exposed supporting roots at their base. The leaves are long, thin and often pointed.

Pandanus is sometimes called 'pandanus palm' or 'screw pine' but is neither a palm nor a pine, belonging instead to the Pandanaceae family.

Traveller's Palm can dominate vast areas of savannah-like habitat

1 Iconic fan shape

2

Most species have a spiny trunk (*above*) and exposed supporting roots (*below*)

1 Octopus tree Didiereaceae [11 species]

M Sogno
F Arbre Pieuvre

DISTRIBUTION: Formerly thought to comprise a Malagasy endemic family, although some continental African species have recently been placed in this family. In Madagascar, there are four genera and 11 species, all found in the spiny forest of the southwest.

| Height: | <15 m \| 50' |

WHERE TO SEE: One of the dominant tree families in the spiny forest.

ID: One of the most striking components of Madagascar's unique spiny forest. All species have spines and small leaves that grow close to the main trunk. The 'classic' species, including the widespread *Didierea madagascariensis*, have a profusion of tentacle-like trunks reaching toward the sky.

2 Pachypodium *Pachypodium* spp.

M Vontake

DISTRIBUTION: Most of the world's 25 or so species are endemic to Madagasacar. They grow mainly in dry and rocky places, and thrive in the southwest.

| Height: | <6 m \| 20' |

WHERE TO SEE: Southwestern spiny forest, for example around Toliara and Ifaty. Also prominent around Isalo.

ID: Succulent plants with variable, but generally unusual structure. The trunks of some species have a swollen base, while others have a bottle-like shape. Many are covered in spines, which serve to condense fog that runs down and waters the plant.

Some pachypodiums have bottle-shaped trunks

1 Didierea madagascariensis

2 Pachypodium rosulatum

Six of the world's nine baobabs are endemic to Madagascar. They are found in dry parts of the southwest, west and north, and lose their leaves during the dry season.

ⓔ ① Western Baobab* *Adansonia za*

M Za
F Baobab Za*

DISTRIBUTION: Dry forest of the west and southwest. Found at elevations up to 800 m (2,600'). The most widespread Malagasy baobab.

ID: Large, with grey bark, fairly straight trunk and rounded crown. Fruit is variable in shape, but is always somewhat oval and never round. See Grandidier's and Northwestern Baobabs for separation from those species.

NEAR THREATENED	
Height:	<30m | 100'

WHERE TO SEE: Berenty, Toliara area, Zombitse-Vohibasia NP, and Kirindy Forest.

No living Malagasy animal is capable of dispersing baobab seeds; it is likely that the 'gorilla lemurs', prior to their extinction, were the main dispersers of the seeds of these huge trees.

ⓔ ② Grandidier's Baobab *Adansonia grandidieri*

M Reniala
F Baobab de Grandidier

DISTRIBUTION: Fairly small distribution in the southern part of the west.

ID: Huge, stately, columnar baobab with pale grey bark. Similar to Western Baobab, but has a different shape: a long, bare trunk with a flat array of straight branches at the top, whereas Western has branches starting just above the middle of the tree, and some of these branches hang down irregularly. Grandidier's Baobab has an oval-shaped fruit, more rounded than the elongated oval fruit of Western Baobab.

ENDANGERED	
Height:	<30m | 100'
Diameter:	<3m | 10'

WHERE TO SEE: Around Morondava, most famously at the 'Allée des Baobabs' northeast of town.

The Malagasy name for Grandidier's Baobab is 'Reniala', meaning 'mother of the forest'.

ⓔ ③ Northwestern Baobab*
Adansonia madagascariensis

M Bozy
F Baobab du Nord-ouest*

DISTRIBUTION: Dry forest of the northwest and north.

ID: Medium-sized baobab with smooth grey bark. Often tall and thin. Best separated from Western Baobab by its round rather than oval-shaped fruit.

NEAR THREATENED	
Height:	<20m | 65'
Diameter:	<3m | 10'

WHERE TO SEE: Ankarafantsika and Ankarana NPs, and around Diego-Suarez.

It is difficult to age baobabs, but some African specimens have proven to be well over 1,000 years old.

1 Grey bark and straight trunk

2 Tall and majestic, with smooth grey bark

Often very tall and thin

3

❶ ① Diego-Suarez Baobab*
Adansonia suarezensis

M Bozy Diego*
F Baobab de Diego-Suarez*

DISTRIBUTION: Tiny range in dry forest around Diego-Suarez, in the far north.
ID: A beautiful baobab with burgundy bark, and often a 'T'- or 'Y'-shaped form, with heavy branches spreading from near the top of the tree. Elongated oval fruits.

Perrier's Baobab *Adansonia perrieri* (not illustrated) is a rare northern species that can be seen in Ankarana National Park.

ENDANGERED	
Height:	<25 m | 80'
Diameter:	<2 m | 7'

WHERE TO SEE: On the slopes of Montagne des Français, along the road between Diego-Suarez and the beach town of Ramena.

❶ ② Fony Baobab* *Adansonia rubrostipa*

M Fony
F Baobab Fony*

DISTRIBUTION: Found in dry forest below 300 m (1,000') elevation, from central western Madagascar to the northern part of the southwest.
ID: The smallest and most distinctive baobab: reddish bark, round fruit, serrated leaves and usually a bottle-shaped trunk.

NEAR THREATENED
Height: <20 m | 65'

WHERE TO SEE: Common around Toliara and Ifaty.

The famous baobab in Mahajanga, in the middle of the roundabout (traffic circle) where the town's main road reaches the coast, is actually an African Baobab *Adansonia digitata*, not a Malagasy species.

Baobabs bloom at the beginning of the rainy season and have large and spectacular flowers.

Baobabs have hard fruits covered in fine hair. They vary in shape from round to oval depending on the species.

Maroon bark

Reddish bark and bottle shape

Glossary of terms

aestivate	to go into a state of torpor similar to hibernation
Afrotropics	ecozone that includes sub-Saharan Africa and all the Indian Ocean islands of the Malagasy region. Sometimes also considered to include the southern part of the Arabian Peninsula and small parts of Iran and Pakistan
arboreal	living in trees
arthropod	invertebrates with exoskeletons, segmented bodies and jointed appendages. They include the insects, spiders and crustaceans, and make up the phylum Arthropoda
bare parts	parts of a bird not covered in feathers, namely legs, bill and any exposed skin around the eye and the base of the bill
call	shorter and simpler bird vocalizations that are used mainly for communication between birds: to stay in touch, warn of predators, or to share food sources (see also **song**)
carrion	flesh of dead animals
caruncle	an odd type of **bare part** shown by asities, an endemic Malagasy bird family
casque	hard, helmet-like projection on the head of some chameleons
CL	carapace length: the standard length measurement used for turtles, terrapins and tortoises
Comoros	islands lying in the Indian Ocean northwest of Madagascar. Geographically, Mayotte is part of the Comoros, although politically it is part of France, whereas the other Comoran islands comprise their own country
dabble / dabbling	a feeding strategy in which the bill is moved around in shallow water. Often to refer to 'dabbling ducks' which feed on the surface of the water as opposed to 'diving ducks' which dive to feed
diurnal	active during the day
dry season	the portion of the year that is cooler, with lower rainfall. Generally between April and October in the east. The rains are shorter, more sporadic, and usually arrive later in the west. In the southwest they can fail altogether
epiphyte	a plant that grows on another plant, but which does not parasitize it
Europa	small island off the coast of southern Madagascar. Politically part of France, although claimed by Madagascar
gallery forest	band of forest that grows along a watercourse, usually in dry country
Glorieuses	French possession consisting of a group of tiny islands northwest of Madagascar. Also known as the Glorioso Islands

Gondwanaland	the southern of two supercontinents formed by the breakup of Pangea. It contained present-day South America, Antarctica, Arabia, Africa, Australia and peninsular India
high plateau	elevated part of central Madagascar comprising the contiguous area with an elevation above 800 m (2,600'). Divided from the northern Madagscar highlands by an area of lowlands. Often referred to by its French name: 'Hauts-Plateaux'
invertebrate	animal lacking a backbone
Kirindy Forest	privately owned forest reserve that is part of a former logging concession. Properly referred to as Kirindy CNFEREF, and not to be confused with Kirindy-Mitea National Park, which lies south of Morondava
Malagasy Region	Madagascar, the Comoros (including Mayotte), the Seychelles, the Mascarenes, a few remote outlying islands, and the surrounding waters
Mascarenes	the islands of Réunion, Mauritius and Rodrigues, which lie east of Madagascar. Réunion is part of France, while Mauritius and Rodrigues make up their own country
Mayotte	island lying northwest of Madagascar. Geographically part of the Comoros, but politically part of France
MNP	Madagascar National Parks, the Malagasy government agency responsible for the management of the national protected area system
Neotropical	the tropics of the New World: southern Mexico, the Carribean, central America and much of South America
nocturnal	active at night
NP	national park
occipital lobe	a flap of skin at the back of the head, possessed by some chameleons
Old World	Europe, Africa and Asia
onomatopoeia	the formation of a word that imitates a natural sound. Some bird names are onomatopoeic, reflecting their voice (*e.g.* cuckoo)
Pandanus	A genus of palm-like plants. Sometimes called 'screw pine' or 'screw palm'
primary (forest)	old forest that has never been cut or suffered significant disturbance. Sometimes also called 'virgin forest' or 'old-growth forest'
rainforest	forest with high rainfall, in which most trees stay green and retain their leaves year-round. This term is sometimes reserved for lowland humid forest, but in this book is used for all humid forest, from sea-level up to the treeline
riparian (forest)	along the banks of a river or stream

Sambirano forest	forest type in far northern Madagascar, which resembles eastern rainforest. Some of this forest is on the west coast, providing an exception to the general rule of Madagascar's east being wet while its centre and west are dry
secondary (forest / habitat)	forest or other habitat that has regenerated after the destruction of the original, primary forest or other habitat
Seychelles	a nation of 115 islands that lies northeast of Madagascar
SNR	Strict Nature Reserve, a type of protected area that is manged by Madagascar National Parks (**MNP**)
song	a longer and more complex bird vocalization whose primary purposes are to attract a mate and defend a territory (see also call)
spiny forest	arid, scrubby habitat found in southwestern Madagascar. Sometimes called 'spiny thicket' or 'spiny desert'. It is not arid enough to be truly considered desert, but lacks the closed canopy of true forest. Prominent vegetation includes baobabs and octopus trees
Sub-Saharan Africa	the portion of the African continent that lies south of the Sahara Desert
SVL	snout-to-vent length. This measurement is often used for reptiles, many of whose tails are variable in length, often curled up, and/or prone to being shed
taxonomy	the scientific study of naming species and classifying the relationships between them
terrestrial	dwelling on or in the ground
TL	total length. For most animals, this is the length from the tip of the nose to the tip of the tail
tsingy	Malagasy word used to describe a landscape of eroded limestone pinnacles
underparts	the part of an animal between the chin and the vent, including the breast and belly
western dry forest	the predominant type of forest in western Madagascar. Also found locally in the north. Much more open than rainforest, and seasonally very dry. This is a deciduous forest: meaning that many trees lose their leaves during the dry season
wet season (rainy season)	the portion of the year that is warmer, with more rainfall. Generally between November and March in the east. The rains are shorter, more sporadic, and usually arrive later in the west. In the southwest they can fail altogether
wingbar(s)	on birds, one or more distinct bands across the coverts, at the top of the wing
WS	wingspan (used as a measurement for butterflies and bats)

Further reading and useful resources

Mammals
Les Carnivora de Madagascar (2012) by Steven M. Goodman. Association Vahatra.
Les Chauves-souris de Madagascar (2011) by Steven M. Goodman. Association Vahatra.
Lemurs of Madagascar (2010) by Russell A. Mittermeier *et al.* Conservation International.
Mammals of Madagascar (2007) by Nick Garbutt.
Yale University Press.
Les Petits Mammifères de Madagascar (2011) by Voahangy Soarimalala and Steven M.
Goodman. Association Vahatra.

Birds
The Birds of Africa: Volume VIII (2013) by Roger Safford and Frank Hawkins. Christopher Helm.
Birds of Madagascar (1998) by Pete Morris and Frank Hawkins. Yale University Press.
Birds of the Indian Ocean Islands (2013) by Ian Sinclair and Olivier Lagrand. Struik Nature.
Guide to the Birds of Madagascar (1990) by Olivier Langrand. Yale University Press.

Reptiles and amphibians
Les Amphibiens des Zones Arides de l'Ouest et du Sud de Madagascar (2014) by Franco Andreone, Gonçalo M. Rosa, and Achille P. Raselimanana. Association Vahatra.
Complete Guide to Scientific and Common Names of Reptiles and Amphibians of the World (1996) by Norman Frank and Erica Ramus.
A Field Guide to the Amphibians and Reptiles of Madagascar (2007) by Frank Glaw and Miguel Vences.

Butterflies
Butterflies of South Africa (2012) by Steve Woodhall. Struik Nature.

Plants
Baobabs de Madagascar (2012) by Andry Petignat. Arboretum d'Antsokay.
Guide des Plantes Succulentes du Sud-ouest de Madagascar (2009) by Andry Petignat and Blaise Cooke. Arboretum d'Antsokay.

General
Les Animaux et Ecosystèmes de l'Holocène Disparus de Madagascar (2013) by Steven M. Goodman and William L. Jungers. Association Vahatra.
Atlas of Selected Land Vertebrates of Madagascar (2014) edited by Steven M. Goodmand and Marie Jeanne Raherilalao. Association Vahatra.
The Natural History of Madagascar (2007) edited by Steven M. Goodman and Jonathan P. Benstead. University of Chicago Press.

Online resource
The IUCN Red List of Threatened Species. www.iucnredlist.org

Acknowledgements and photo credits

Malagasy local guides and biologists have been instrumental in our exploration of their country and learning about its wildlife. Some of the most important of these have been RAJERIARISON Emile, RAJERISOA Luc, RALAHY Andriamasy (Ndrema), RATSISAKANANA BESOA Maurice, RAZAFIMANANTSOA Angeluc and TAREHA Sylvain Christian.

Steve Goodman reviewed the bird and mammal sections and provided invaluable input.

The assistance and expert review of Devin Edmonds, Gonçalo M. Rosa and Mark Scherz was essential in allowing us to cover reptiles and amphibians. Likewise, butterflies could not have been so thoroughly or accurately covered without the help of David Lees.

Josh Engel, Iain Campbell, Charley Hesse, Christian Boix, Derek Schuurman, Nivo Ravelojaona and Ian Sinclair provided various forms of help and advice over the years.

Janet Behrens and Chris and Judith Gibson reviewed and edited the entire manuscript.

This book would not have been as attractive or complete without the support of many contributing photographers, to whom we extend our sincere thanks. All the photographers are listed in the following photo credits section.

We enjoyed the company of many different Tropical Birding clients while guiding tours in Madagascar. Several of these have allowed the use of their photos in the book.

Robert Kirk of Princeton Univeristy Press believed in the concept for this guide. Rob Still, Rachel Still and Andy Swash of **WILD***Guides* put the book together. Their patience, long hours, and desire to make everybody involved in the project satisfied with the end product is much appreciated.

PHOTO CREDITS

Photographs not taken by Ken Behrens are gratefully acknowledged and each image is listed, together with the photographer's initials, as follows: **Nick Athanas** (antpitta.com) [NA]; **Keith Barnes** [KB]; **Steve Blain** (steveblain.blogspot.com) [SB]; **Iain Campbell** (iaincampbell.smugmug.com) [IC]; **Roger and Liz Charlwood** (worldwildlifeimages.com) [RLC]; **Leslie Clapp** [LC]; **Greg and Yvonne Dean** (worldwildlifeimages.com) [GYD]; **Devin Edmonds** [DE]; **Charley Hesse** [CH]; **Andrew Hollander** [AH]; **Rob Hutchinson** [RH]; **Chris Krog** [CK]; **Markus Lagerqvist** (pbase.com/lagerqvist) [ML]; **David Lees** [DL]; **Sandrine Martinez** (flickr.com/photos/msandrine) [SM]; **Pete Morris** (birdquest-tours.com) [PM]; **Gonçalo M. Rosa** [GR]; **Daniel Rosenberg** (flickr.com/photos/cowyeow) [DR]; **Rob Schell** (flickr.com/photos/robschellphotography) [RS]; **Dubi Shapiro** (pbase.com/dubisha) [DS]; **Dave Smallshire** (flickr.com/photos/davesmalls) [DSm]; **Tom Stephenson** [TS]; **John Sullivan** (wildherps.com) [JS]; **Kristian Svensson** (flickr.com/photos/macronyx) [KS]; **Andy and Gill Swash** (worldwildlifeimages.com) [AGS]; **Warwick Tarboton** (warwicktarboton.co.za) [WT]; **Nigel Voaden** (flickr.com/photos/nvoaden) [NV] and **John Wilkinson** [JW].

Images sourced via the photographic agencies **Agami** (agami.nl), **Naturepl** (naturepl.com) or **Shutterstock** (shutterstock.com) are credited in full. Images reproduced under the terms of the Creative Commons Attribution-ShareAlike 3.0 Unported license, or the GNU Free Documentation License, Version 1.2 or any later version published by the Free Software Foundation, are also credited in full (these are indicated by "/CC" after the photographer's name in the list); in this respect we would particularly like to acknowledge **Frank Vassen** (flickr.com/photos/42244964@N03) who provided many images. Images that are in the public domain are credited to the source followed by "(public domain)".

Introduction

16 Rufous Mouse Lemur [Ryan M. Bolton/ Shutterstock]; Giraffe-necked Weevil [KB]; Comet Moth [KB].
18 Landscape [Frank Vassen/CC (Flickr)].
18 Cream-lined Swallowtail [SB]; White-fronted Brown Lemur [Frank Vassen/CC (Flickr)].
19 Speckled Day Gecko [GR].
21 Green Sea Turtle [Wouter Hagens/CC]; Bottlenose dolphin [NASAs (public domain)]; Lesser Frigatebird [RLC].
22 Landscape [KB].
22 Coquerel's Sifaka [KB].
23 Leaf-nosed snake [GR].
24 Landscape [KB].
29 Green Bright-eyed Frog [reptiles4all/ Shutterstock].

Mammals

33 Mouse lemur (1c) [Frank Vassen/CC (Flickr)].
34 Dwarf lemur (1c) [NA].
37 Coquerel's Giant Mouse Lemur (1a) [SM]; Northern Giant Mouse Lemur (1b) [Russell Mittermeier/CC].
38 Small-toothed Sportive Lemur [KB].
39 Milne-Edwards' Sportive Lemur (1f) [SB]; White-footed Sportive Lemur (1c) [KB].
40 Greater Bamboo Lemur (feeding) [KB].
44 Ring-tailed Lemur (main photo) [SB].
45 Ring-tailed Lemur (in tree) [KB]; (group on ground) [KB].
47 White-fronted Brown Lemur (female) [KB].
49 Red-bellied Lemur (male) [KB].
51 Mongoose Lemur (male) [CH]; (female) [David C. Azor/Shutterstock].
52 Black-and-white Ruffed Lemur [LC].

53 'Northern' Black-and-white Ruffed Lemur [Frank Vassen/CC (Flickr)].
55 Masoala Woolly Lemur (1a) [ML]; Eastern Woolly Lemur (1b) (with baby) [KB].
57 Verreaux's Sifaka (dancing) [IC]; Coquerel's Sifaka [KB].
59 Diademed Sifaka [RH].
63 Indri (hanging) [KB].
64 Aye-aye [javarman/Shutterstock].
67 Ring-tailed Vontsira [DS]; Spotted Fanaloka [DSm].
68 Fosa [SB].
70 Madagascar Flying Fox [KB].
71 Madagascar Flying Fox [KB].
73 Mauritian Tomb Bat (two together) [Frank Vassen/CC (Flickr)]; Commerson's Leaf-nosed Bat [JW].
76 Common Tenrec [SB].
79 Eastern Red Forest Rat (1b) [SB]; Black Rat [CSIRO/CC]; Western Tuft-tailed Rat [Nick Garbutt/ Naturepl].
80 Bottlenose Dolphin [Truncatus (public domain)].
81 Bottlenose Dolphin [NASAs (public domain)].

Birds

83 Scaly Ground-roller [AGS]; Blue Vanga [KB].
85 Red-billed Duck (main photo) [CH]; White-faced Whistling-duck (main photo) [JW].
87 Madagascar Partridge (female) [NA].
89 Grey Heron (main photo) [KB]; Madagascar Heron (main photo) [DS].
90 Black Herons [KB].

91 **Purple Heron** (main photo) [NV], (flight) [KB]; **Black Heron** (main photo) [WT].
92 **Great Egret** (inset) [KB].
94 **Madagascar Pond Heron** [SB].
95 **Squacco Heron** (main photo) [JW].
96 **Black-crowned Night Herons** [KB].
97 **Black-crowned Night Heron** (adult) [KB].
99 **Madagascar Buzzard** (main photo) [NV]; **Madagascar Harrier-hawk** (adult) [AGS].
101 **Black Kite** (main photo) [KB]; **Frances's Sparrowhawk** (perched female) [KB].
103 **Madagascar Crested Ibis** (both photos of bird) [RH].
105 **Common Moorhen** (main photo) [KB].
109 **Greater Sand Plover** (main photo) [AGS], (flight) [Daniele Occhiato/Agami].
113 **Whimbrel** (main photo) [AGS], (flight) [Dave Montreuil/Shutterstock].
115 **Crab-plover** [Adrin Shamsudin/ Shutterstock].
118 **Red-tailed Tropicbird** [KB].
119 **Lesser Frigatebird** (male and female) [RLC].
121 **Feral Pigeon** (main photo) [KB].
127 **Madagascar Coucal** (inset) [TS].
130 **Blue Coua** [AGS].
133 **White-browed Owl** (right) [SB]; **Barn Owl** (main photo) [CK].
135 **Madagascar Nightjar** (main photo) [DS]; **Collared Nightjar** (main photo) [Frank Vassen/CC (Flickr)].
137 **Mascarene Martin** (perched) [NV].
139 **Madagascar Malachite Kingfisher** (left) [DS].
141 **Broad-billed Roller** (left) [DS], (right) [AGS].
143 **Pitta-like Ground-roller** [DS]; **Rufous-headed Ground-roller** [NA].
145 **Scaly Ground-roller** [DS].
147 **Long-tailed Ground-roller** (main photo) [KB].
149 **Schlegel's Asity** (male) [JW]; **Common Sunbird Asity** (female) [CH], (male) [DS].
151 **Pied Crow** (main photo) [Ralph Griebenow/ Shutterstock].
153 **Madagascar Bulbul** [KB].
155 **'Amber Mountain' Forest Rock Thrush** [DS].
156 **Subdesert Brush Warbler** [AGS].

161 **Rand's Warbler** [PM].
163 **Long-billed Tetraka** (male) [KB]; **Spectacled Tetraka** [AGS]; **White-throated Oxylabes** [PM].
165 **Souimanga Sunbird** (breeding male) [DS], (transitional male) [KB], (female) [KB]; **Madagascar Green Sunbird** (male) [TS], (female) [KS].
167 **Red-tailed Vanga** (male) [DS]; **Chabert Vanga** (main photo) [DS].
169 **Blue Vanga** (female) [NA], (male) [DS]; **White-headed Vanga** (female) [NA], (male) [GYD].
171 **Nuthatch Vanga** (female) [DS]; **Crossley's Vanga** (male) [DS].
175 **Tylas Vanga** (right) [KB]; **Pollen's Vanga** (female) [DS]; **Madagascar Cuckoo-shrike** (female) [NA].
177 **Madagascar Starling** (male) [CH], (female) [NA].
179 **Sakalava Weaver** (female) [KB].

Reptiles

181 **Madagascar tree boa** [KB].
183 **Flat-tailed Tortoise** (2a) Frank Vassen/CC (Flickr)]; **Madagascan Big-headed Turtle** (3a) [Ryan M. Bolton/Shutterstock].
185 **Green Sea Turtle** [Bthv/CC]; **Hawksbill Sea Turtle** [LC]; **Nile Crocodile** [KB].
187 **Minute Leaf Chameleon** [GR].
189 **Brygoo's Leaf Chameleon** [GR]; **Elongate Ancient Leaf Chameleon** [Axel Strauss/CC].
191 **Parson's Chameleon** [KB].
192 **Jewelled Chameleon** [IC].
193 **Jewelled Chameleon** (male) [GR], (female) [KB].
194 **Big Nose Chameleon** [Frank Vassen/CC (Flickr)].
195 **Perinet Chameleon** (male) [Gavinevans/CC]; **Big Nose Chameleon** [CH].
197 **Cryptic Chameleon** (male) [Frank Vassen/ CC (Flickr)]; **Short-horned Chameleon** (male) [Frank Vassen/CC (Flickr)].
204 **Rhinoceros Chameleon** [SM].

Index

This index includes the English and *scientific* names of all the species included in this book.
Bold text is used to highlight a main species account.
Grey text is used to indicate 'groups' of species which have a main species account.
Regular text is used for species, or 'groups' of species, that are not subject to a full account.
Italicized numbers relate to pages where a photograph may be found, for those species that do not have a full account.